The Revolt of the Black Athlete

SPORT AND SOCIETY

Series Editors
Randy Roberts
Aram Goudsouzian

Founding Editors
Benjamin G. Rader
Randy Roberts

A list of books in the series appears at the end of this book.

The Revolt of the Black Athlete

50th Anniversary Edition

HARRY EDWARDS

With a New Introduction and Afterword

UNIVERSITY OF ILLINOIS PRESS
Urbana, Chicago, and Springfield

First Illinois paperback, 2018
© 1970, 1969 by The Free Press
© 2017 by the Board of Trustees
of the University of Illinois
Reprinted by arrangement with the author.
3 4 5 6 7 C P 6 5 4 3
♾ This book is printed on acid-free paper.

The Library of Congress cataloged the cloth edition as follows:
Names: Edwards, Harry, 1942– author.
Title: The revolt of the Black athlete / Harry Edwards.
Description: 50th anniversary edition. | Urbana : University
    of Illinois Press, 2017. | Series: Sport and society | Includes
    bibliographical references and index.
Identifiers: LCCN 2017000461 | ISBN 9780252041075 (hardback)
Subjects: LCSH: African American athletes—History—20th
    century. | African American athletes—Political activity—
    History—20th century. | African American athletes—
    Social conditions. | Sports—Social aspects—United States
    History—20th century. | Sports—Political aspects—United
    States—History—20th century. | Sports—United States—
    History—20th century. | Discrimination in sports—United
    States—History—20th century. | BISAC: SOCIAL SCIENCE
    / Ethnic Studies / African American Studies. | SPORTS &
    RECREATION / History. | HISTORY / United States / 20th
    Century.
Classification: LCC GV583 .E36 2017 | DDC 796.089/96073—dc23
    LC record available at https://lccn.loc.gov/2017000461

Paperback ISBN 978-0-252-08406-5

Contents

Dedication

In Memory of Muhammad Ali, 1942–2016

I first met him just before my freshman year at San Jose State. Ali—then Cassius Clay—was training for the 1960 Rome Olympics and the boxing coach, Julie Menendez, was also the boxing coach at San Jose State. Both Julie and I were from East St. Louis, Illinois, and he invited me over to meet some of the boxers, especially the younger ones. (Ali was born in January of 1942, I was born in November of that same year). Julie warned me that he couldn't "stop Clay from talking," and he was right. Upon meeting him, I thought at the time that Cassius Clay was "nuts." Of course, he wasn't nuts, just an extremely talented, brashly confident, wonderfully unique and iconoclastic personality, especially for a "Negro" athlete in those times. There was no way that I could've anticipated that our paths would intersect as they ultimately did over the years or the auspices under which that would happen. And now it is done.

It is only when a giant passes from among us and we stand blurry-eyed and blinking in the glaring reality of our loss that we come truly to appreciate the extent to which we all really had just been living in his shadow. So it is with Muhammad Ali. Though it is too early to tell what the full scope and significance of his life contributions have been, some aspects of his legacy are already evident: he was an athlete of unparalleled brilliance, beauty, and bravado at a time when Black athletes (other than the Globetrotters) were expected to be seen, not heard—silent, self-effacing producers, not loquacious, verbose, entertaining performers who attracted attention to themselves. In the broader popular culture, he almost singlehandedly deepened our understanding of religious freedom as something more than an American historical and political cliché. He influenced, even provoked people from the most powerful (Dr. Martin Luther King Jr., Robert Kennedy, among others) to the most naïve among college students and draft-vulnerable youth in communities across this nation to rethink their positions on the issue of war and peace. He was the model and measure of validity for generations of athletes relative to their activist engagement of issues emerging at the interface of politics and sports, from those activist athletes involved with the Olympic Project for Human Rights in 1968 to the University of Missouri Black football players who threatened a football boycott in support of students protesting against racism on that campus in 2015, to the 2016 kneeling protest gesture of San Francisco Forty Niners quarterback Colin Kaepernick during the playing of the National Anthem, to the call during the 2016 ESPYS Awards show by NBA players LeBron James, Carmelo Anthony, Chris Paul, and Dwyane Wade for less talk and "tweets" and more activism focused on social issues on the parts of professional athletes, to the Seattle Seahawks "locked arms" gesture of unity in opposition to injustice in society.

He taught us all by word and example that there can be no "for sale" sign, no price tag on principles, human dignity, and freedom; and, in fighting both in the boxing ring—literally—and beyond for the legitimacy of his Muslim name, Muhammad Ali, he succeeded in expanding the American cultural acceptance, even the embrace of nontraditional names to the point that a Black man named Barack Hussein Obama could be elected president of the United States—not once, but twice. Is Muhammad Ali *The Greatest*? Compared to whom, compared to what—of his era or any other? The Greatest, even within the context of what we already know and understand about his life's journey, does not begin to truly capture the magnitude and significance of his broad scope contributions and legacy.

He stood astride the last four decades of the twentieth century like a bronzed colossus, the most recognizable human face on earth—one foot firmly planted in the sports arena, the other in the world beyond, eventually dwarfing all but the most globally illustrious among us in both. His athletic brilliance long since faded, now his very physical presence among us will be missed, but his indomitable spirit of principled courage, commitment, and sacrifice will always be with us because he has so deeply penetrated our perceptions of our potential as a people and validated our most positive visions of what we should and in fact could be as a society and as a nation. It was a blessing and profound privilege to have known him.

Well done, Champ, and Godspeed, my Brother!

Rest in Peace!

Introduction to the 50th Anniversary Edition

During the week of September 22, 1967 (initially with the support of one graduate student, a former athlete, Ken Noel) I organized a rally in protest of institutionally entrenched, demonstrably anti-Black racism and discrimination in the policies, operations, hiring practices, student recruitment patterns, and overall academic and campus culture at San Jose State College (S.J.S.C.)—now San Jose State University—in California. As an S.J.S.C. scholarship athlete and a sociology honor student with an already well-developed interest in relationships at the interface of race, sport, and society, even as an undergraduate I had become keenly aware of the ever-more-central and critical role of the Black athlete in the revenue-producing sports of collegiate football and basketball.

No less important—and against the background ideologies, strategies, and momentum of a full-blown, society-wide movement to compel enforcement of Black people's civil and human rights across America—I had come to understand the unintended, largely unanticipated, and unacknowledged "externality" of an emergent "power potential" inherent in the tragically exploitive circumstances and position of the Black collegiate athlete. It was under the auspices of this awareness that I determined to "leverage" Black athlete power potential as *the* central strategy of an effort to force progressive institutional change in the circumstances and outcomes of Black people overall—including Black athletes—in relationship to S.J.S.C.

Demands were posted, several campus rallies were held, and I threatened to orchestrate a Black-player boycott of the S.J.S.C. season-opening football game against Texas Western University (now the University of Texas at El

Paso) that would be backed by mass community-based Black picketing and demonstrations at the game—which then would have to be played between teams made up of only *White* players (symbolically important), since the Black players from Texas Western had also publically stated that they would not cross a picket line to play a game that was being boycotted by Black S.J.S.C. players in support of a struggle against racism at the school. Ultimately, and in unexpected short order, the S.J.S.C. administration acceded to most of the posted demands and offered other concessions. Nonetheless, due to a range of emergent factors and forces beyond the control of those immediately involved in efforts to resolve the situation at S.J.S.C., the Texas Western football game was cancelled, marking the first time in National Collegiate Athletics Association (N.C.A.A.) history that a Division I sports event had been cancelled due to racial turmoil at a member institution.

Over the ensuing five decades, it largely has been the threatened Black player boycott and the cancellation of the football game—when this S.J.S.C. history has been noted at all—that have commanded the attention and interests of journalists and academics. These sports chroniclers, researchers, and analysts, with a few noteworthy exceptions, have ignored the details of the history that predisposed the S.J.S.C. revolt, and likewise have paid scant attention to the institutionalized conditions that precipitated and drove the movement and threats of a player boycott and mass demonstrations. But still, word of developments at S.J.S.C. and the changes they spawned spread rapidly through Black collegiate circles. In consequence, similar efforts sprang up on more than one hundred "nominally desegregated" campuses across the nation. This was not altogether unexpected, since the race-related continuities and contradictions at S.J.S.C. were by no means unique to that campus. Rather, they conformed to patterns of interracial relations and institutional arrangements evident at most Division I majority-White colleges and universities then in the process of building their "athletic brands," reputations, and competitive records and fortunes in revenue—producing sports through the ever-greater exploitation of and dependence on Black-athlete talent. As with the S.J.S.C. history, the social-political risks, liabilities, and vulnerabilities inherent in this tack relative to a range of interests of the institutions involved have been over the years largely ignored by sports journalists, academics, and even the institutions themselves—in the last case, essentially the equivalent of "whistling past the cemetery," or worse, denial.

It was therefore, no surprise to me when the sports establishment, sports journalists, and academics for the most part were not only "caught off guard" and in many cases *astonished* when Black players at the University of Missouri

(U. of M.) "tweeted" a group photo of themselves attached to a pledge to boycott all football activities—practice and games—until the demands of U. of M. Black student protestors were met, including a demand for the resignation of the president of the university. A few sports journalists and students of developments at the interface of sports, race, and society saw in the U. of M. situation the history of the 1967 S.J.S.C. saga being repeated. Most, however, were unaware that there was any history to *be* repeated. And in fact, notwithstanding their levels of awareness, virtually all were analytically off the mark and far afield in terms of a valid comprehension of Black athlete activism in the past or currently, including at the U. of M.

Two of the admonitions traditionally attributed to Spanish philosopher and essayist George Santayana concerning history declare that, "Those who do not learn from history are doomed to repeat it," and alternatively, that, "Those who do not remember history are condemned to relive it." I suspect that Santayana did not author both of these (and still other) variations on his essential theme regarding a price inevitably exacted for a failure to grasp and be guided in human affairs by the lessons of history. Such variations more likely have been enunciated over time by others trying to encompass a more fundamental and seminal question: *Why* do populations and societies so often fail to learn from, remember, and be directed by the past? Not discounting at all the well-documented human capacity for outright stupidity, there are other factors that potentially inhibit a reasoned, functional grasp of history. First, populations and societies sometimes *choose*—out of fear, rage, cultural convention and tradition, or under the influence of demagoguery—to *ignore* the lessons of history. Even the most egregious—and sometimes vehemently regretted—violations of otherwise deeply held moral, legal, and political principles can recur. What we have long acknowledged to have been substantially genocidal government policies of herding Native American populations onto "reservations" during the "Indian Wars" of the eighteenth and nineteenth centuries in America did not stop the U.S. government from *choosing* in the twentieth Century to consign Japanese-Americans to "relocation camps" on the West Coast during World War II. Neither has the internment of Japanese-Americans behind barbed wire-topped cyclone fences under military guard in the 1940s, now almost universally condemned, deterred certain segments of the U.S. population and certain political interests from advocating that more than 11 million reportedly undocumented Latinos currently in this country be rounded up, transported to the U.S.–Mexico border, and released on the Mexico side of a wall specifically built and heavily patrolled to keep them there. Nor has the regrettable and often blatantly racist history of selective exclusion of certain nationalities from immigration to the United States tempered vehement demands by some that there be a ban on all Muslim immigration to the United States "until we figure out what's going on with the recruitment and placement of terrorist cells within our country." These are instances of a failure to learn from history—by *choice fueled by fear and demagoguery*.

Second—as alluded to above in my mention of journalists' and academics' handling of the S.J.S.C. movement and of the Black athletes' revolt during the 1960s overall—at least partially at issue relative to the question of *why* history so frequently goes unheeded is the matter of *authorship* or, simply put, *who* is deemed to have a legitimate prerogative to define *what is relevant and what constitutes history*, and to *create the narrative* chronicling and memorializing it. On these questions there seems a curious reality: the concept of history has a great deal in common with concepts such as "profit" and "progress"—at some level it comes down to who is keeping the books. To this degree, the "history" deemed worthy of being *learned* and *remembered* does not just *organically* recommend itself. Rather, it is *selected* and *edited* for emphasis and propagation by the authors of that history. In consequence, peoples and even entire societies are often rendered all but completely oblivious to certain features of history, including their own, because these features have been "de-selected," distorted, denied, forgotten, ignored, or lost in the process of creating a selected historical narrative. A classic illustration of my point relative to the issue of who legitimately exercises the prerogative of determining what is "history" and of chronicling that history is my characterization of both collegiate and professional sports in the 1960s as "slave systems" of control and exploitation of Black athlete talent. In fact, the very first chapter of the 1969 edition of *The Revolt of the Black Athlete* is substantially focused on presenting a narrative on the Black athlete's situation as analogous to being enslaved. In 1967, when I first made the accusation that the N.C.A.A. and its member institutions were running a "plantation system" of Black-athlete exploitation in the revenue-producing sports of basketball and football in particular, my main detractor at the time, N.C.A.A. Executive Director Walter Byers, denounced my remarks out of hand as patently absurd and labeled me as a "Black Militant agitator." But by 1995, in his memoir, *Unsportsmanlike Conduct: Exploiting College Athletes*, Byers himself mocked the N.C.A.A.'s concept of "amateurism," calling it "a modern day misnomer for economic tyranny." Furthermore, as noted by Joe Nocera and Ben Strauss in their 2015 publication "*The Inside Story of the Rebellion against the N.C.A.A.*," Byers went on "to compare college sports to 'the plantation' two decades before Taylor

Branch made the same analogy." In his article, published in *The Atlantic* in 2013, Taylor Branch, the Pulitzer Prize–winning author, did indeed make the case not only that the majority of athletes who play elite college football and men's basketball are African American, but that the N.C.A.A.'s control and oversight of those sports "lets off the unmistakable whiff of the plantation."

Now, the point here is that neither Byers, Branch, nor Nocera and Strauss cite the fact that *the "plantation analogy" is not new*; quite the contrary. Rather, the authors call Byers remarks "one of the most stinging indictments of college sports ever written." And, relative to Branch's use of the "plantation" analogy as an apt description of the circumstances of Black athletes in revenue-producing colleges sports, the authors state the following: "Walter Byers had used the same word in his 1995 autobiography, but the country hadn't been ready to hear it. In the months after his article came out (in *The Atlantic*), *Branch was the country's most visible N.C.A.A. critic*" [emphasis added]. The fact, of course, is that America had been deaf to admonitions regarding the plantation structure and operation of revenue-producing elite collegiate sports for at least two and a half decades before either Byers or Branch ever launched their critiques.

Still, the real problem in all of this is not the fact that what is characterized as a "stinging indictment" was nothing *new*; nor is it that almost fifty years after the "plantation analogy" was applied to the Black collegiate sports experience, an author—who was essentially recycling the concept—could be regarded as "the country's most visible N.C.A.A. critic" with no mention of the fact that his criticism was *old news*. The real tragedy is that both in 1995 and in 2013, the "slave plantation" concept *still* applied because so *little* had changed since the 1960s—due, I believe, in no small part to the fact that this characterization of the history of the Black collegiate athlete's experience during that era of rapidly expanding desegregation of theretofore White locker rooms was denounced, denied, ignored, and ultimately, apparently lost to national cultural narrative and memory.

No less potentially significant is a third consideration: the idea that there is some inevitable "Ground Hog Day"-level repeat and recapitulation of history as the price of not knowing or forgetting otherwise actionable historical knowledge is at best an illusionary notion. Only under almost unimaginably extraordinary circumstantial consequences of detail and dynamics could there be any possibility that history literally could be "repeated" or "relived," a potential that exists at the same level of impossibility as literally stepping twice into the "same" flowing river. The relationships and forces generating history simply are too complex, dynamic, and perpetually "emergent" to be precisely and exactly reiterated from one historical event, much less from one historical *era*, to another. What we can't discern, what we can't detail or comprehend and, therefore, cannot validly deconstruct, we tend to fill in with culture-based presumption and "disciplinary imagination," and with "theory" that imposes continuities and patterns that bridge historical gaps and blind spots. So, though the movements at S.J.S.C. fifty years ago and at the U. of M. in 2015 share some important features and similarities (for example, the leveraging of the power potential of Black athletes; achieved outcomes and concessions to similar demands; the ultimate resignation of the president of the institution; appointment of a high-level administrative official charged with monitoring, managing, and reporting upon the racial climate and culture of the campus; and a barrage of negative and largely unanticipated consequences of the *successes* of the movements), what happened at the U. of M., accurately and strictly speaking, is *not* S.J.S.C. history repeated or relived.

On the other hand, certain substantive similarities in strategy, demands, and outcomes aside, what we should learn from and remember regarding the S.J.S.C. movement, reiterated in the U. of M. effort, are the dynamics and processes at the interface of sport, race, and society that framed and fueled both histories: race-related institutional and cultural continuities, contradictions, and conflicts evident in sport, education, and society that spawn activist reactions and responses, reactions and responses that turned on considered calculation, sometimes incomplete and limited comprehension, and—more often than I would've been willing to admit during the S.J.S.C. effort—utter chance developments that could have been neither anticipated, orchestrated, nor controlled (for example, Muhammad Ali's refusing military induction on April 28, 1967, or the April 4, 1968 assassination of Martin Luther King Jr.). In organizing the S.J.S.C. effort and the subsequent "Olympic Project for Human Rights" (O.P.H.R.) movement, my focus recurrently was forced back to the tasks of distinguishing and trying to understand *how* and the *extent to which* these dynamics and processes came into play relative to any particular development and to a consideration of the consequences for any or all of what I regarded—back then—to be the "five imperatives" of organizing a successful social movement. (I had arrived at the substance of these "five imperatives" during the course of my study of intergroup relations and social organization and change under Professors Robin Williams and William Foote Whyte, respectively, at Cornell University):

1. *A substantial and organically sustained pool of aggrieved plaintiffs seeking redress.* The focus cannot be on uniquely *individual problems,*

challenges, or even *gross injustices* if there is to be development of an effort beyond a "cause celeb" stage to a full-blown "movement." Similarly those collectively seeking redress must be bound together by *enduring* and *largely inescapable* definitions of "mutual connectedness"—definitions such as race, gender, ethnicity, religion, sexual identity, and the like. So at S.J.S.C., though I was well aware that White athletes, too, were being exploited on many levels in the collegiate athletic enterprise (a point made subsequent to the S.J.S.C. revolt by writers such as Dave Meggassy in his book *Out of their League* and Jack Scott in *The Athletic Revolution*), my strategy and intent was only to speak to and organize around the circumstances and outcomes of *Black athletes*. These athletes shared the circumstances of Black students beyond the arena in the broader campus community and they were substantially impacted by racist continuities and contradictions that extended to and were expressed in their sports environment.

2. *A relentless and expanding demand for change, legitimized not only by the aggrieved population but also by collaborating "outside" interests and even, unwittingly, by some detractors.* The statement then, so often expressed by detractors during the S.J.S.C. effort, "I agree with your goals but not with your methods," constituted a tacit, unintended measure of *support* of the demands levied. There was just some disagreement over means.

3. *A threatened "establishment interest" that makes the changes demanded more reasonable and appealing to the establishment in terms of cost-reward outcomes than maintaining the status quo.* The *existential threat* of a boycott by Black football players and supporting mass demonstrations not only imperiled the opening football game, these actions also potentially threatened the ability of all S.J.S.C. athletic programs heavily dependent on Black athletic talent—which would subsequently be associated with an institution that had an image and reputation for anti-Black racism—to recruit Black athletes in the future. Though this additional "leverage factor" was "emergent" and not part of my initial strategy, it became clear over the course of the movement that S.J.S.C. officials—and particularly Athletic Department personnel—were *even more* concerned about this only faintly comprehended, unanticipated, long-term potentiality than they were about the immediate threat of a Black football player boycott alone.

4. *Substantively factual arguments and supporting ideological "scaffold-ing" and "framing" to successfully surmount and overcome two charac-teristically employed adversarial "ploys":* first, an adversarial penchant for portraying the established structure of power and control as the *real* aggrieved party, for projecting the "system" and its minions and "hand maidens" as unjustly accused and challenged; and second, a tendency to paint the circumstances of those protesting—particu-larly Black athletes—as having been instituted either in their best interests or as necessary and unavoidable. In the case of the S.J.S.C. movement, there were repeated claims that the Athletic Department did everything it could to "protect Negro athletes academically" and to show that it did not share in and had no part in perpetuating any racial concerns at issue between Negroes and the larger S.J.S.C. com-munity. Of course, it was a simple matter to debunk such claims by persistently pointing out the facts of a lack of Black personnel of *any* status in the Athletic Department outside of the locker room; the dis-parate graduation rates of Black athletes; the channeling of Black ath-letes into courses geared to keep them eligible, but that contributed little or nothing to either their education or their progress toward a college degree; and the list goes on. The contradictions between demonstrable fact and Athletic Department claims were as stark and glaring as the continuities that existed between racist policies and discriminatory practices in the broader S.J.S.C. campus community and within its athletic programs. And both spheres of university life were grounded in a White supremacist ideology that defined certain areas of merit, and therefore of opportunity, to be exclusively the privilege and purview of Whites.

5. *A sustaining ideology beyond that professed by adversaries and that legitimizes goals and means that enable vigorous "push back" against tendencies toward definitional hegemony and retrenchment relative to compelled changes.* So long as ideological definitions controlled and imposed by adversarial interests are the principal basis for framing contested issues, for resolving those issues, and for appraising the extent of goal achievement and change relative to those issues, those interests will continue to effectively define *what* are legitimate goals, *which* methods are legitimate to achieve those goals, and *when* those goals have been sufficiently achieved to "rein in" or even to cease outright the struggle for change.

This is why I felt that both the S.J.S.C. and the O.P.H.R. movements had to be strategically and directly identified with the broader civil rights struggle in general and with the Black Power movement in particular. To a great extent, movement effectiveness turned on the inability of adversarial interests to *presume* that all sides perceived, framed, defined, and analyzed contested issues and proposed remedies within the same ideological context. A substantial part of both the S.J.S.C. and O.P.H.R. efforts involved propagating the ideological framing and definition of these struggles as legitimate and necessary components and manifestations of the broader society-wide civil rights and Black Power movements. Without this transformative ideological scaffolding, the perception and understanding of our efforts would have been substantially controlled and projected by adversarial interests beginning with the fact that what we saw as *first steps* and *initial* corrective measures would likely have been defined as "final concessions," terminal to the movement and any further goal achievement.

Throughout the book, aspects of both the S.J.S.C. and O.P.H.R. movements reflect persisting efforts—sometimes stated, sometimes only implied—to meet and manage the challenge of one or more of these five imperatives.

I believe that over the last fifty years, the facts, the relationships, and the conclusions drawn from them as portrayed in the original edition of this book—characterized as irresponsibly radical and militant at the time—have held up well, especially if considered within the context of the times and as historical prologue. Throughout the pages that follow this introduction, there are insights and analyses that to this day continue to illuminate issues at the interface of race, sport, and society.

Early on, it became abundantly clear that simply being "right" in terms of our portrayal of issues and developments at the interface of race, sport, and society was far from sufficient to persuade people—even many among our own people—to our side of the arguments involved, much less to support the actions that we were advocating. From the outset, then, I had to cope with severe criticism from all sides while still keeping my eyes on the prize and continuing to articulate and pursue movement goals.

So, when Robert (Pappy) Gault, a Negro coach with the United States Olympic boxing team in 1968, denounced the O.P.H.R. as "misguided" and me as a "militant trouble maker" bent on destroying all that had been achieved for Negroes through sports, it was of no concern, just part of the struggle. When he put a U.S. flag into George Foreman's hand following his Olympic heavyweight boxing victory (demonstrably proving that the Olympics were political), it was of no consequence—that again, was just another sad contradiction of the Black struggle. In the case of the boxing team, I never really had any expectations of support in the first place. The O.P.H.R. didn't approach a single Black boxer seeking support. I mean, if not one of these Olympic boxers came out in support of former Olympic and then World Heavyweight Champion, Muhammad Ali, as had the O.P.H.R., why would the O.P.H.R. harbor any hope or expectation that they would support our movement efforts? George Foreman has often said over the years since the 1968 games that he "didn't care then about what the O.P.H.R. was trying to do," and that he "couldn't care less now"—despite often having complained about how he was treated upon his return from the games. He has stated that he was called (and quite wrongly so) everything from an "Uncle Tom" to a "traitor to his race," and worse. Things got to the point that, as he recalled, he "was ashamed" to show off his Olympic gold medal. I felt badly for George and hated to hear that. But, like the consequences of "Rope-a-dope" during his "Rumble in the Jungle" championship fight against Muhammad Ali, his were largely "self-inflicted wounds." Not only did the O.P.H.R. never politically solicit or target George Foreman concerning anything, personally I have always respected and been quite fond of him and wished him all the best. And why wouldn't I? In waving that flag in the ring, he proved the point that the O.P.H.R. had made all along: *the Olympic Games are political!* In fact, to this day, in a prominent place in my home, I have a token of George's most significant and enduring contribution not only to Black people, but to American culture and society more generally: the George Foreman Greaseless Hamburger Grill. (Now that is a contribution! I mean, think about the potential health consequences—suppose that we Americans just gave up a little bit of the grease that we ingest annually?)

Similarly, Stan Wright, the track coach at Texas Southern University in 1968 and the sprint coach of Jim Hines, Olympic 100-meter champion, was extremely caustic in his attacks on the O.P.H.R. and on me personally. He, too, alleged that my urging Black athletes to boycott and demonstrate at sporting events undermined generations of "Negro advancement through sports," and that urging a Black boycott of the 1968 Olympics could *never* be justified. (Ironically, subsequent to his statements, Stan Wright himself threatened to boycott the 1972 Munich Olympics after he was "passed over" for the position of head coach of the U.S. Olympic track team and was appointed sprint coach instead. He only agreed to attend the Munich Games as an assistant coach after he was assured that he would be the head U.S. Track and Field Coach in 1976 at the Montreal Olympics—where, by the way, he ultimately became the "fall guy" after two American sprinters and medal contenders missed their races due to a communication failure regarding the times of their events.)

And then there is the case of Will Robinson, the high school coach of basketball star Spencer Haywood. Unlike Lew Alcindor (now Kareem Abdul Jabbar), Haywood decided to participate in the 1968 Olympics as a member of the U.S. basketball team. He had been a stellar high school player in Mississippi and had subsequently emerged as the best junior-college basketball player in the country. Because there was so much discussion among Black Olympic athletes—including basketball players—about the Olympic Project for Human Rights in the wake of the Smith-Carlos demonstration following the 200-meter event, the U.S.O.C. sent Will Robinson to Mexico City to admonish the Black basketball players in general—and Spencer Haywood in particular—not to engage in any form of protest activity, not even to make any statement in support of such protests or of the athletes involved. Robinson's stated position was, "You are at the Olympics to represent America, not Black people. We can deal with our race problems after the games are over." Haywood became the star of the championship U.S. Olympic basketball contingent and returned home as the most-sought-after collegiate basketball prospect in the country. He ultimately enrolled at the University of Detroit—where his high school coach and U.S.O.C. sycophant and "go between," Will Robinson, was also promised a job as assistant coach. In the end Robinson didn't get the job because, according to him and at least one University of Detroit staffer, "the University of Detroit refused to hire Black coaches"—a development about which he remained bitter for the rest of this life, so much so that two weeks before his death, he made a tape recording reprising his disappointment and denouncing the University of Detroit's actions. Ironically, *one of the central demands of the O.P.H.R. was that Black coaches be included in the candidates' pool for assistant and head coaching jobs at least in the sports where we predominated as athletes: basketball, football, and track and field* (see Appendix E). As I put the issue at the time, "Why should we play as athletes where we can't work as coaches?"

Pappy Gault, George Forman, Stan Wright, Will Robinson, Jesse Owens, and a host of other sports figures who adamantly and often angrily disagreed with the goals and methods of the S.J.S.C. and O.P.H.R. struggles were simply dismissed as Negro detractors who, again, taught us early on that it was not enough simply to be right, even when it came to some of the very people on whose behalf we were struggling.

There are also a number of outright embarrassing mistakes and miscues in the book. Mostly, these were due to the failures in effective collaboration between me and the assigned book editor, or to outright editorial "heavy handedness," or to what I suspected for years might even have been a deliberate effort to editorially undermine the book. Ultimately of course, whether the issue was one of editorial competence or lack of commitment to the book, it is always the author who bears responsibility for the contents of a book—all of it. But nonetheless, there are lessons to be learned even from these missteps and errors. After reading the uncorrected galley proofs of *The Revolt of the Black Athlete*, making corrections and sometimes arguing in person and over the phone about changes that I wanted or corrections that were needed, I did not read the book again until after publication. It was only then that I found that the editor had not made many of the changes and corrections that I had asked for, and also that, unbeknownst to me, I had apparently "lost" a number of the arguments that I'd had over certain changes. For example, on page 4 of the book (page 13 in this edition), there is this statement: ". . . Institutions such as Hampton in Virginia, Lincoln University in Missouri, Tuskegee in Alabama, and Howard in Washington, D.C. became models for similar schools all over America. Most of them followed the 'George Washington Carver dictum of separate as the fingers, but like one as the hand.'" I had argued with an editor that attribution of the "separate as the fingers . . ." dictum was incorrect, that it should be correctly attributed to Booker T. Washington, *not* to George Washington Carver, whom he insisted was the author of the phrase. His last comment on the issue was that he'd "check it." He may have checked it, but as it turned out, he never changed it.

A similar expression of disregard and/or heavy-handed control is evident in the editor's book placement of a poem by the noted Black poet don l. lee. I had instructed him to place the poem, titled *Black Runners / Black Men*, immediately after chapter 5, "Mexico City 1968." I wanted the poem included, first, because of its content and its author. Second, artists were playing seminal roles in all aspects of the struggle in the 1960s: Maya Angelou, Nikki Giovanni, Nina Simone, Lorraine Hansberry, James Baldwin, don l. lee (Haki R. Madhubuti), and Leroy Jones (Amiri Baraka) among a great many others. Amazingly, the editor had argued that the poem really didn't "have a place in the book," and that in any event, he couldn't put it immediately after chapter 5. I argued strongly for the poem to be included. In the end, he did include the poem in the book—just barely, as the very end page of the book following the subject index! (The poem appears in my afterword, on page 173, in this edition.)

In yet another editing misstep, on page 23 (page 26 in this edition), the names of Jackie Robinson and Oscar Robertson are co-mingled, conflated, producing the name "Oscar Robinson," both in the text and in the index to the book. During this era, the 1960s, when relatively few Black athletes were accorded high profile star publicity and billing in White mainstream sports culture, one Black star athlete was often confused by Whites with another (in much the same way that Whites who knew few Blacks often assumed that all Blacks must know each other, meaning that if you were Black and from California, you had to know their "Black friend from California"). This White "compression" of Black identity and Black life space was like the editorial control that I wrestled with—symptomatic of the times. Even those Whites who were willing, even eager to work collaboratively with Blacks often came to such tasks afflicted with sometimes subtly, sometimes brazenly expressed presumptions of White superiority—superiority in *information*, superiority in *insight*, superiority in *judgement*, and most certainly superiority in *control* and *power*. I have little doubt that, to at least some extent, this ubiquitous American social-cultural affliction of White supremacy—which was then far less hidden beneath patinas and façades of political correctness—was at the foundation of some of these errors. For years, and despite several inquiries from publishers regarding my interest in updating and re-issuing *The Revolt of the Black Athlete*, I resisted doing so because I did not feel comfortable with the idea, I did not feel requisite ownership and authorship over the book. I have decided to collaborate with the re-publication of the book at this time because of the resurgence in Black athlete political activism, because of the approaching fiftieth anniversary of the S.J.S.C. and O.P.H.R. movements, and because I believe there is much to be learned from that history—all of it. For this reason, I also have decided to reissue the book with all of the original text in place and uncorrected because I believe that even the mistakes in the book speak in a way to the character of those times.

Along with acknowledgement of some mistakes and missteps, there is one glaring omission that must be addressed: the lack of due attention paid to the status, circumstances, outcomes, and contributions of Black women— either as athletes or in the struggles for change more generally. The 1960s were pre–Title IX and pre–*Roe v. Wade* years, the two greatest factors giv- ing impetus to the development of women's collegiate sports opportunities and programs. (Title IX, of course, mandated parity in the allocation of resources and funding between men's and women's athletic programs at all collegiate institutions receiving federal funds, while *Roe v. Wade* provided institutions with some assurance that the women recruited as athletes and coaches would have access to affordable and accessible healthcare and medi- cal services—including family planning, thereby substantially mitigating a pervasive and enduring rationalization for excluding women from not only athletic scholarship opportunities and coaching positions but from equal access to jobs more generally in the academy.) Therefore, almost all of the

Black female 1968 Olympians came from H.B.C.U.s, which had long demonstrated a much more "gender inclusive" disposition relative to women
based on their mission and mandate from the outset of employing sports
as a "health and well-being regimen" no less than a competitive enterprise.
But this also meant that in 1968, those Black women athletes were subjected
to the same admonitions and threats as their Black male athlete peers from
H.B.C.U.s. Any effort to recruit them into the O.P.H.R. movement, therefore, seemed futile. In sum then, relative to Black female Olympians' role or
participation in the O.P.H.R. movement, at the time of the initial publication of this book, there was essentially, and regrettably, no effort to get them
involved or to secure their support.

And the tremendous commitment and contributions of women behind
the scenes of both the S.J.S.C. and O.P.H.R. movement for the most part
went similarly unacknowledged—except for some brief mention literally in
the "Acknowledgements." Like other movements of the day, the movements
in sports tended to focus on the circumstances and outcomes of Black *men*
and on securing *their* advancement opportunities—the largely unspoken and
unacknowledged, even unconscious presumption being that when the racial
issues afflicting Black men were mitigated or resolved, the issues impacting
the circumstances and outcomes of Black women likewise would be mitigated and resolved automatically. Sadly, to far too great an extent, we simply
did not perceive and could not appreciate, much less act upon, the fact that
a great deal of what negatively impacts Black women—both then, much
as now—does so not because they are Black, but because they are women.
And so, because we relegated women and their gender-based sports issues
to the background, there evolved a "slippery slope" of neglect leading to the
consignment of women themselves and their contributions to the struggle
to "secondary significance"—when either was acknowledged at all. And this
misogynistic tendency was not just a characteristic associated with "male-
focused" sports-related activist movements, such as the O.P.H.R.; it was characteristic of Black civil and human rights struggles more generally during
the 1960s. Without the "behind the scenes" work of Sandra Boze, her sister
Gayle, Mary East, and Rochelle Duff—four among the few Black women
enrolled as students at S.J.S.C. as undergraduates—the day-to-day pursuit
of S.J.S.C. and O.P.H.R. goals would have been much more difficult, if not
impossible. The work that they did was invaluable, even if unacknowledged.

Let me also briefly address the issue of the relevance of certain characterizations in this book and how these typically reflected the dynamics of racial
nomenclature and politics of the era. Here, I want specifically to clarify the
distinctions made between "Black," "White," and "Negro."

In the mid-1960s the overwhelming majority of people now designated "African Americans" still referred to themselves as "Negroes," some even as "Colored." Thanks largely to the influence of Malcolm X and the sloganeering of militant youth movement leaders such as Stokely Carmichael, *Negroes* and *Colored* people had begun to eschew those characterizations of themselves in favor of the designation "Afro-American." At this point in the evolution of ethnic-racial name changes, the word "black," while no longer a pejorative, was not yet used as a purely racial designation. It was used more in reference to a worldview, a social-political outlook, a cultural disposition. So it was not so much an issue of *being* black, racially, as it was of *thinking* black, of *acting* black. The issue of "who was blacker than whom" was a recurrent theme of debates among even the most militant youth groups. (The echoes of that era are heard even today in questions such as whether President Barack Obama is "Black enough" or whether Bill Clinton was America's first "Black" president—as writer Toni Morrison has stipulated.) So it was only later in the "name change game" that *Black* came to designate biogenetic racial heritage.

In chapter 2 on the mass media, I distinguish between "black," "Negro," and "white" reporters. Without the above understanding and appreciation of the dynamics of changing racial identity and nomenclature during that era, that discussion would seem, within the context of today's more or less "settled" *Black* and *African American* self-designation, to have been rather gratuitous, if not *insane*.

And finally, let me address my hubris, my strident tone, and the sometimes angry temperament that I project in parts of this book. In a 3000-page Federal Bureau of Investigation (F.B.I.) file of dispatches, official S.J.S.C. and University of California, Berkeley documents, book pages, published articles and academic papers, and transcribed lecture notes that I accessed in 1977 through the *Freedom of Information Act*, there was an F.B.I. dispatch from 1968 that states in part:

> Harry Edwards joined the San Jose State faculty in 1966. He was considered an outstanding teacher by the office of the Academic Dean, having an I.Q. of 168. . . . The White colleagues at S.J.S.C., while they remembered Edwards as an undergraduate athlete and scholar, they told a news reporter that they did not know him anymore. They felt that Edwards had been on his way to becoming a successful Negro. They believed that when he went to Cornell as a Woodrow Wilson fellow and undertook a study of race relations in the U.S., he apparently reopened old wounds long suppressed. When he returned to S.J.S.C., it was in the role of *antagonist* [emphasis added]. The White faculty felt there might not be any accommodating Edwards in the future.

And, of course, my former professors didn't know me—they never did. They had presumed to know me all too thoroughly and too soon based on too little information and too little awareness and observation—an ironic array of errors for a sociology faculty. They presumed to completely know the star athlete and honor student whom they encountered in their race-relations "comfort zone." But I also lived every day as one of those Negro students on campus who was shut out, isolated, and alienated; who was humiliated and insulted everyday by the very sight of the unstated but evident "Whites only need apply" fraternity and sorority "rush" and activity tables set up in the middle of campus; who was starkly aware of the paucity of Black faculty, of no Black coaches, no Black administrators, and of the dearth of non-athlete Black students; who was the target of "nigger" and "coon" epithets shouted from the upper-floor windows of "fraternity row" student housing—where some of my White basketball and track and field teammates often lived; who was sometimes only within "ear shot," sometimes the intended audience of "Sambo" and "jungle bunny" jokes told by White teammates and classmates with the best of humorous intentions. I was one of those Black students on campus who endured the White stares, the looks of befuddlement and even anger, who took note of the White gritted teeth occasioned anytime a Black male had the temerity, the effrontery to return the greeting of a White coed who had the simple decency to say hello—a violation of campus racial etiquette that was seldom tolerated, and if you were aware as a Black student-athlete, seldom repeated. Any suspicion or allegation of an interracial dating relationship could get your athletic grant-in-aid rescinded.

On another level, my White colleagues' assessment that I had been well on my way to "becoming a successful Negro" was not only based on incomplete information, it was an understatement. I had arrived in California from the Black "underside" of the "Southend" in East St. Louis, Illinois, and had risen to become both a star athlete and an emerging scholar. By the time that I was a twenty-one-year old college senior, I held a national discus record and the school records at both S.J.S.C. and the community college that I had been compelled to attend owing to poor high school grades, and I would have been a legitimate 1964 U.S. Olympic trials prospect had I chosen to prepare for the discus event and try out. I was also on the draft boards of the N.F.L. Minnesota Vikings, the (then) A.F.L. San Diego Chargers, and I had been scouted by the N.B.A. Los Angeles Lakers (though a Lakers scout later informed me that they were only interested in me as a rebounder and defender because I "had no left hand"). Academically, I was about to graduate from S.J.S.C. with "High Honors" and had been awarded Woodrow Wilson and Cornell

University fellowships, and was awaiting financial details of scholarship and fellowship awards from four other top universities. In short, I was not only on a path to becoming a "successful Negro," I was on a path to achieving the "American Dream" even by *White* male standards: a twenty-one-year-old Negro on the draft boards of professional teams in both basketball and football, a potential Olympic prospect who held a national record in at least one sports event, and a scholar and prestigious fellowship awardee en route to pursuit of an Ivy League Ph.D.—in the early 1960s? Little wonder that my White former professors and, later, colleagues in the S.J.S.C. Sociology Department felt that they no longer knew me.

In fact, what they did not know, what they could not have envisioned was the fact that all along, I was traveling a path paralleling that of the "successful Negro" and the "American Dream." This was the path channeling Negroes into what Malcolm X called "the American Nightmare." And my sojourn along that path, through that nightmare was not only never "suppressed," it was *lifelong* and *inescapable*.

Because Black peoples' "American nightmare" experience tends to enshroud virtually every aspect of their lives (which is what James Baldwin was referencing when he declared, "To be Black and aware in America is to live in a constant state of rage!"), it is difficult to say exactly when I might have initially become consciously aware of being on this nightmare path. But I believe that this awareness probably dawned with the lynching of Emmett Till and my seeing the photos taken at his funeral in 1955. Emmett Till, a fourteen-year-old Negro boy from Chicago visiting relatives in Money, Mississippi, was abducted from his great-uncle's cabin and savagely beaten and murdered, supposedly for "getting fresh" with a White woman in a local "mom and pop" store. In September 1955, *Jet* magazine carried a full-page, up-close photo of Till lying in a casket, his mutilated, swollen, and savagely beaten head and face displayed—as his mother had wanted, "to show the world what had been done" to her son. I was thirteen years old at the time—only a year younger than Emmett Till—and I was badly shaken by the photo and the story behind it. I took that copy of *Jet* home to my father—more than anything else, in an adolescent way, probably in search of reassurance and affirmation that what happened to Emmett Till was a horrific criminal aberration, a monstrous but rare and exceptional act of barbarity that would be quickly and severely punished, an atrocity that could never happen to me. If anyone could reassure me, could affirm that this vicious killing of a boy *who was just like me* would not go unpunished, it was my dad. I thought at the time that my father was the biggest, baddest, strongest man in the world. He was 6'3" tall, weighed about 225 pounds with a 33-inch waist; he had been a boxer, a sprinter—both while serving ten years at Joliet State Prison in Illinois. He was tough! He had a deep, resonant bass voice that reminded me of Paul Robeson, William Marshall, or James Earl Jones today. But when I handed him the magazine and asked him why this had happened and what would happen to the people who did it, he stared at the page with Emmett Till's photo, but he never looked up—this from the man who had *always* admonished me to look people in the eye when I was talking to them, "especially about important stuff." And this was important stuff. Then, in almost a whisper, he said, "It happens all the time down there. It happened to him because it has always happened. That's why I never went back Down South. And *nothin'* is going to happen to the people who did it. That boy shouldn't have ever been down there." When he did finally look up, there was brow-wrinkling pain on his face and a deep sadness in his eyes. But mostly what I detected in my father's countenance was something I'd never seen there before—*fear*, fear for himself and fear for me. I was never able to see my father again as I had seen him up to that point because for the first time in my life it became crystal clear to me that there were things going on in this country that not even my daddy, as big and strong as he was, could save me or himself from—such as being lynched like Emmett Till. And as the years passed my distrust of and enmity toward America's arrangements and disposition relative to racial issues grew, particularly after I enrolled at the newly integrated East St. Louis Senior High School. There, I heard racial epithets hurled at and about Negro students and in reference to the two Negro teachers on staff so casually and so often that I soon came to take little notice of such incidents, just in order to get through the day. "I heard but didn't hear" them. That was one of my first lessons learned at East Side High.

Beginning in 1960, my college years were framed and informed by the hopes of the Civil Rights Movement, beginning with the student lunch counter sit-ins in the South. I had grown up with segregated downtown lunch counters in East St. Louis, and I very much identified with the young College students who were engaged in that struggle. And when some of them ended up at S.J.S.C. after being expelled from Negro colleges in punishment for their efforts, I rushed to meet and talk with them. I was also deeply impressed by the continuing "freedom ride" campaigns being waged throughout the South and with the collaborative efforts of Negroes and Whites—and particularly the young college students among them—to end segregation in public transportation.

Then, on June 12, 1963, Medgar Evers was killed in Jackson, Mississippi—an act that brought the horror and injustice of the Emmett Till case rushing vividly back to mind (and again, true to my dad's expectation, it would be decades before anyone was even charged with the crime).

The March on Washington and Dr. Martin Luther King Jr.'s "I Have a Dream" speech of August 28, 1963 (the eighth anniversary of the Emmett Till murder—August 28, 1955) for me again raised the banner of hope for this country and for Negroes. Then on September 15, 1963—a little more than two weeks later—the Sixteenth Street Baptist Church in Birmingham, Alabama, was bombed, killing four little girls attending Sunday School and injuring twenty-two other people—again, with no one charged or prosecuted in the case.

On June 21, 1964—two weeks after I graduated from S.J.S.C.—James Chaney, Andrew Goodman, and Michael Schwerner, three young people aged twenty-one, twenty, and twenty-four, respectively—again, my age group, and students—were lynched by White supremacists in, again, Mississippi. They had been actively registering Black voters during what was called "Freedom Summer." And, again, true to my dad's expectation, no one was immediately charged or brought to justice for the crime at the time (though the F.B.I. arrested eighteen men on suspicion of conspiracy to commit murder, a conspiracy between Neshoba County law enforcement and the Ku Klux Klan). It was not until 2005 that someone was tried and sentenced for the three murders—a man, who by then was eighty years old and reputed to be the ringleader of the conspiracy, was convicted of three counts of manslaughter, forty-one years after the crime, and sentenced to sixty years in prison.

In the summer of 1964, a month or so after the time of the Chaney, Goodman, and Schwerner murders, I headed to Cornell to get a jump on my graduate work there. I knew that I wanted to focus on race and intergroup relations in America and was interested in studying and perhaps writing my M.A. thesis on "the Black Muslim family." After settling in at Cornell, I took several trips to New York City to attend gatherings of Malcolm X's "Organization for Afro-American Unity" (Malcolm by then had broken with the Nation of Islam). I even got to speak with Malcolm briefly on one occasion and to meet with one of his aides about possibly interviewing some families affiliated with the organization, believing as I did that the success of any Black Nationalist cultural movement would have to be founded on a strong foundation of family relationships. Both Malcolm and his aide seemed interested in the proposal. Then, on February 21, 1965, a little more than six months later, Malcolm X was assassinated. Similarly, on January 17, 1968, I met with Dr. Martin Luther King Jr. in New York City to hold a press conference to publicize his endorsement of the Olympic Project for Human Rights. We spoke by phone once after that press conference, in late February, and promised to keep in touch as the 1968 Olympic Games approached. But we never spoke again—on April 4, 1968, a little more than two months after our phone conversation, Dr. King was assassinated in Memphis, Tennessee. And this was not the end of the death and carnage that for me paved a path into the depths of an American nightmare and so vividly impacted the course of my political perspectives and development.

On June 6, 1968, I was working with a small group of S.J.S.C. students constructing placards and banners in preparation for a San Francisco Bay Area "Bobby Kennedy for President" rally to be held the next day. At the time Kennedy was speaking at a campaign rally in Los Angeles and earlier had spoken by phone to some of his Bay Area organizers expressing his hope for a massive and diverse turnout. Kennedy needed the votes of Blacks and other minorities to win. He was running on an anti–Vietnam War platform. Along with Dr. King and most other more militant left-of-center Black activists and leadership organizations, I was also adamantly opposed to the War. Bobby Kennedy was our candidate. But he never made it to the Bay Area. He was murdered as he left the hotel following the Los Angeles campaign rally.

From Emmett Till through Bobby Kennedy, I was deeply and indelibly impacted by the violence attendant to intergroup relations and politics more generally in America. And as much as anything else, it was this cascade of violent events from my adolescent years through the time that I became of age as an athlete, as a student, and as a young adult that set the trajectory of my life. The violence of one year in particular, 1963, seemed to set the tone and tenor of things: that year ended with the assassination of President John F. Kennedy on November 22, 1963—my twenty-first birthday.

All that followed through 1968 I regarded largely as validation and affirmation of my perspectives on and experiences of an American nightmare.

It was to some substantial degree my efforts to resolve the contradictions between these two paths that I was traveling—the American Dream and the American Nightmare—that came to be expressed, at least partially, through my activism and, most particularly, through my stridency and often angry rhetoric. I made it a point to set doubt, fear, and cautiousness aside. I remember talking once with Huey Newton, co-founder of the Black Panther Party, in 1967 at an antiwar rally and laughing about the sentiment so often expressed by White radicals: "Don't trust anybody over 30!" We had a more basic concern: *We didn't expect to live to be 30!* In my case, the three-hundred–plus death threats that I received in letters, on postcards, and over the phone between the cancellation of the S.J.S.C. football game and the 1968 Mexico City Olympic Games made that expectation feel more and more like a certainty. If I was going to avoid being immobilized, I had to set aside all fear—*all fear*. (Not that I didn't take precautions—I never drank out of water provided to me at speaking events, and only ate at self-serve, "smorgasbord" type restaurants, for example. If no one knew that I was coming, they couldn't poison my food.) And I took my models in regard to dispensing with fear not just from Dr. King and from Malcolm X but also from people I saw, talked to, and worked with more regularly—Huey Newton, H. Rap Brown, Stokely Carmichael, James Foreman—who were probably the most *fearless* people I had ever encountered. (In fact, Huey and Rap were so fearless that more than once I heard other people in the movement wonder aloud if one of them or the other was completely sane!) None of these activists were insane—and neither was I. Still, from time to time people took note of my angry disposition and that—as my friend of fifty years, football legend Jim Brown, once said—I "could get way out there!" Dr. King made me promise that no athletes would be hurt or injured during the course of the O.P.H.R. campaign. Likewise, the father of the woman who would become my wife of nearly fifty years asked me, shortly before his death, to promise that I would not get his daughter killed." That fearlessness—born of a sense that I, like others in the movement, was "on the clock" anyway relative to my survival chances—gave rise to a burning urgency in everything that I did and said that was movement related. There was no room or time for subtlety, for nuance, for compromising understatement. And there was also this: since the onset of Jackie Robinson's tenure with the Brooklyn Dodgers, the media, both Negro and White, had propagated the notion that sport in America was evolving as an "institution apart," as an institution on a trajectory of racial equality and justice that contrasted starkly with the racist traditions of the society at large. In consequence of such propaganda, the sports establishment, in effect, had a "headlock" on Americans in general and Negroes in particular when it came to the issue of the status, circumstances, and outcomes of Negroes in sport. Having been a three-sport athlete in "desegregated locker rooms" since high school, and having become an ardently dedicated student of "sport, race and society," I understood that a society with such strong currents of racist and discriminatory traditions as American society could no more evolve a nonracist sports institution than a chicken can lay a duck egg. A society that evidences such deeply rooted and thoroughly engrained racist proclivities will organically generate and propagate only that which it is structurally and functionally amenable to producing—unless it is compelled to do otherwise through committed struggle. And even then, the tendency will be for any compelled changes to be relentlessly, continually, and both subtly and vigorously opposed, always with an enduring pressure toward obstruction and retrenchment, toward reestablishing the traditional structure and functioning of the race-based hierarchy. Major goals of my rhetoric were to fearlessly, even stridently challenge and demonstrably prove the fallacy of prevailing definitions portraying the character of race relations in American sport, to establish as unimpeachable fact that Negroes had no more "made it" in sport than in any other sector of American society and, therefore, that Black athletes had the same obligation to fight for change as Black people in other arenas of American life.

In sum, then, I believe that there is much to be learned and remembered from the processes, dynamics, and portrayal of the history chronicled on the pages that follow. It is my hope that for those reading—and, in some cases, rereading—*The Revolt of the Black Athlete*, my tack of reissuing the book largely as initially published (mistakes, omissions, hubris, fundamental arguments included) will enable a better and more complete grasp of the events of that era.

On a more personal level, what follows also reflects the vision, the commitment, and the audacity of a Black twenty-five-year-old former star athlete and honor student who became a "scholar-activist" who cared enough about Black people and his country to undertake a quest to advance both through changing their perceptions and understandings of the games they play—while, not at all coincidentally, struggling also to resolve the contradictions of his own life experiences with the "American Dream" and the "American Nightmare"—those dual realities, that "double consciousness" that he was living and wrestling with every day as a consequence of being Black and aware in America.

Harry Edwards
January 3, 2017

The Revolt of the Black Athlete

Foreword

Professor Harry Edwards, architect of the Olympic boycott, is no stranger to me. I first knew him as an athlete at San Jose State College, especially as a basketball player. However, little did I know then how much organizational genius, dogged determination, and dedication to principle lay within that 6'8" frame. But the Professor is that way. He would be the last person in the world to flaunt his talents and abilities.

During the year 1968 Harry Edwards, virtually alone, confronted the combined forces of the U.S. Olympic Committee, the U.S. political establishment, and racists of all kinds from all corners of the earth, including white and Negro racists in the mass media. His opponents pictured him as a demon, a two-headed monster, a mere opportunist. He had shaken them all with his call for justice for the black athlete.

The Olympic Project for Human Rights (the Olympic boycott) was directed against the 1968 Olympics in Mexico City. Edwards' primary move, however, was against all athletics. For years black people and whites have lived under the delusion that athletics is one sure road to racial equality in this country. It is Edwards' contention that in many ways the lot of black athletes is just as bad today as it was before Jackie Robinson integrated baseball in 1946. Edwards' charges and activities have led to national magazine articles on the plight of black athletes. The athletic departments of over a hundred colleges and universities have been shaken to their foundations. The fire has been started and the match was applied by Harry Edwards. For it all started at San Jose State College when black athletes rebelled against unspeakable housing conditions and vile discrimination.

Edwards' promise to disrupt the San Jose State—University of Texas at El Paso football game set off a shock wave throughout the nation. It upset the city of San Jose so much that President Robert D. Clark of San Jose State cancelled the game, against the wishes (or orders) of Governor Ronald Reagan and Superintendent of Schools Max Rafferty. Reagan and Rafferty had said that they would turn out the militia before they would see the game cancelled. From this moment on, Edwards' theme was written. The desire, the motivation, all centered around one word—"justice"—justice for the black man; justice for the black athlete—BY ANY MEANS NECESSARY!

The Olympic boycott movement was really not new. Political satirist-comedian Dick Gregory had proposed the idea before the 1960 Olympics, but people had merely laughed at him then. He made the same proposal again in 1964. At that time he did get a few people to go along to picket the Olympic trials in Los Angeles. But Harry Edwards moved the struggle out of a local, national context and made it an international issue.

I often laugh to myself when I reflect over the fact that throughout the year 1968, Harry Edwards operated the entire project out of a camper. The publicity and the ability to carry out the proposed boycott took money. The funds came out of Edwards' own pocket and from those who believed in the justice of the project. If the donations had matched the amount of hate mail that Edwards, Tommie Smith, Lee Evans, and John Carlos received, Harry could have thrown away his camper and bought a bus. Smith, Evans, and Carlos could best be characterized as the "Three Musketeers" during this period in 1968. They are three unique individuals. Tommie Smith holds eleven world sprint records; Lee Evans is considered to be the greatest quarter-miler of our time; John Carlos is the listed world record holder in the 200 meters. Smith and Carlos long will be remembered by black people throughout the world for their victory-stand demonstration in Mexico City. Although Evans was unable to bring himself to demonstrate as dramatically and nobly as Smith and Carlos, he did endure the hardships and the emotional strain connected with the boycott for some nine months prior to the games.

Edwards' approach in this book will be enlightening even to his severest critics. He highlights the political, economic, and social implications of the Olympic boycott movement and the revolt of the black athlete and stresses the need for black athletes to think politically regarding the plight of black people in general rather than to view athletics as an opportunity to fulfill their own personal and selfish goals. Edwards is a revolutionist, a modern Nat Turner, Malcolm X, and Paul Robeson all rolled into one. A semi-high school dropout, Edwards found his destiny late in his academic career—the search for justice for black people. He is presently finishing studies for his Ph.D degree at Cornell University in Ithaca, New York, and continuing his fight.

This revealing book brings out the many personal hardships, tribulations, and trials the author encountered during that long, long year of 1968. Included are the attempted $100,000 bribe, the role of the former Vice President Hubert H. Humphrey, that of the late assassinated Robert Kennedy, and other politicians, in the Olympic Boycott movement.

In a rebellion, the kid gloves come off and only the bare knuckles remain. Such is the case here. Certain Negro athletic "heroes" are placed in a different perspective with regards to their contribution to the revolutionary struggle of black people in the United States today. Edwards peels off the covers and exposes the myth of fair-play and *esprit de corps* in sports as a giant trap for black athletes who have been charmed from without and strangled from within.

This book can perhaps best be described by saying, as we would in the ghetto, that the brother tells it like it is. He gets right down to the "nitty gritty." Undoubtedly it will have black people wondering to themselves and inquiring of Professor Edwards: "Where have you been so long Brother, your people have had need of you for so long a time."

God Bless you Harry Edwards.

SAMUEL J. SKINNER, JR.
Sports Director
KDIA Radio

Preface

> It's beyond me why these people would allow themselves to be misled by fanatics like Harry Edwards and H. Rap Brown. These athletes are seen by millions of people on nation-wide and world-wide television, they have first-string-starting assignments at white schools, and they are invited to all the big athletic events. Why our Niggers right here at the University have never had it so good.

This statement was made by the Director of Intercollegiate Athletics at one of America's major universities, later to be "white-listed" by the Olympic Committee for Human Rights during the Spring, 1968, track and field season. He was speaking to the sports editor of one of America's leading weekly news magazines. His remarks are typical of the sentiment of many of the athletic administrations that determine policy in the world of intercollegiate, amateur, and professional athletics in America. Equally typical was the response of the sports editor. He merely shook his head, indicating that he, too, could not understand such ingratitude, and then went on about the business of obtaining a *publishable* story for next week's issue. All too often too many of these self-proclaimed guardians of the morals and ethics of the sports world lend tacit approval to such racially corrupt and hypocritical attitudes, thus further degrading and violating the basic human dignity and intelligence of black athletes.

Recreation and athletics have traditionally been billed as essentially therapeutic measures—measures that cure faulty or deteriorating character, that weaken prejudice, and that bind men of all races and nationalities closer together. The evidence does not support the theory. Athletic and recreational centers set up in high-crime or delinquency areas have become merely convenient meeting places for criminals and delinquents.[1] Recreational and athletic activities, far from inhibiting crime, actually have spawned it in both the amateur and professional areas. As for eliminating prejudice, whites may grudgingly admit a black man's prowess as an athlete, but will not acknowledge his equality as a human being. In athletics, where the stakes are position, prestige, and money, where intense competition prevails and a loser is anathema, a white racist does not change his attitude toward blacks; he merely alters his inclination to abuse him or discriminate against him overtly.

Recreational patterns in America widen and perpetuate racial separation. Recreation is exclusive, compounded of all sorts of considerations, not the least of which are racial and economic. There is, therefore, usually little opportunity for recreation to narrow the gap between white and black Americans. Moreover, there is absolutely nothing inherent in recreation that would change attitudes. Recreation simply refreshes the mind and body and gives old attitudes a new start and a fresh impetus.

At an athletic event, by no means are all the bigots and racists sitting in the stands. They also are on the field of play.

The roots of the revolt of the black athlete spring from the same seed that produced the sit-ins, the freedom rides, and the rebellions in Watts, Detroit, and Newark. The athletic revolt springs from a disgust and dissatisfaction with the same racist germ that infected the warped minds responsible for the bomb murders of four black girls as they prayed in a Birmingham, Alabama, church and that conceived and carried out the murders of Malcolm X, Martin Luther King, and Medgar Evers, among a multitude of others. The revolt of the black athlete arises also from his new awareness of his responsibilities in an increasingly more desperate, violent, and unstable America. He is for the first time reacting in a human and masculine fashion to the disparities between the heady artificial world of newspaper clippings, photographers, and screaming spectators and the real world of degradation, humiliation, and horror that confronts the overwhelming majority of Afro-Americans. An even more immediate call to arms for many black athletes has been their realization that once their athletic abilities are impaired by age or injury, only the ghetto beckons and they are doomed once again to that faceless, hopeless, ignominious existence they had supposedly forever left behind them. At the end of their athletic career, black athletes do not become congressmen, as did Bob Mathias, the white former Olympic decathlon champion, or Wilmer Mizell, ex-Pittsburgh Pirate pitcher. Neither does the black athlete cash in on the thousands of dollars to be had from endorsements, either during his professional career or after he retires. And all his clippings, records, and photographs will not qualify him for a good job, even in any of the industries that supposedly produce the breakfast foods that champions feed on. These are only the most obvious of the inequities faced by the black athlete. Others are less obvious but no less humiliating and they have no less a devastating effect on the black athlete's psyche. Like other blacks, black athletes find housing, recreational facilities, clubs, and off-season jobs closed to them (unless the coach passes the word to a prospective employer or renter that the candidate is a "good" Negro, the implication of course being that most black people are in some mysterious fashion not "good").

In essence then, the black revolution in America has not been carried into the locker room, as one sportswriter has stated. What has happened is that the black athlete has left the facade of locker room equality and justice to take his long vacant place as a primary participant in the black revolution. Underlining the importance and significance of the political and social status of this new generation of black athletes is the fact that candidates for political offices at the local and national levels in both major political parties worked vigorously in 1968 to secure the endorsements and active support of black athletes. Where the athletes' amateur status would have been jeopardized by such public commitment, statements were sought from them regarding their approval of some particular candidate's program (for instance, that of Hubert H. Humphrey) to establish equality in amateur athletics or to give the athlete more say in settling disputes between such competing athletic organizations as the National Collegiate Athletic Association and the Amateur Athletic Union. Robert Kennedy with Rosey Grier and Rafer Johnson, Hubert H. Humphrey with Ralph Metcalf, Richard Nixon with Wilt Chamberlain, and Nelson Rockefeller with Jackie Robinson attest that the stupid, plow-jack stereotype of the black athlete is no more. Whether they made a truly significant contribution to black progress or merely prostituted their athletic ability for the sake of other aims is a matter of keen debate among politically conscious blacks.

In this book we will analyze the newest phase of the black liberation movement in America. Within the context of that movement we will define the goals that underlie the athletes' protests and clarify what has been portrayed as the substantially elusive and irrational tactics and direction of their efforts. The statements we will make are not the rantings of some sideline journalist, but the documentary facts of the movement from the perspective of a man who himself was victimized by the American athletic structure, who helped plan, direct, and implement the revolt, and who intends to continue the fight until the goals of that revolt have been achieved.

The exploitation and suffering of the black athlete in America is no more a recent development than is the inhumanity and deprivation suffered by Afro-American non-athletes. Nor do these recent athletic protests mark the first instances of black athletes speaking out. The difference in this instance is that they are speaking out not only on their own behalf, but on behalf of their downtrodden race, and the world and the nation are listening. America's response to what the black athlete is saying and doing will undoubtedly not only determine the future course and direction of American athletics, but also will affect all racial and social relations between blacks and whites in this country.

Hopefully this book will be read and understood by many people, but particularly by those who control athletics and exert political and economic power in America. For it is the latter who have the power to correct the injustices that beset the American sports scene before they spawn conflict. And by some means, somewhere along the line, these injustices shall be corrected.

February, 1969
H. E.

Note

1. For a brief discussion of value, delinquency, and organized recreation and athletics, see A. W. Green, *Recreation, Leisure, and Politics,* McGraw-Hill Book Company, New York, pp. 98–105.

Acknowledgments

There are many people who deserve to be mentioned in this note, but it is possible to name only a few. First of all, I would like to acknowledge the invaluable clerical aid and moral support of Mrs. Regina Skinner throughout the trying days when the strategies of the revolt were being formulated and this book was being organized and written. Miss Sandra Boze and Miss Rachelle Duff were invaluable sources of encouragement and intellectual inspiration, as were Ken Noel and James Edwards, who not only served as chief implementors of strategy in many phases of the revolt of the black athlete, but also contributed courageously and unselfishly to the development of that strategy. Mr. Louis Lomax was both an indispensable ally and a source of invaluable contacts. Without his collaboration, the initial phases of the revolt would have been far less effective. Eddie Sims provided an enthusiasm and determination that contributed significantly to the maintenance of morale among those key members of the movement who were based at San Jose State College. Horace Whitehead's confidence and optimism made the disappointments and problems much less burdensome. I would like also to acknowledge the contributions of those who have given courageously and unselfishly of themselves in all areas of the black liberation struggle and who reaffirmed their determination to make justice and freedom a reality for all Americans during the revolt of the black athlete: the late Rev. Dr. Martin Luther King, Jr., Mr. Stokely Carmichael, and H. Rap Brown. And last, a word for the support and contributions of all those persons who gave freely of their most precious and in many cases their only assets—an undying faith in the present generation of black youth and an undeniable determination to obtain justice and freedom in every sphere of life for the frustrated and oppressed black masses of America.

H. E.

1

The Emergence of the Black Athlete
in America

The Development of Black Athletics After Slavery

Prior to the enactment of the Emancipation Proclamation, most black people in America engaged only in recreational activities. Afro-Americans, those few blacks who supposedly enjoyed full citizenship during slavery, participated to some degree in actual athletic activities but these instances were, by all evidence, rare relative to the lack of participation by the masses of blacks. The full impact of black athletes upon American athletics awaited implementation of the provisions of emancipation and more particularly, the establishment of Negro educational institutions.[1] With emancipation also came the development of black athletic clubs and colleges.

The major impetus to the development of Afro-American athletics during slavery and after emancipation were the racially and economically discriminatory practices of white Americans. Blacks were excluded from white athletic clubs, so they established their own. The reasons given for the exclusion were the same tired rationalizations and racist cover-ups that are so prevalent today in athletic circles. Some coaches felt that their "racially pure" white players would not play beside a black man. And although this assumption may have been true, few coaches ever tried playing blacks with whites in an effort to substantiate or disprove their feelings. Others claimed that their fans would not have attended games played by a biracial team. Still others simply believed that blacks were not capable of playing with the same degree of sophistication as white players. And many envisioned tremendous difficulty in scheduling games involving a mixed team. Whatever the reasons for black exclusion may have been, they were based on speculations heavily seasoned with white-supremacist leanings rather than facts. Yet these and other similar attitudes were so pervasive that Afro-Americans, caught up in the same drive toward increasing athletic participation that possessed whites in the late nineteenth and early twentieth centuries in America, set about establishing their own clubs. Although it is difficult to document the playing histories of black athletic clubs, what evidence there is tends to show that they performed as well as white teams, and in some cases, better. All-black baseball and basketball teams and leagues proliferated, and in later years they served as springboards into "big league" professional sports. In some instances, all-black teams did play all-white teams with, as might be expected by an unbiased observer, mixed results. They won some and they lost some. It is clear, however, that black teams fared much better than had been expected in these biracial contests. In 1928, for example, the all-black Renaissance Five defeated the famed all-white Celtics—the leading white basketball team of the time—and several other all-white aggregations. And these victories were not atypical, although they seemingly went unnoticed by the white sports-reporting establishment of the day.[2]

Much of the same was true of black baseball teams. Although they played mostly against one another, occasionally they challenged all-white teams or were challenged by them, the whites feeling fairly certain that they could "beat the niggers." Such was not always the case. Here again black teams held their own, winning some and losing some.

Boxing, however, was to be the sport most heavily infiltrated by blacks, for it was the first American sport to permit widespread competition between blacks and whites, at least at the lower club levels. There had been black boxers for decades preceding the twentieth century, but it was not until the 1900's that contending blacks were given shots at America's white-dominated championship titles. Devout racists such as John L. Sullivan staunchly refused to fight black contenders, even as great a one as Peter Jackson in 1889.[3] Even though there were several "Colored Boxing Champions of America," the first black champion recognized by America and the world was Jack Johnson, who won the heavyweight championship from Tommy Burns on December 26, 1908. The breakthrough was a long time coming, considering the fact that blacks had been boxing by the same rules as whites and supposedly had been citizens of the same country as had many of the white champions for at least three to four decades.

The same circumstances surrounding the participation of Afro-Americans in baseball, basketball, and boxing pertained also to other club sports such as track, football, and tennis. Yet despite the racial and economic limitations, the black athletic clubs and the black boxers managed to survive and, to some extent, athletically, they even managed to prosper. It was the Negro colleges, however, that were most influential in bringing the Afro-American athlete into numerical prominence. And here, too, it was the enduring American institutions of racism and economic discrimination that determined the direction of this development.

The Negro Colleges and the National Emergence of the Black Athlete

Growing out of the ever increasing pressures toward racial segregation in America and the awesome need to educate the millions of newly-freed Afro-Americans, Negro colleges sprang up all over the United States. Such institutions as Hampton in Virginia, Lincoln University in Missouri, Tuskegee in Alabama, and Howard in Washington, D.C., became models for similar schools all over America. Most of them followed the George Washington Carver dictum of "separate as the fingers, but as like one as the hand." These institutions, which were generally supported by philanthropic whites or by state funds controlled by racist government officials, endeavored to develop "safe" educational programs—meaning, of course, those that were non-threatening to whites. This plan was followed out of fear of loss of financial support, ignorance on the parts of school administrators, or just plain "Uncle Tomism." At any rate, the result was the same. Courses in agriculture, mechanical skills, music, and physical education were over-represented in the curricula. Subjects dealing with abstract use of intellectual skills were singularly scarce. Many Negro colleges emphasized agricultural, mechanical, and industrial skills in their names. Such schools as Tennessee A. & I. State University (Agricultural and Industrial) and Arkansas A. & M. College (Agricultural and Mechanical) were, and are today, typical of colleges whose names designated their central educational focus. From the intellectual standpoint, these colleges might well have been renamed, substituting "Athletics and Ignorance" for "Agricultural and Industrial" and "Athletics and Music" for "Agricultural and Mechanical" (or "Athletics and Tomism" for "Agricultural and Technological"). For, as we mentioned, these colleges provided little in the way of intellectual substance for their students. White racist government administrators and often the philanthropists themselves felt that black people were happiest singing and dancing, working with their hands, and playing games. And not only would blacks be happier thus occupied, but white racists could feel much safer. Negro college administrators and faculties operated these colleges in ways that conformed to racist desires much as they do today. In fact, the persistence of these deplorable educational conditions, over a hundred years after emancipation, led black students on several predominantly Negro college campuses in the late 1960's to revolt and demand the de-emphasis of athletics, music, and other non-intellectual endeavors in favor of more appropriate educational concerns. Typical of these uprisings were those occurring on the campuses of Grambling College in Louisiana, Howard University, and Stillman College in Tuscaloosa, Alabama, where black students actually shut down the institutions over these issues.

Yet despite their educational shortcomings, or maybe because of them, Negro colleges have provided an avenue to athletic prominence for many black athletes. Not that no black athletes competed for white schools. Some predominantly white schools enrolled Afro-Americans from their inception. Others, such as Amherst, Harvard, and Tufts College, as well as other liberal New England schools, have histories of Afro-American participation in sports dating back many years.[4] This statement should be qualified to some extent, however, for blacks were not always welcome to participate in all the athletic activities available. For instance, it is fairly common knowledge that Afro-Americans were, until very recently, unwelcome as basketball players on the courts of most "Big Ten" schools, particularly those of Illinois, Indiana, and Iowa, because basketball lagged behind football as a big-money sport and the drawing power of black basketballers thus was a minor consideration. And in some cases, this attitude toward black basketball players in the Big Ten Conference persists today, even though it is now socially and financially expedient that it be submerged.[5] But notwithstanding long histories of token integration, most black athletes today, as in the past, play out their careers in predominantly Negro colleges.

America went through a depression and two world wars with its black-white collegiate separation unbroken. But with the end of World War II and the new orientations that this catastrophic event wrought, hitherto all-white schools began to reassess their policies of excluding black students in general and black athletes in particular. America, as one of many countries attempting to erase the scars left by war, turned enthusiastically and increasingly to organized athletics as diversion. With this growth in spectator interest and the resulting financial rewards from rising attendance figures, white schools could no longer afford to sit idly by and allow Negro colleges to siphon off potentially valuable black athletic prospects merely because of an accident of birth. Many of these white schools went into the South and actively recruited black athletes. Football players in particular were prime commodities, because football then, as today, has a greater finance-producing potential than any other sport. In this regard, it was no accident that when lily-white schools moved to integrate their athletic activities, football was usually the first sport involved. Some athletic clubs soon followed the lead of the colleges, but only a few.

So thanks to the impact of a world war, the Supreme Court decision outlawing separate educational facilities in the nation's schools in 1954, and the urge on the part of whites once more to exploit blacks economically, Afro-Americans at long last were allowed to venture into big-time college athletics in significant numbers. (Parenthetically, but understandably, given the sub-par educational status of the Negro colleges, this integration was unidirectional, with many black athletes going to white schools but with few white athletes entering Negro schools.) From these integrated teams were to come many black athletes who were destined to achieve fame and fortune in professional sports. Negro colleges also continued to produce their share of athletic greats. But as far as most of America's sports enthusiasts were concerned, unless an athlete achieved fame in one of the big-name, predominantly white institutions, he counted for little. And in this regard, the attitudes of the Afro-American public differed hardly at all from those held by the white majority. Even the most avid black follower of sports in America would have been hard pressed to name the selections to the "Negro All-American" first teams during the years of the late 1940's to the middle 1950's, except for those few blacks who made it big in pro athletics. But publicly, for all intents and purposes, blacks had finally been accepted as equals by whites—or at least those blacks who were superior enough to make first string ostensibly were accepted. So thoroughly has this myth been perpetuated that athletic excellence, even today, looms second only to education as a prescribed path for blacks to follow in escaping the humiliations and drudgery of their "second-class" citizenship. But what has integration really meant to the black athlete? What has this move really meant psychologically, socially, and educationally for him? Is the Afro-American athlete significantly better off in predominantly white schools than he was in all-black institutions?

Black Athletes in Predominantly White Colleges:
The Shame and the Glory

With the emergence of racially mixed athletic teams, black athletes found themselves in refreshingly new but sometimes brutally dehumanizing educational and athletic environments. Not infrequently the black athlete approaches life and athletics on a predominantly white college campus with all the excited anticipation of a child at a carnival, but also with many misgivings. He was in the past, as he is today, usually somewhat unsure of his abilities—social, athletic, educational, and otherwise. He often feels during his first few weeks on campus that perhaps he has misjudged his athletic potential. Perhaps he has savored too long and too eagerly the cheers of his home town high school fans. Threatening his pride, his narcissism, is the gnawing fear that grips most prospective college athletes—he has perhaps chosen a school at which he is doomed to "ride the pines" for four solid years. Questions involving education also are a source of almost constant concern. Many black athletes come to predominantly white schools under "special adjustments" usually instituted on their behalf at the request of the coach at the college. Will they be able to make the grade academically—even with the help of the tutors promised them by the athletic department, and with the "Mickey Mouse" courses prescribed for them by their coaches—"just until they find their study legs?" Will they be able to write acceptable term papers and pass examinations in order to maintain their eligibility? What faces them if they fail? Such doubts and fears, as we have indicated, also plague white athletes. But compounding the black athlete's concern is the question of his social life. When he is not in class or practicing, what will he be doing, how will he, a black athlete, spend his time? Will he be invited to join other students in typical college-centered activities? Indeed, will he even want to? His questions will be answered quickly and clearly, often shockingly.

The question of his athletic ability is usually the first of the black athlete's questions to be answered, for it was athletic ability that brought him to the attention of the coaches in the first place. Before official practice even starts at most college campuses, the coaches of the various sports always make certain that their newly-recruited freshmen and transfer athletes have access to the necessary equipment to carry on "informal workouts on their own." And the integrated, predominantly white colleges were not in the past, nor are they today, any different. Under the watchful, searching eyes of the coaches, the black athlete goes through his paces in football drills, pick-up basketball games, and batting and fielding drills on the diamond—and sometimes over the course of an academic year, he does all three. For the black athlete in the predominantly white school was and is first, foremost, and sometimes only, an athletic commodity. He is constantly reminded of this one fact, sometimes subtly and informally, at other times harshly and overtly, but at all times unequivocally. The black athlete is expected to "sleep, eat, and drink" athletics. His basketball, football, or baseball (depending upon the season) is to be his closest companion, his best friend, and in a very real sense, the symbol and object of his religious concern.

A black athlete generally fares well in athletic competition relative to other incoming athletes at a white-dominated college. The cards are somewhat stacked for him, however, because few black high school athletes get what are typically classified as second- and third-string athletic grants-in-aid. One simply does not find black athletes on "full-rides" at predominantly white schools riding the bench or playing second- or third-team positions. Second- and third-team athletic grants-in-aid are generally reserved for white athletes. A second-string black athlete is under infinitely more pressure than his white counterpart. For everyone expects a black athlete to excel athletically, and if he does not, he has let down the coach, the school, and the entire "Negro" race. He is suspected of "goldbricking," breaking training, lacking concern for his teammates. (This central fact of the black athlete's life will be discussed in detail later in this chapter.) Physically, black college athletes have stood the test in spite of the incessant, sometimes brutal, mental strains they have been forced to bear.

Educationally, black athletes have not been much better off at white schools than they would have been had they attended Negro colleges. And as much as white racist coaches and athletic directors would like to attribute the alleged lack of intellectual incentive among some black athletes to inherent racial failings, such is simply not the case. The fault lies in the "Mickey Mouse" courses into which black athletes are inevitably herded and with the coaching staffs at white schools who not only coach the black athletes, but often counsel them on academic matters. From the perspective of many white coaches and athletic directors, the world does not need black doctors, sociologists, chemists, dentists, mathematicians, computer operators, or biologists. Moreover, such lofty academic goals might jeopardize a black athlete's college career and thus wipe out the colleges' financial investment in him. What is more, how many black doctors, sociologists, chemists, dentists, or biologists, does the average white coach (or the average white man) know? Not many, if any at all; and so, his thinking goes, black people must not possess the necessary intellectual capacity to rise to such heights. So, the coaches conclude—when they think about it at all—why subject the "boy" to any more pressures, why add any additional strain to his load. Outline for him a four-year academic program that will qualify him for a B.S. degree (not necessarily designating Bachelor of Science) in basketweaving, car-washing, or gymnasium maintenance. Not many accredited schools offer degrees in such educationally dubious areas, however, and still fewer jobs are available for persons possessing such credentials. As a result, proportionately few black athletes graduate from predominantly white schools within the four-year time period covered by their span of collegiate eligibility. In fact, many never graduate at all. Having neither the personal funds to finish school after their athletic eligibility has expired nor the necessary academic background to qualify for aid on scholastic grounds, the black athlete simply falls by the wayside or takes his press clippings, trophies, awards, and his four years of irrelevant education and looks for any job he can find. If he is extremely lucky, he may be tapped by some professional team, but turning pro often opens up a whole new world of disappointment and frustration for him, as we shall see. By and large, most black athletes simply return to the ghettos and resume the life of drudgery and humiliation they knew before they went off to school.

Between 1957 and 1967 only seven out of twenty black football players graduated from the University of Washington; at the University of Oregon in the last three years, only six of eleven. Similarly dismal statistics prevail at the University of California at Berkeley, at Minnesota, at Michigan State, and so on and on. Wilt Chamberlain and Gale Sayers, among others, never graduated from Kansas U. In the 1966 N.C.A.A. basketball finals, none of the five black starters for the University of Texas at El Paso (then Texas Western) graduated. In essence, then, black athletes traditionally have received an almost criminally fraudulent deal educationally in practically all predominantly white colleges—from Harvard University right on down.

Perhaps the grimmest, most dehumanizing experiences for black athletes arise from the dismal and repressive social conditions they encounter on white campuses. Particularly relevant here are the restrictions—formal and informal—involving participation in fraternity and sorority life, school dances, parties, and decisions affecting utilization of tuition fees and funds.

Officially, a black athlete on a white campus is a duly registered member of the academic community and is therefore entitled to all the rights and subject to the responsibilities thereof. This is his "official" status. Unofficially, vast areas of college life are closed to him. Foremost among the areas off-limits to blacks—athletes and non-athletes—are the fraternities and sororities. With a few notable exceptions, a black athlete at a white college never becomes a big enough name, athletically or otherwise, to breach the formal and informal discriminatory and racist policies followed by most fraternities and sororities on America's white-dominated college campuses. In areas where integrated white schools and black schools exist in close proximity, it is not unusual to find black athletes from the white college joining fraternities at the black schools because the white-dominated fraternities on their own campus exclude them. Many of the black athlete's white teammates may and usually do belong to these racist clubs. I can recall clearly how puzzled and enraged I became when white teammates of mine at San Jose State, after avoiding me all week and closing their fraternity doors in my face, still could have the unmitigated nerve to talk to me about "team spirit" on Saturday. But that was perhaps the most naive period of my entire college life. I soon found out, as do most black athletes at white schools, that white "teammates" can practice with you five days a week for hours on end yet at night refer to you as "coon," "nigger," and "jiggaboo" and then jump all over you on Saturday afternoons talking about team spirit.

From all indications, my experiences at San Jose State were not dissimilar to those encountered by other black athletes at white schools. I had several fights with white teammates who called me "nigger" and "coon." I "walked into" numerous conversations between whites in the locker room involving "jiggaboos" and "night-fighters." And not all these whites were athletes. Some were coaches, team managers, and trainers.[6] A black person never adjusts to these things. He either fights, and risks being branded a trouble-maker, or he ignores such humiliations. During my collegiate athletic days, I did both.

Fraternities, then, having their origins primarily in the South and maintaining what may be construed as distinctively southern prejudices, are the exclusive domains of whites on most large college campuses. They facilitate the social adjustment of the incoming white student, but also serve as drawing cards to be utilized by coaches attempting to recruit white athletes of college potential to their schools. In fact, the first humiliation to which a black athlete is subjected comes during the recruiting stage, before he is even enrolled in school, and the sorority-fraternity situation again is a factor.

Typically, recruitment—the modern-day equivalent of the slave trade—is carried out by first inviting a prospective athlete to the college campus to look things over and to get a feel for the school. A day is generally selected when an important sports event is scheduled, such as homecoming. Both black and white athletes are invited and shown around the campus. They are all there to see for themselves and to hear of the advantages of attending this institution rather than another. This "togetherness" comes to a screeching halt, however, when the time for the inevitable socializing arrives. The coach, after all, does not want his new recruits to feel that at his school things are all business and no play. What generally happens at this point is that the prospective athletes are separated—by the coaches—along racial lines. The prospective white athletes are assigned to white athletes already enrolled at the school, varsity men whenever possible and in the sport for which the incoming athlete is being recruited. Inevitably, some of these campus stars are members of fraternities and are able to line up dates for the recruits, take them to parties and dances, and generally to initiate them into the social life of the institution. Black recruits also get a realistic feel for the social life and college spirit on campus-but from a different perspective. As is the case with the white prospects, black recruits also are escorted around by currently enrolled black athletes. But here the similarity between the experiences of the white recruit and the black recruit ends.

First of all, the incoming black athlete is not always escorted by someone engaging in the same sport for which he is being recruited. For not all sports on white campuses were integrated at the same time. As a result, a basketball prospect may be escorted about the campus by a football player or track man. Second, the black escorts do not have access to fraternities and sororities and so cannot escort their charges to parties, dances, and other "after game" activities that might be scheduled. And woe unto him who is naive enough or who has gall enough to go, uninvited, to a social gathering sponsored by a white fraternity or sorority, even though all his white teammates and their guests might be there. In lieu of such niceties, the coach will generally give the black recruit's escort ten or fifteen dollars and bid them farewell until some specified time the following day. And since there usually are few, if any, black females on the campuses (and they are not six feet eight inches tall and are not experts at dribbling basketballs, kicking footballs, and hitting baseballs-and therefore get no scholarships) the black recruits' days on campus become singularly boring, monotonous, miserable. For the fortunate, there are sometimes ghettos not too far from the campus or "tourist" towns such as Juarez, Mexico, which is practically adjacent to the campus of the University of Texas at El Paso, where companionship and entertainment can be found.[7] For the less fortunate, as was true in my case, the time is spent having dinner in a second-rate restaurant, viewing a third-rate movie, and then returning to a dull, depressing room in some isolated corner of the campus to talk sports or exchange banalities and wait for another day that promises more of the same.

And how does a white coach usually justify this double standard of treatment for incoming black and white athletes? Once again we encounter the same set of rationalizations. Some believe that "Negroes feel more comfortable with their own." Others say that to mix the men socially would alienate the white players and their dates. Still others justify their actions by saying that things have always been done this way. And, if all else fails, the white coach "cops out" by pleading ignorance of the situation. Under any circumstances, however, the resultant damage to the psyches of both the recruit and his escort is incalculable.

A related but somewhat different problem centers around the choice of dating partners on a white campus. If there is any aspect of the informal social codes of white college campuses that apply most emphatically and almost singularly to black males it is the one covering interracial dating. And the warning of "Don't be caught even talking to a white girl, much less dating one," has been driven solidly home to the black athlete. This dictum is prescribed by white coaches and enforced by white teammates, who often report to coaches any incidents of interracial dating between black athletes and white females. White team members also will belittle and slander white females who date Afro-Americans. For it is commonly alleged among many white men, regardless of their station in life, that any white female who even talks to a black male, much less dating him, must be engaged in some sort of lewd and licentious affair, or at the very least is obsessed with the supposed sexual prowess of black men in general.

Outside the athletic arena then, the life of the black athlete is lonely, monotonous, and unrewarding, even before he enrolls at the white school. He may be a big hero on the field or on the court, but in street clothes and even in the team locker room, he resumes his status as "just another nigger." These conditions then are part of the shame and the glory that fall to black athletes on predominantly white college campuses. But his problems are just beginning; they increase once he has made the "big team."

Profit, Property, and the Black Amateur Athletic Machine

Once he is on campus, a black athlete does in fact become part of the big team, and an important part. As the head basketball coach at San Jose State College, Dan Glines, once emphatically stated, "Without the black athlete, you don't have a chance in this game. You don't draw fans, and you don't win." But a black athlete also finds that his equals are not his white teammates, but the basketballs, baseballs, jockey straps, and other forms of property and equipment—all of which, like him, are important and vital to sports. Like a piece of equipment, the black athlete is used. The old cliché about "You give us your athletic ability, we give you a free education" is a bare-faced lie, concocted by the white sports establishment to hoodwink athletes, white as well as black.

First of all, there is no such thing as a "free" ride. A black athlete pays dearly with his blood, sweat, tears, and ultimately with some portion of his manhood, for the questionable right to represent his school on the athletic field. Second, the white athletic establishments on the various college campuses frequently fail to live up to even the most rudimentary responsibilities implied in their half of the agreement. As we have seen, the educational experiences of most black athletes on white college campuses would insult the intellectual aspirations of an idiot. At one large California school, a black athlete merely had to pass out the basketballs and volley balls for a coach who taught two "techniques of teaching" athletics courses to get four units of credit toward the twelve he needed to maintain his athletic eligibility. None of the four units counted toward his degree requirements. Few schools provide the tutors so often promised to black athletes prior to their enrollments. Usually the coach, rather than supplying tutors, simply obtains copies of tests for his black athletes. (This also happens upon occasion with white athletes, but not very frequently. Sometimes it is not even necessary for a coach to get a test for his academically vulnerable white athletes, because they may have already secured the test from the files of their fraternity house.) And if he is injured or if he fails to live up to the coach's expectations, a black athlete may be required to work at various campus jobs to "help balance things out."

Gradually, most black college athletes begin to realize that his white employers, his teammates, even his fellow students, in spite of the cheers and adulations they shower upon him, regard him as something akin to a super animal, but an animal nevertheless. He is expected to run faster, jump higher, dribble better, pass fancier, and play longer in general than any of his white teammates. The black halfback in football who has only average speed does not play. The black basketball player who cannot jump, dribble, run, *and* shoot does not play. A black athlete on a white campus cannot afford to make mistakes or perform occasionally at a mediocre level. If he does, he does not play. He is expected to be tireless. If he slows up, it is because he is not in shape. He is always supposed to go at top speed and if he doesn't, he has let the entire Negro race down. He is expected to be better in general than his white teammates. In fact, he has to be to play at all.

A common practice on many white college campuses is to "stack" black players in one position or another in order to limit the number who actually make the team. It is a *de facto* quota system. As we mentioned, only the top black athletes are offered grants-in-aid to the big-name schools from the outset. This situation, combined with the public pressures on black high school stars to go to big schools and the fact that white players do not have to be, nor are they expected to be, as good as black athletes, means that theoretically most of the positions on predominantly white college athletic teams could in fact be manned by black players. So, the black players are stacked at one position or another—such as halfback or end in football, or center or guard in basketball—and left to fight among themselves for the positions on the team that are open to them. The results are usually the same. A few blacks make the team, usually in first-string positions. Other blacks with athletic abilities far and above those of many of the whites who make the team are summarily dismissed or told that they can stay on the team but only if they agree to a cut in their financial support or consent to give it up altogether.

Other techniques for maintaining the quota system on predominantly white teams are equally as simple, and as effective. At most white schools, certain positions are reserved exclusively for whites. Take the position of quarterback. You could count the number of quarterbacks who have played intercollegiate football for predominantly white colleges without taking off your shoes—Ron Burton at Colgate, Jimmy Raye at Michigan State, Sandy Stevens at Minnesota, Wilburn Hollis at Iowa, and a few others. Many coaches and athletic establishment members feel that blacks lack the necessary intellectual equipment to become quarterbacks, that they will be unable to remember plays or formations and pick apart a defense, that running things on the field would be "too much for the coon's mustard-seed brain to handle," as one trainer stated to another during a football game at a large Mid-western university in 1966.

If, then, so many white college coaches, white athletes, and white students in general so deplore and are repulsed by the presence of black athletes, why are they recruited? The answer is obvious. We have already alluded to it. One has only to read the minutes of the congressional hearings on the dispute between the National Collegiate Athletic Association and the Amateur Athletic Union to understand that amateur athletics in America is big business. One element in the dispute between the N.C.A.A. and the A.A.U. centers around the control of ten million dollars presently held in banks and investment capital by the A.A.U. The N.C.A.A. maintains that a sizable proportion of these funds was put there by college athletes affiliated with the N.C.A.A. and that therefore the N.C.A.A. should have a cut of the booty.[8] Individual schools also fare handsomely from amateur athletics. Athletic receipts have provided funds for constructing many new buildings on many college campuses throughout the country.[9] A player such as O. J. Simpson is worth approximately three million dollars in gate receipts and television rights to the University of Southern California. Much the same can be said of Lew Alcindor at the University of California at Los Angeles. Every white coach who recruits a black athlete hopes that he has uncovered a potential O. J. Simpson or Lew Alcindor, because that would mean money for his school and prestige, and money, for him. And what do the black athletes receive in return? Most often, with few exceptions, their walking papers as soon as their eligibility is up. They join the ranks of has-beens, who never really were.

Why then do black athletes go to white schools, if they find nothing but humiliation or at best toleration from the time of their recruitment until they remove their uniforms for the last time? The answers to this question are as varied as the dreams and hopes of all black athletes who yearly leave the ghettos and poverty to attend predominantly white schools. Perhaps a more pertinent question would be, Why do they stay? Black athletes stay on racist white college campuses because of a driving obsession to prove themselves and because, in the black community itself, a heavy stigma attaches to the black athlete who goes to a big-name school and "fails to make the grade." If he fails academically, he is ridiculed; but if he quits, he is despised. For he has not taken advantage of "the chance that his parents didn't have." He has failed those who had faith in him. He has added validity to the contention held by whites that black people are lazy, ignorant, and quit when the going gets rough. In essence then, he is despised because he has failed to prove himself to whites. He has failed to demonstrate unequivocally that he can take it. A black athlete himself may feel guilty even about the thought of quitting. But what he doesn't realize is that he can never prove himself in the eyes of white racists—not, at any rate, as a man or even as a human being. From their perspective he is, and will always be, a nigger. From their perspective the only difference between the black man shining shoes in the ghetto and the champion black sprinter is that the shoe shine man is a nigger, while the sprinter is a fast nigger.

The black athlete on the white-dominated college campus, then, is typically exploited, abused, dehumanized, and cast aside in much the same manner as a worn basketball. His lot from that point on does not differ greatly from that of any other Afro-American. His life is riddled with insults, humiliations, and all other manner of degrading experiences. The coach will no longer call a racist landlord and request that he rent to the former black athlete because he is a "good Negro." Few white coaches work to get black athletes respectable summer jobs or their wives full-time jobs during their eligibility; one can imagine what the efforts amount to after the athletes' eligibility has expired. Then the athlete is finally and desperately on his own. Then, and only then, do most of them realize the degree to which they have been exploited for four long years. As a result, some simply give up on the society and join the armed forces. Others attempt to cling to the one commodity that they have been able to peddle, however cheaply—their athletic abilities. These pathetic, brooding, black figures can be seen playing in hunch games and city-league games in any college town. And then, when they are invited, there is always the periodic return to the old college campus to play against the new recruits and relive some of the old excitement. These former athletes seldom tell new black recruits the truth about the "big team." They avoid the issue partly because they do not wish to face humiliating questions about why they themselves stayed on for four years in the face of such conditions. Partly, it is because they want the new young recruits to look up to them as heroes, as black men who had proven themselves in athletic competition where, as they say, each man is rated according to his courage, his ability, and his winning record. But most of all, the former black athlete does not tell the new black recruit the truth because, at a time when he is trying to salvage and preserve whatever masculinity he has left, he also wants to maintain as much as possible the fantastic delusion that in some way his four college years had been everything that he had wanted them to be. For him, the future looks dismal and hostile and the present is a farce. The only phase of his life that he can control is the past, and this he attempts to do through deluding himself, by rationalizing, and by lying to the new black recruits at his alma mater.

The Black Professional Athlete

Every black amateur athlete dreams of "turning pro." In his mind it is almost as if the natural progression of things is to play high school sports, receive an athletic grant-in-aid to some big-name college, and after four years of collegiate stardom, to sign a whopping bonus contract with some professional team. Of course, for the vast majority of both black and white athletes, this "natural" progression never fully develops. But what about those black athletes who make professional teams? What is life like for the black "play-for-play" athlete?

By and large, the same humiliations and degradations that plague the athletic careers of black amateurs also haunt black professionals. All professional athletes—black and white—are officially and formally classified as property. They exist to make money for the club owners. But here the similarities between black and white professionals cease. Racism and discrimination are the exclusive lot of the black professional. And, unlike the amateur scene, practitioners of hate seldom are subtle.

In professional athletics, blacks and whites of similar abilities are paid vastly differing salaries. Whites, in a word, make more on the average than blacks. The super-stars such as Bill Russell, Wilt Chamberlain, Willie Mays, and Jimmy Brown, of course, rank as exceptions. The same pattern holds with regard to salary increases. Whites have much less difficulty obtaining raises than do blacks. So, in much the same way that the black amateur is cheated and short-changed on the educational return that he is supposed to receive as a result of his athletic exploits, the black professional is generally short-changed on the financial returns that would normally accrue from his athletic ability. This economic discrimination is compounded by the practice of excluding most black professional athletes from the thousands of dollars to be made from endorsements of commercial products. A black professional athlete might triple his income simply by recording or filming testimonials to the effect that he drinks Brand X or that he drives Brand Y. Willie Mays shows off knee-length socks and drinks Coke; Wilt Chamberlain blesses Volkswagens and cries for his Maypo; Bob Gibson futilely tosses baseballs against shatter-proof glass—but these are exceptions. As one black basketball player once put it, "You would think that we would at least be able to endorse tooth paste. We are supposedly famous for those shining 32's." He was years ahead of Madison Avenue in his thinking. How many black athletes have ever endorsed toothpaste? Emerson Boozer, Matt Snell, and ———. Every form of excuse is used to justify this discrimination. "Black men cannot endorse razor blades because their five o'clock shadow won't show up on T.V." Yet everyone knows that Oscar Robinson and Gale Sayers shave. "Black people can't speak correctly." Yet Dizzy Dean and Casey Stengel have endorsed products and they certainly are no paragons of grammar. Who could sell fried chicken better in racist America than a black man with a brown paper bag and a southern drawl? Ad men will tell you that for years an unwritten but virtually sacrosanct law of their business ran—"If a black man peddles it, regardless of who he is, whites won't buy it."

Black men are similarly discriminated against where speaking engagements are involved. Bill Russell once ran up against such an instance. An official of a social club had called the Boston Celtics' office and asked about the availability of Bob Cousy as a guest speaker. The honorarium offered was fifteen hundred dollars. Upon finding that Cousy was unavailable, they asked for Bill Russell. The offer to him was five hundred dollars, even though Russell had been the team's leading player during the past season and had been voted the league's most valuable performer.

The black pro, like his amateur counterpart, must constantly struggle for decent living accommodations. For as many black professional athletes have found out, any time a black man is south of the Arctic Circle, he is down

South as far as housing is concerned. He is even segregated when he is traveling with his team. As of fall, 1967, only one professional football team had a policy of not discriminating along racial lines in assigning athletes to rooms away from home. That team is the Green Bay Packers. But perhaps I object too much. There was a time not too long ago when black athletes were left behind on road trips, and in those days, athletes were paid by the game.

All professional athletes' problems do not originate off the field. As is the case with black amateurs, the vast majority of the irritations and abuses suffered by black professional athletes are inflicted by their own teammates and their coaches.[10]

The Black Professional Athlete as a Machine

All professional athletes, as we have said, are the property of the various white-owned professional athletic franchises throughout America. But unlike black athletes, white athletes are not reduced to a slave-with-pay status, completely devoid of human or masculine characteristics. On the field, a black athlete dare not make a mistake. If he does, the roof caves in on him. Very often he will be ridiculed and badgered by both his white teammates and his coaches. If he does well, that is what is expected of him, that's what he is being paid to do.

Fans, too, are the source of cruel, pitiless abuse. Black cats released on the playing field, choice epithets like "nigger" floating down from the stands, are all too familiar to dwell on. What, perhaps, is not so well documented is the simple fact that the same fan that pays a dollar and a half to $4.50 to get into a stadium or gymnasium to see Willie Mays or Wilt Chamberlain play would not give either one of them a drink of water if he owned the Pacific Ocean. After Chamberlain won the "Most Valuable Player" award in the National Basketball Association, he was promptly turned down when he tried to buy a home in cosmopolitan San Francisco, then the home city of his team. Willie Mays suffered a similar affront in the same city—and San Francisco has a reputation of being the most liberal city in the country. The black professional is slurred by his teammates, discriminated against by the public, humiliated and harassed by the fans, and emasculated by his coaches. And if he isn't smart, he winds up broke to boot. In this last instance, the black professional boxer comes most readily to mind.

It is common knowledge that a significant proportion of the black boxers who have held championships have ended their careers in the grips of financial disaster. Jimmy Carter, the light heavyweight champion of the late

1940's, grooms poodles for a living. Joe Walcott, a popular former heavyweight champion, is a juvenile affairs officer. Sugar Ray Robinson, perhaps the greatest boxer of all time regardless of weight category, is a dance instructor and has filed bankruptcy petitions on several occasions. "They'll never have to hold any benefits for me," Robinson often boasted. The list could go on and on. In general, few if any former black boxing champions own their own businesses, or homes, or hold executive jobs in private or public businesses. Most of them end up on welfare, in state hospitals, in prisons, or working at menial jobs. Perhaps the most pathetic image of the black athlete in all sports annals, however, is that of the beaten, scatter-brained, broke, black ex-boxer. Some of the greatest of the great have ended up as physical and emotional wrecks and/or the victims of con men, larcenous managers and promoters, gangsters, and their own ineptness at handling money. The names and achievements of these former black champions would do justice to any boxing hall of fame.

The black athlete in professional athletics is regarded by most of his white comrades and owners as a machine—a machine to be used as white men see fit and then discarded after youth has gone or injury has reduced it to the point where cost has surpassed production. Then the "machine" is simply traded in for a newer model (as is the case when an aging player is traded for a future draft choice in football or basketball) or he is just cast aside.

After their playing days are over, few black athletes become managers or coaches in the major professional leagues. Blacks virtually never receive offers to coach at any of the many colleges that yearly employ former professional athletic greats. By and large, these are rewards for meritorious service given and for expertise acquired, but are reserved for whites only.

This, then, is the lot of the black athlete who has the "fortune" to turn professional. How does he respond to these racist challenges and affronts to his dignity and manhood?

The Bitter Pill of Accommodation

Like the black slave who sang songs and hummed tunes as he toiled in the fields, the black professional athlete has, too, traditionally accommodated himself to the discrimination and racism he has encountered in professional sports. And, as was the case with the black slave, so successful has his masquerade been that many naïve, ignorant, or openly racist whites actually believed that the black professional athlete was in fact not humiliated or enraged by the treatment he received. Just as many southern "crackers" and "red necks" will swear even today that "Our darkies have always been happy—even during slavery," so in the same manner many northern and other southern whites felt for years that the professional black athlete was actually genetically predisposed to being non-violent, always was inclined to turn the other cheek. Black men, engaged in violent, aggressive, competitive sports actually were regarded as hereditarily non-violent! Moreover, black athletes were expected to be submissive. After all, they were lucky to be on the field with white folks at all, lucky to be paid for their efforts.

Black men, of course, take no more kindly to racial slanders and slurs than do men of any other race. Many a black lip has been bitten in suppressed rage, many a black head has been turned away to thwart the urge to smash every white face within reach. Many a black professional athlete has accommodated to the abuse, intolerance, and ignominy heaped upon him by whites. And why? Because it was necessary for them to survive athletically and, more particularly, financially. Taking a page from the slave's book on survival tactics, the black pro learned to tum the other cheek when his impulse was to kill, to smile when his impulse was to curse, to answer respectfully and deferentially questions that would insult a cheap call-girl. This mass withdrawal, the feigned indifference, actually was encouraged and even ordered by many professional team managers and coaches. For as many a black professional was told, white America was not yet ready to accept black men in sports, particularly black men who challenged affronts to their manhood and their very humanity. For Jackie Robinson to challenge a white pitcher who may have bean-balled him or to go after a white fan who may have spit on him or insulted him was unthinkable. Such behavior would have branded him an "uppity nigger" or at the very least with having a chip on his shoulder. White athletes could sling bats at heckling spectators or rough up a pitcher suspected of throwing a spit ball at them, but not Jackie Robinson, the infinitely patient and understanding Negro. For had he lost control of himself, he also would have lost his job and Mr. Rickey's experiment would have failed. Jackie Robinson took it—and then returned to the locker room to wonder if it really had been worth it.

Black athletes breaking into other professional sports also took it, accepted the insults and humiliations that inevitably confronted them at every step. Today, their attitudes are changing. They are less willing to accommodate, to knuckle under, but they are not yet completely free to respond as men, as the recent case of John Wooten, a lineman for the Cleveland Browns professional football team, illustrates. Wooten, in response to an instance of overt racial discrimination by some of his white teammates involving an annual team social event, angrily and publicly denounced the action as racist and patently detrimental to team unity. The white player responsible for organizing the event responded by calling Wooten overly sensitive and a trouble-maker. Both Wooten and the white player were promptly dismissed from the team. The white player was just as promptly picked up by another National Football League team, but Wooten suddenly found himself without any offers. He was picked up by an N.F.L. team only after the Olympic Committee for Human Rights held a press conference on the matter and threatened to "... disrupt by any means necessary every home game played by the Cleveland Browns until Brother John Wooten is reinstated, at full salary, into professional football." The means are justified if in the end they guarantee to black professionals the rights and privileges hitherto reserved for white professionals—to express themselves freely, to maintain their dignity, to preserve their masculinity.

The plight of the black athlete has not received the public exposure and coverage that the situation warrants. And even when the subject has been taken up, the dehumanizing, demoralizing aspects of the black athlete's experiences rarely have been emphasized. Instead, most reporters—white reporters in particular—have dwelled upon how meekly, how submissively black athletes have handled ugly situations or how gentlemanly they have been under explosive pressures. Humiliating incidents, if mentioned at all, usually are subordinated to issues such as the super-human qualities—on the field of play—of black athletes. Thus, most sports reporters have helped perpetuate the injustices that have been heaped upon black athletes. Why has this pattern become established? What motivates these priests of the sports world, the guardians of the morals and ethics of athletics? What actually has been the nature of sports reporting from the black perspective?

Notes

1. Here I make a distinction between Negro and Afro-American, or black. "Negro" here is used as being synonymous with "nigger." It carries the same negative connotations. It is felt that white racists created Negroes as they did niggers.

2. See Edwin B. Henderson, *The Negro in Sports,* The Associated Publishers, Inc., Washington, D.C., 1949.

3. *Ibid.,* pp. 18–20.

4. *Ibid.,* pp. 100–123.

5. This attitude on the part of white coaches and fans in Mid-western conferences in particular was verified by the statements made to me by several athletes during my visits to Big Ten schools as a prospective college athlete in 1958 and 1959 and also by the findings of others. For further discussion of this point, see *Ibid.,* p. 160. See

also Jack Olsen, "The Black Athlete—A Shameful Story," *Sports Illustrated Magazine,* July 1, 1968, Volume 29, No. 1, pp. 15–27.

6. For similar experiences suffered by black athletes at the University of Washington in Seattle, see Jack Olsen, "Pride and Prejudice," *Sports Illustrated Magazine,* July 8, 1968, Volume 29, No. 2, pp. 18–31.

7. For a detailed discussion of the life of the black athlete in residence and black recruits at the University of Texas at El Paso, see Jack Olsen, "In An Alien World," *Sports Illustrated Magazine,* July 15, 1968, Volume 29, No. 3, pp. 28–41.

8. For a detailed look into the N.C.A.A.-A.A.U. fracas, see "NCAA-AAU Dispute," Hearing before the Committee on Commerce United States Senate, Eighty-ninth Congress, First Session, August 16–27, 1965. United States Government Printing Office, Washington, D.C., 1965.

9. For a detailed description of how athletic receipts have helped to build one college campus, see Jack Olsen, "In An Alien World," *Sports Illustrated Magazine,* July 15, 1968, Volume 29, No. 3, pp. 28–41.

10. For a detailed discussion of the typical treatment of the black professional football player at the hands of his white coaches and teammates, see Jack Olsen, "The Anguish of a Team Divided," *Sports Illustrated Magazine,* July 29, 1968, Volume 29, No. 5, pp. 20–35.

2

Sports and the Mass Media

The mass media in America, particularly television, have done a great deal to bring about a greater awareness on the part of whites regarding the problems and life circumstances of Afro-Americans. There is little doubt but that the various desegregation drives in the South would have failed were it not for the fact that through television the grim realities of "southern hospitality" were brought into America's living rooms. It is also true that, through all forms of the mass media, many Americans have become for the first time aware of the depths of the frustrations and anxieties suffered by black people in white America. This is not to say, however, that the newspapers, television reporters, and radio announcers have been unfailingly fair to Afro-Americans. In fact, with fortunately many individual exceptions, the mass media has on frequent occasions been harsh, insensitive, and indifferent to the plight of black people. It has acted upon many occasions as an unofficial arm of the establishment in America—particularly with regard to the phrasing of news stories and the general slant of the coverage. Rather than assessing or clarifying public opinion, the press, television, and radio frequently have catered to public opinion in phrasing and presenting news reports. A network television program on urbanization fixes on ghetto "riots" as its main theme, for example. And in a white racist society this practice can be and has been extremely detrimental to the interests of black people. Most news reporters in America, however, are towers of morality, ethics, and truth when compared to this country's sports reporters.

The White Sports Reporter

The large majority of white sports reporters in America have remained aloof from the problems of racial justice and injustice in the United States. As a group, they have seemingly been singularly unmoved by the frustrations and fate of black people, even of black athletes. With few exceptions—such as Howard Cosell and Jerry Eisenberg—many white sports reporters approved or stood mute as Muhammad Ali was immorally, unethically, and illegally stripped of his heavyweight boxing title. Not a single white sports reporter to my knowledge ever bothered to mention that John Wooten, in the incident mentioned in the last chapter, had been shunted aside.

The reasons behind this insensitivity on the part of white sports reporters are many. First of all, when a white American becomes a journalist, he does not all at once become a citadel of racial and social objectivity. A racist white man who becomes a journalist becomes nothing more than a racist white journalist, in much the same sense as a racist who becomes a cop becomes merely a racist cop. Reporters come from the same racially intolerant climate responsible for the denial of the American dream to black Americans for three hundred and fifty years, and in general their racial attitudes reflect that fact. These attitudes are inevitably reflected—either through omission or commission—in their work. I am not implying that all white sports reporters are dedicated racists. What I am saying is that many are simply insensitive to the magnitude and impact of the social problems that are festering beneath their very noses. In short, many are either racist or ignorant. Or worse, they are indifferent.

Another factor that determines the present state of sports reporting in America is that sports reporters must be responsive to the desires and needs of the sports industry. This is roughly analogous to a situation where the jury is chiefly responsive to the needs and desires of the criminal. Unfortunately, in sports reporting, considerations of social justice and moral responsibility often are of secondary consideration or fall by the wayside completely. This is essentially because athletics still are regarded by most people as primarily recreational-as all fun and games. And the sports establishment would love to keep it that way. But the very word "establishment" belies the claim. Sports in America is big business, and has a significant social, economic, and political impact on both the national and international levels. To many white sports reporters, it is unthinkable that anyone would want to upset the "happy, socially peaceful, and racially tranquil world of sports" by exposing some of the racial or social injustices, the recruiting and slush fund scandals, or the naked exploitation that tarnish the fanciful picture. Even if he were so inclined, the average sports reporter would probably be dissuaded in the end by the fact that he must have access to sports figures-including coaches, managers, and owners-if he is to present anything more than box scores under his by-line. These captains of the sports industry have demonstrated upon many occasions that they can make the life of an unpopular sports reporter miserable. This in turn could affect the reporter's livelihood, because a sports reporter with no access to sports figures is of little value to any newspaper or network.

Along similar lines, many reporters are responsible, again not to society or to justice, but to their sports editors. These men, like the mass media they serve, tend to be of a conservative bent in social and political matters. Many a significant and worthwhile sports story has been "deep-sixed" because the slant of the story clashed with the political and social attitudes of the sports editor. The dictum handed down from above runs "Your job is to report the sporting news, not to initiate a crusade." So usually, the only element that detracts from the fun-and-games syndrome in most sports reporting is the sad fact that for every winner, there has to be a loser.

Public opinion studies have shown time and time again that people will not buy or read anything with which they disagree. Americans are no exception. We tend to read only what reinforces our own attitudes. Newspaper reporters, editors, and publishers are keenly aware of this tendency. They have to be. For most newspapers operate to make money. Most do, however, try to strike a happy medium between service and profit. (The results of this, in the case of sports reporting, is that significant social injustices in the athletic arena are typically slanted to minimize embarrassment to the sports establishment, are mis-stated, or simply are ignored.) For no segment of the American mass media, basically a capitalistic enterprise, is going to risk financial disaster for the sake of principle—not even when that principle is the basic right of all United States citizens to social, political, and economic justice. And in this racist society where the vast majority of American citizens see sports as primarily a recreational activity, not too many sports reporters are willing to risk their personal futures in an effort to bring those instances of injustice based upon race to the attention of the public.

Consequently, the sports world in America (on the basis of a few exploitative "breakthroughs" such as Jackie Robinson's entering white-dominated professional baseball) has been portrayed as a citadel of racial harmony and purity, and this distorted image has been fostered primarily by sports reporters and by persons who control the media through which sports news and activities are communicated to the public. The simple truth of the matter is that the sports world is not a rose flourishing in the middle of a wasteland. It is part and parcel of that wasteland, reeking of the same racism that corrupts other areas of our society.

Not all of the guilt, however, should be thrust upon the white reporter and his white employers. Negro reporters and Negro-owned media too are responsible, for they have deluded many of their own followers with fanciful myths that belie the truth about the world of sports.

The Negro Sports Reporter

Negro sports reporters in many ways reflect the same orientation—and hence the same inadequacies—as most white reporters. Access to sports personalities, economic considerations, and lack of control over what they can and cannot write are sources of constant frustration for many. But many others destroy their effectiveness completely through crippling individual and personal tendencies. Many simply are "Uncle Toms" who have been crawling and shuffling for white people for so long that they have misplaced completely all sense of responsibility and loyalty. Such persons categorically denounce any reporting about black athletes that is "social" or "political." Their chief concerns are to keep everyone happy, though deluded. Most of the time they are too busy looking the other way, keeping the boat steady, to report objectively and with conviction. Baleful the day when they find themselves in a position of having to side with black people against a racist or patronizing white establishment.

A publication, of course, is no better than the people who write for it—black or white. Many high-circulation magazines that purport to speak for America's blacks actually are more concerned with maintaining a "respectable Negro image," meaning the image that portrays black people striving as hard as possible to be like white folks. At the very best, such publications take a middle-of-the-road position when it comes to approaching and handling critical racial questions. Invariably, in their worst guise they fill their pages with irrelevant, defensive drivel about the social life of the bourgeois Negro, the latest wig crazes, the experiences of the "only big-time Negro hunting master," the only Negro airline pilot, and so forth. But when it comes to socially, politically, and economically relevant issues, most of them play it right down the middle, or worse. For they have their white advertisers to consider, who buy pages of space to advertise bleaching creams, hair straighteners, wigs, and other kinds of racially degrading paraphernalia. In the area of sports, one generally encounters innocuous stories about Willie Mays' ability with a bat or the speed of halfbacks Walt Roberts and Nolan Smith, little men in a big man's game. But seldom, if ever, has the truth about the sports industry in America and the situation of black athletes found its way to the pages of these publications. There is, however, a rising new face on the sports reporting scene—the sensitive, socially conscious black sports reporter.

The Black Sports Reporter

Unlike Negro and white reporters, the black sports reporter possesses certain qualities that tend to place him outside of, and in many instances in opposition to, the sports establishment. He differs significantly from his white and Negro colleagues in his attitude, philosophy, and guts level. And neither the designation "black" nor the differentiating qualities are necessarily directly related to skin color or racial heritage. On the contemporary sports scene, the black sports reporter is typified by Sam Skinner of San Francisco's *Sun Reporter,* Dick Edwards of the *Amsterdam News,* Bob Lipsyte of *The New York Times,* Jerry Eisenberg of the Newhouse syndicate, Pete Axthelm of *Newsweek Magazine,* and Dave Wolfe of the Life-Time syndicate. The last-mentioned four just happen to be white.

The black sports reporter writes not only about developments on the field of play, but also of those influences that might affect athletes off the field. He does not pause to consider how the sports establishment will respond to his story. If his editor refuses to print it, he may soften it, but he always presses to maintain its central focus. The black reporter is undeterred by risks to his job or personal attacks against his reputation. For him such considerations are secondary to justice, fair play, and personal character and conscience. For the black reporter actually believes in all the principles and ethical considerations supposedly fostered by sports. His fight is against those who have violated these standards and sought to profit from their debasement. It will be men of dispositions and persuasions such as these who will write the true history of American athletics.

Perpetuating the Myth of the Black Athlete

As we intimated above, many Negro and white sports reporters in America have contributed to the conditions in the athletic industry that have prompted the revolt of the black athlete. Much of their influence comes through their omission of relevant social, political, and economic conditions within sports, but they also have been active perpetrators of discrimination and unfairness. (Although Negro reporters are less guilty in this regard, many Negro reporters have succumbed to pressures from above to color and dilute their stories. In some instances they have actually authored reports more biased than those that a white reporter would write in order to show that they are "part of the team.") Many black athletes have felt at one time or another that they were discriminated against. Aside from the money, prestige is the greatest incentive to professional sports participation. In amateur athletics, it is the main incentive, along with love of the game. Prestige is typically accrued and measured by the frequency and general tone of publicity that an athlete receives in the various reporting media. Black athletes as a whole feel that many sports reporters have not always given credit where credit was due. In a pro grid game not too long ago, a black flanker had scored on an end-around play and caught passes from his quarterback and halfback for two more scores. Next day he was outraged to find out that the reporter covering the game had heaped praise on the white quarterback for his masterful game-calling while the flanker himself was barely mentioned in passing. Were this an isolated case, we could dismiss it as merely the complaint of a disgruntled glory seeker. But it is not an isolated case. It reflects a state of affairs that exists at the high-school level and extends on into professional sports. This type of reporting perpetuates the myth that black athletes are not capable of leading or inspiring a team to victory. In the minds of many spectators, particularly white spectators, black athletes are excellent performers—once they are told what to do. But for them to spark a team to victory or, through their own individual performances to raise the competitive morale of their teammates, is simply beyond them. There have been very few black quarterbacks; therefore, blacks are not intelligent enough to play quarterback, or to coach, or to manage an athletic team, so the thinking goes and the myths are continued.

3

Mounting the Revolt

The revolt of the black athlete in America as a phase of the overall black liberation movement is as legitimate as the sit-ins, the freedom rides, or any other manifestation of Afro-American efforts to gain freedom. The goals of the revolt likewise are the same as those of any other legitimate phase of the movement—equality, justice, the regaining of black dignity lost during three hundred years of abject slavery, and the attainment of the basic human and civil rights guaranteed by the United States Constitution and the concept of American democracy. It was inevitable that this revolt should develop. With struggles being waged by black people in the areas of education, housing, employment, and many others, it was only a matter of time before Afro-American athletes, too, shed their fantasies and delusions and asserted their manhood, faced the facts of their existence. The revolt was as inevitable as the rising of the sun. Within the context of the overall black liberation struggle, the revolt of the black athlete has its roots and draws its impetus from the resistance of black people in the dim and distant past to brutal oppression and callous exploitation. The movement for black liberation dates from the first moment that a black captive chose suicide rather than slavery. More recently, lynchings, murders, and beatings have served only to heighten this resistance and to give the movement new force and direction. And now, at long last, the black athlete has entered the arena as a warrior in the struggle for black dignity and freedom.

The Undercurrent of Revolt

The first publicly acknowledged indications that a revolt by black athletes was imminent came with the publication of Bill Russell's book *Go Up for Glory*. Unwilling to communicate the same old tired clichés, glittering generalities, and distortions, Russell in the book attempted to put the real sacrifices a famous black athlete endures and the rewards he receives in proper perspective. The consequences for Russell were severe. He was lambasted by the nation's leading Negro and white sports reporters; he was accused of being ungrateful and egotistical; and, of course, he was charged with the old ungrateful bit—"But look what sports, and coaches in particular, have done for you. Why, if it were not for basketball, you wouldn't be what you are today." But at least part of Russell's theme was that perhaps if it were not for him, basketball would not be all that it is today. His concern was not only for what basketball had done for him, but what white coaches and white-controlled amateur and professional basketball had done to him. This approach represented a radical departure from the fun-and-games, win-some-lose-some style of autobiography typically ghost-written for Negro and white sports stars.

Other early rumblings of revolt revolved around the issues of segregation and social discrimination. For instance, in the late fifties and middle sixties, there were numerous cases where black athletes refused to participate due to discrimination in spectator seating at athletic events or because of discriminatory practices encountered by the athletes themselves. A firm indication that the revolt was brewing appeared in 1965 when the black athletes chosen to play in the American Football League's East-West All-Star game banned together and refused to play in New Orleans, Louisiana, because several of the Afro-American stars had been refused entrance to some of the city's social clubs. As a result of the athletes' threat to boycott the event, Joe Foss, then commissioner of the league, had the game moved to another city. This incident marked the first time in modern athletic history that a sporting event had actually been changed to another site because of discrimination against Afro-American participants. And the threat succeeded largely because of the unity among the black athletes involved, a unity forged from their firm conviction that they were men and that they in fact were going to be treated as such. From that time on, the days when black athletes would play the role of unthinking machines on the field and submissive sub-humans off the field were definitely numbered.

In the realm of amateur athletics there had been rumblings too. In 1960, someone suggested to Rafer Johnson that he boycott the Olympic games of that year in order to protest the treatment of black people by the police during the civil rights protests in the South. Johnson laughed the whole notion off and walked away. But the incident reached the press and was, from that day on, irrevocably planted in the minds of black people as perhaps yet another tool to use in dramatizing the gravity of the plight of Afro-Americans in racist white America.

In 1963, Dick Gregory, black human-rights activist, politician, and comedian, attempted to organize a boycott of the Russian-American Track and Field meet by black athletes. The boycott itself failed, but the brief movement gave impetus to the whole idea of utilizing amateur athletics as a means of dramatizing racial injustice. In 1964, Gregory once again put forth the notion of boycotting an athletic event, this time the 1964 Olympic games that were to be held in Tokyo. The boycott idea once again found little support among the athletes, but Gregory did manage to get about a dozen people to picket the United States Olympic trials.

Once the black athletes who competed in the 1964 Olympic games arrived at Tokyo, there were new indications of the rising tide. There were rumblings in the American Olympic quarters centering around the treatment of the black Olympians on the U.S. team, treatment involving social activities, athletic assignments, and housing accommodations. The incidents were quickly settled, however, and the whole affair was hushed up by the press. But after the 1964 games, what hitherto had been merely rumblings turned into full-throated roars. The American press went to great ends to quiet the furor, but to no avail. At every major track meet that followed the games black athletes got together and talked about the possibility of a black boycott of the 1968 Olympics to be held in Mexico. They discussed the justifications for the move and also the possible ramifications.

Then, in the fall of 1967, two events occurred that brought all the talk and discussion to a head. First, Tommie Smith, in Tokyo for the University Games, casually commented that some black athletes would perhaps boycott the 1968 Olympics. He merely gave a simple answer to an equally simple inquiry. A Japanese sports reporter had asked, "Do I understand correctly that there is talk in America about the possibility that black American athletes may boycott the 1968 Olympic games at Mexico?" Smith answered, "Yes, this is true. Some black athletes have been discussing the possibility of boycotting the games to protest racial injustice in America." The effect of Smith's brief and noncommittal statement was immediate and its repercussions were enormous. The major American wire services and most of the country's sports pages carried the story, proclaiming that Tommie Smith had stated that there was considerable sentiment among black athletes favoring a boycott of the Olympic games in order to protest racial injustice. Of course, Smith at that time had made no such statement.

The second event was a revolt of black students and athletes at San Jose State College in California, which just happened to be the institution at which Tommie Smith and a number of other "world-class" athletes were matriculating. The significance of this event was that sixty of the seventy-two Afro-American students on campus (out of a college enrollment of 24,000) had banded together and for the first time in history utilized collegiate athletics as a lever to bring about social, academic, and political changes at an educational institution. The whole plan for the revolt originated from a discussion between me and Kenneth Noel, then a master's degree candidate at San Jose State. He, like most of the black males on the campus, was a former athlete. Most of the Afro-American males on San Jose State College's campus were former athletes who no longer had any college athletic eligibility left but who had not yet graduated for precisely the reasons discussed earlier. Ken was one of the three who had graduated after a six-year term as an undergraduate and then continued on for a Master of Arts degree. Our rather casual conversation centered around the old and the new aspects of life at San Jose State for black students. After talking for about an hour, it suddenly dawned on us that the same social and racial injustices and discrimination that had dogged our footsteps as freshmen at San Jose were still rampant on campus—racism in the fraternities and sororities, racism in housing, racism and out-and-out mistreatment in athletics, and a general lack of understanding of the problems of Afro-Americans by the college administration.

Our first move was to approach the administration. We were promptly referred to the Dean of Students, Stanley Benz. It did not take him long to make it crystal clear that, where the interest and desires of the majority whites were concerned, the necessities of black students were inconsequential. At this point, we felt that we had no alternative but to move into the public arena. So we called a rally to commence at noon on the opening day of classes for the fall, 1967, semester. We had circulars printed and placed them in all the college's departmental mail boxes. These circulars essentially served notice that the rally would be held and that the topic would be the elimination of racism at San Jose State College. We invited all faculty members and administration officials.

The rally began on time with, at first, only about thirty-five black students and about a hundred whites in attendance. The faculty was sparsely represented and only a handful of the college's more than fifty administrative officials was present. But as the rally gained momentum, more and more people came out to see what was happening. At its height, there were over 700 people in attendance, including the president of the college, Robert Clark, and representatives from various black community organizations. As soon as it was clear to us that no more people were coming, we outlined a list of demands and stated publicly what our strategy would be if our demands were not met. We, in effect, declared that we would prevent the opening football game of the season from being played by any means necessary. Most observers felt that this was an inconsistent and self-defeating strategy. Why stop the football game? Why attack the only area that had granted black people full equality?

Our strategy was basically a simple one. First of all, we recognized something that perhaps the casual observer did not—that athletics was, in fact, as racist as any of the other areas of college life. Second, we felt that we had to utilize a power lever that would bring the community and student body as well as the administration of the college into the pressure situation. We had seen, all too often, the spectacle of black people demonstrating and picketing groups, organizations, and institutions of limited concern to people in positions of power. We therefore decided to use something more central to the concerns of the entire local community structure—athletics. What activity is of more relevance to a student body than the first football game of the season? What activity is of more relevance to a college town after a long and economically drought-stricken summer than the first big game? And what is of more immediate importance to a college administration than the threat of stopping a game that had been contracted for under a $12,000 breach of contract clause and the cancellation of all future competition commitments if the game were not played? The faculty also was deeply involved in the affair, particularly the faculty of the Department of Men's Physical Education and Intercollegiate Athletics. For some of the black athletes had threatened to boycott the game if the black students were forced to try to stop it.

The rally was a success and immediately afterward an organization was formed, the United Black Students for Action. It was composed chiefly of Afro-American students, but there were also some white faculty members in advisory capacities. Negro faculty members on campus refused even to attend the rally much less help in developing an organization to implement the ultimatums and directives resulting from the rally. Our demands were as follows:

U.B.S.A. DEMANDS

We the affiliates of United Black Students for Action, hereby put forth the following *DEMANDS:*

1. Public deliberation of *all* problems and proposed solutions relevant to the situation of minority groups at SJS.

2. Publicly announced pledges from the SJS Administration that housing—*approved, unapproved, fraternities,* and *sororities* not open to ALL SJS students will not be open to *any* student. In conjunction with this pledge the following *DEMANDS* are put forth:

    a. That those housing units discriminating are to be *off limits* to all students under 21 years of age—this holds also for *fraternities* and *sororities* that refuse to desegregate.

    b. That *any* student *insisting* on living in segregated housing be *suspended* from SJS until such time as he conforms to the moral and ethical codes of this college. And this too refers to sororities and fraternities that refuse to desegregate.

3. That the highest authority (local and/or national, whichever is more appropriate) of *any* and *all* social and political organizations be required to stipulate *in writing* before November 1, 1967, that its particular organizational branch on the SJS campus is open to *all* students, and secondly, that *any* and all such organizations *not* conforming to this requisite be dissociated from the college on November 2, 1967.

4. That *any* and *all* organizations providing the above stipulation *prove* by the first day of instruction of the spring semester 1968 that they have ceased all racist discrimination at SJS.

5. That the Dept. of Intercollegiate Athletics organize and put into operation *immediately* an effective program that provides the same treatment and handling for all athletes including visiting prospective athletes.

6. That the Dept. of Intercollegiate Athletics make a public statement denouncing the racist principles upon which the present fraternity system functions and secondly, that they publicly dissociate themselves and their dept. from this system.

7. That the college administration either work to expand the 2% rule to bring underprivileged minority group members to SJS as students at least in proportion to their representation in the general population of California or that the administration utilize this 2% rule *solely* for the recruitment of minority group students.

8. That a permanent commission be set up to administer and operate a "tutorial" type program aimed at the recruitment of minority group members, and, secondly, that this commission show *proof* by the deadline admission date for the spring '68 semester that it has worked effectively to make the student minority group population at least proportionate to the representation of the various minority groups in the general population of the State of California.

9. That the administration take steps to insure that student government is representative of the total population of the college and not just an organized, affluent, but corrupt group of racists from 11th Street [Fraternity Row].

Due to the seriousness of the present situation, U.B.S.A. urges all parties empowered to act upon these DEMANDS to do so immediately.

PROFESSOR HARRY EDWARDS
Coordinator United Black Students for Action

The end result of the confrontation was that the college administration moved to meet our demands, but not before tension had reached such a pitch that the game had to be called off. Both the college administration and the faculty had visions of incidents occurring similar to the soccer riots in Argentina and Peru that had left hundreds of people dead and hundreds more maimed and injured. Adding to the chaos was the doubt surrounding the question of whether or not the black players from either team would compete, even if the game were held. There was considerable communication back and forth between the two schools involved—the University of Texas at El Paso and San Jose State. The athletic directors of both schools finally decided to adhere to President Clark's decision and not play the game at all. There had been some discussion of the possibility of playing the game on the Texas campus, but word got around that if the decision to cancel the game were ignored by the schools' athletic departments, the San Jose State College stadium would be burned to the ground. All totaled, the cancellation of the football game had cost the San Jose community and the college somewhere in the neighborhood of $100,000 in direct game receipts and anticipated business income. The black students were relatively unconcerned about the cancellation, because they had been low on the college's educational totem pole for years. What is a cancelled game relative to acquiring the basic human rights due any citizen of this country and the regaining of one's black dignity?

So we had carried the confrontation. But more than this, we had learned the use of power—the power to be gained from exploiting the white man's economic and almost religious involvement in athletics.

Meanwhile, the furor surrounding the statements allegedly made by Tommie Smith in Japan continued. White and Negro sports reporters accused him of being ungrateful, childish, and unpatriotic. He began receiving all manner of "fan mail," most of it personally insulting and racially or politically derogatory. All the paraphernalia of threat and intimidation was directed against him. Typical of the hate mail that Smith received were the following two letters written in the early Fall of 1967:

Yokohama, Japan
29 Sept. 1967

NIGGER SMITH:

I am a white infantry soldier (draftee) on R&R here in Japan from Viet Nam. Just read an article in the sports section about you. You don't know me and I don't know you, however I have heard that you are a fast nigger.

You said off the track you are just another nigger. Well, I have seen your picture and there is no argument from me on this matter. I don't really know what you niggers want, but let me tell you a few things. We have a high percentage of blacks in my company, and they are as good as the next soldier. However, they are still niggers and that is as far as it goes. We have to work together. The Army requires it.

The Army places us together. We work, eat and sleep in the same areas, but when I have any free time I want to get as far away from a nigger as I can get. The other whites feel the same way. We hope the niggers feel the same way about us. I helped carry wounded niggers to the aid man and I have seen niggers help carry whites to the aid stations. Still, in view of the above we whites do not wish to associate with niggers and we want them to feel the same towards us. The nisei is a fine American. They wish to remain to themselves, their crime rate is very low in comparison to the nigger. They have suffered as much discrimination as the next one, but they are very good Americans. You don't hear of them rioting, burning, looting, stealing, knifing.

For your information & future guidance I am sure that at least 98% of whites (north & south) (and I am from the north) feel the same way.

Don't pay any attention to those white politicians, they only want the nigger vote. Take over a couple of states, run the whites out. Just think you can have your own Governor (Carmichael) and there are many other highly qualified niggers for lesser type jobs. Oh, while you're at it don't forget welfare dept. to handle aid to those Nigger whores that have brought so many bastard niggers into this world.

Now call all your niggers together, plan your action (heroic type) and go out and snatch an elderly white lady's purse, or perhaps break a window out of an old man's shop. You know, do something real brave something you and only you niggers are capable of doing.

Just a YANKEE giving you the straight poop

10/25/67
Mr. Tommie Smith
San Jose State College
San Jose, California

DEAR TRAITOR,

You are not only a disgrace to your College, your Country . . . but to yourself!
Please don't try to win a place on the Olympic Team. I'd rather have our
Country finish last, without you, than first with you.

Yours truly,

Dismayed by the personal attacks, Smith made an appointment to discuss
the whole matter with me. He was taking my course in race relations at the
time. At this meeting, the letters and sports reports were discussed along with
the boycott possibilities. Mention was also made of the resolution that had
been passed at the 1967 National Conference on Black Power that had been
held in rebellion-torn Newark, New Jersey. Out of our discussion came the
decision to check the attitudes of other world-class athletes toward a revolt
of Afro-American athletes over the problems facing black athletes and the
black community in general. A number of black athletes were contacted—
John Carlos, Lee Evans, Lew Alcindor, Otis Burrell, Mike Warren, and Lucius
Allen, among others. We found through our inquiries that not only track and
field athletes, but also Afro-Americans engaged in other athletic activities
had given a great deal of serious thought to the idea of boycotting the 1968
Olympic games in order to dramatize racial injustice in America. Indeed,
some had even committed themselves to such a sacrifice as early as the fall
of 1967. On the basis of this support, we began to mobilize.

The first step was to form an organization that could plan and map strategy for the revolt. To this end, on October 7, 1967, a meeting was held at my
home. In attendance were George Washington Ware, field worker for the
Student Non-Violent Coordinating Committee; Tommie Smith, who at the
time held eleven world track records; Ken Noel, the co-planner of the black
student revolt at San Jose State College; Jimmy Garrett, an excellent organizer
and chairman of the Black Student Union at San Francisco State College; and
Bob Hoover, black political activist and counselor at San Mateo Junior College. Out of this meeting came the Olympic Committee for Human Rights.
It was decided also that the best way to initiate the mobilization was to call
for a workshop and invite as many black athletes as possible to attend. The
task of this workshop would be to spell out formally the direction that the
Olympic boycott phase of the revolt would take. The segment of the revolt

dealing specifically with mobilization to boycott the Olympic games was designated The Olympic Project for Human Rights. Other plans also were proposed—such as the organization of rebellions on various college campuses, the boycotting of racist athletic clubs, and so forth—but our immediate concern was the Olympic Project for Human Rights.

The site chosen for the proposed workshop was the Los Angeles Black Youth Conference, which had as its theme "Liberation is coming from a black thing." This conference, like the original resolution proposing an Afro-American boycott of the Olympic games, issued from the actions and resolutions of the 1967 National Conference on Black Power. This fact, along with the wish of the organizers of the mobilization to get as many segments of the black community involved in the revolt as possible, made the Black Youth Conference a "national" base from which to launch the rebellion. The dates for the conference were November 22 and 23. The time lapse between the organizational meeting and the scheduled date of the Olympic boycott workshop meeting allowed the organizers over a month to get relevant information to as many black athletes as possible and also to urge them to attend.

The first problem confronting the Olympic Committee for Human Rights was financial. There was an immediate need for funds to finance the printing and mailing of information to the athletes. The only source of such funds was my salary as instructor of sociology at San Jose State. Students who had been active in the black student revolt at San Jose State volunteered their time and clerical help and often worked long hours and far into the night in an effort to locate and get information to as many black athletes as possible. We were only partly successful. The main roadblock we encountered in trying to contact the athletes was the common practice at many white-dominated athletic departments of funneling mail for athletes through their respective coaches and not delivering it directly to the athletes themselves. Many coaches at various universities, colleges, and junior colleges throughout the country, for instance, open mail sent to athletes—black athletes in particular. Many athletes, we later discovered, never received the mailings we sent them. But in any event, the movement was on to utilize, for black political ends, the fact of America's dependence upon black athletic talent in order to maintain its competitive edge over other countries in the international summer Olympic games.

The Black Youth Conference

The meeting and agenda of the Black Youth Conference had been well publicized. Workshops were scheduled on the rights of black people under the provisions of the Selective Service Act, the role of black women in the black liberation struggle, the organization of communications networks between black political organizations, and so forth. Also scheduled was a keynote address by James Forman, Director of International Relations for the Student Non-Violent Coordinating Committee. But the event that drew the most attention and interest was the scheduled workshop on the proposed black boycott of the Olympic games. Negro and white reporters hovered about the buildings and facilities of the Second Baptist Church where the conference was held, attempting to obtain information on the number of athletes scheduled to attend, the exact room in which the workshop would be held, and whether or not the press would by allowed to attend the meeting. We succeeded in maintaining the secrecy of the proceedings, however. For black people had long since learned that the less information about Afro-American intentions and plans released to white and Negro representatives of the mass media, the better off black people were. Black newsmen were permitted to attend the sessions, although they were not allowed to bring tape recorders, paper and pencils, or cameras into the' meetings with them. It was decided by the three-man Olympic Committee for Human Rights that because black people did not control to any significant degree any form of the mass media, we would have to guard against "the man's" means of communication being used to our disadvantage. Accordingly, we made up our minds to make the press dependent upon our reports and interpretations of what went on in the workshop rather than permitting them to observe the activities of the workshop at first hand and thus possibly influencing the proceedings by the very fact of their presence.

The conference started on time, as did the Olympic boycott workshop. In attendance were Tommie Smith, Otis Burrell, Lew Alcindor, Lee Evans, and other world-class athletes who were almost certain to make the 1968 United States Olympic team if they chose to enter the trials. Also present was a host of less famous athletes from both the college and high school levels.

By way of starting the proceedings, I introduced myself as chairman of the workshop and then gave a brief half hour résumé of the factors prompting consideration of a proposed boycott of the games. The racist, political, and economic aspects of athletics in America were set forth and then the workshop was thrown open to discussion from the floor. First to speak was Tommie Smith. Briefly, in a five-minute speech, he outlined his reasons for supporting the move to boycott the games. Lee Evans spoke next in a similar vein. Then Otis Burrell took the floor to state his unequivocal support of the proposed boycott. But perhaps the most moving and dynamic statements in behalf of the boycott were those made by Lew Alcindor. His brief and memorable words drew a five-minute ovation from the more than 200 persons who packed the upstairs Sunday School room of the church. "Everybody knows me," big Lew began. "I'm the big basketball star, the weekend hero, everybody's all-American. Well, last summer I was almost killed by a racist cop shooting at a black cat in Harlem. He was shooting on the street—where masses of black people were standing around or just taking a walk. But he didn't care. After all we were just niggers. I found out last summer that we don't catch hell because we aren't basketball stars or because we don't have money. We catch hell because we are black. Somewhere each of us has got to make a stand against this kind of thing. This is how I take my stand—using what I have. And I take my stand here."

But not all those attending approved of the direction and momentum that the discussion was taking. "Deacon" Dan Towler, a former professional football player for the Los Angeles Rams, was the first to voice total opposition to the plan. He pointed out how much sports had done for Negroes and how great a privilege it was for a Negro to compete for America. A chorus of boos greeted his words. Undeterred, he continued, this time attacking the athletes who had previously spoken as being unintelligent and gullible. Finally, as his remarks began to draw threats from the audience, he was shouted down. Other Negroes who had obviously come to try to dissuade the athletes from supporting the movement left the meeting after witnessing the fate of the "Deacon."

At the close of the discussion, a commotion broke out outside the church. An integrated group of pro-communist leftists had attempted to disrupt the meetings and orderly processes of the conference in an effort to take over the movement. They were driven off and some shots were fired, ostensibly by members of the security force in charge of policing the conference, although it was never established conclusively where they came from. The disruption had occurred at a very inopportune time for us inside the church, for we were just about to vote on the proposed boycott and the suggested means of mobilization that had been presented within the context of the floor discussions. Rather than the individual voice vote that we had planned to use, we had to settle for a mass "Yea-Nay" vote, à la the 1968 Democratic and Republican conventions, because of the confusion outside. Only three of the more than two hundred persons in attendance responded with a "Nay," and not one of these was an athlete. After the vote, the workshop was formally and quickly adjourned. The Olympic Committee for Human Rights had gotten the endorsement that it sought and the first step in the mobilization was complete.

As I left the church, Negro and white reporters gathered around. No statement was issued to them. A prior arrangement had been made with a black sports reporter from a Los Angeles paper to record the first official release concerning the decisions reached during the course of the workshop. The statement was brief and lasted only about five minutes. After making the statement, which contained none of the names of the athletes attending the conference, I quickly left Los Angeles to attend the National Conference of Student Body Governments being held in San Francisco. As a result of my initiating the black student revolt on the San Jose State campus, I had been asked to address the conference on the topic "Student Government Responsibility and the Crisis in Race Relations on American College Campuses." Negro and white press reporters had gotten wind of the impending engagement and were waiting at the Sheraton Palace Hotel, site of the conference. A rough statement on the results of the Olympic boycott workshop was hastily prepared and, after giving my talk, I read the statement to the ninety reporters present. Copies of the statement were then passed out to them. The Statement read as follows:

RESOLUTION DRAFTED AT BLACK YOUTH
CONFERENCE, LOS ANGELES NOV. 22, 1967
OLYMPIC BOYCOTT,
HARRY EDWARDS: CHAIRMAN

Whereas: The United States has failed to use its power—governmental or economic—to effectively alleviate the problems of 22 million black people in this country,

Whereas the United States has openly and flagrantly carried out and endorsed acts which have operated—by plan—to the detriment of black people in this country,

Whereas the United States has engaged in acts which constitute a direct affront and humiliation to the basic humanity of black people in this society,

Whereas the United States has hypocritically put itself up as the leader of the Free World while right here in this country we have 22 million black people catching more hell than anyone in any communist country ever dreamed of,

Whereas the United States government has acted in complicity with other racist elements of this society to strip black athletes of their prestige and athletic status based upon mere racist whim,

Resolved: Black men and women athletes at a Black Youth Conference held in Los Angeles on the 22nd of November, 1967, have unanimously voted to fully endorse and participate in a boycott of the Olympic Games in 1968.

New York Athletic Club
Whereas the NYAC has worked effectively and meticulously to maintain within its ranks only white Christians,
Whereas the NYAC has had neither an interest in nor any use for black athletes or athletes of various religious backgrounds until that period of time just prior to the NYAC indoor meet,
Whereas the NYAC has used black athletes in particular to make this meet a financial success for decades,
Black track and field athletes have unanimously voted to boycott anything even remotely connected with the NYAC.
South Africa
Whereas the United States has seen fit to allow the travel within the political borders of this country of persons from countries where black people can neither enter nor escape the slavery thereof,
And whereby the presence of these foreign persons, their participation in any aspect of social, political, or economic activity in this country, and the complicity with which the United States functions in conjunction with such persons all represent an affront to the basic humanity of black people in this country,
Black men and women athletes have voted unanimously to boycott any meet in which participants from two countries in particular might be in participation.
These countries are: 1. South Africa 2. Southern Rhodesia

The immediate repercussions of the decisions reached at the Black Youth Conference were predictable. The evening newspapers and television and radio news and sports shows clearly registered the impact the resolutions had had on the white establishment and its Negro flunkies. Typical of the newspaper headlines were the following:

Los Angeles Herald Tribune:

NEGROES VOTE UNANIMOUSLY TO
BOYCOTT OLYMPICS

New York Daily News:

MOB RULE IN LOS ANGELES: 200 NEGROES VOTE
UNANIMOUSLY TO BOYCOTT GAMES

Los Angeles Times:

NEGRO GROUP VOTES TO BOYCOTT '68 OLYMPICS

During the conference a white reporter intimated in his column that he thought that he had recognized Otis Burrell as one of the black athletes who had participated in the boycott workshop. Burrell was immediately notified that the Christmas vacation job that had been his for three years would be given to someone else. Lew Alcindor was persecuted and vilified for participating in the workshop. More hate mail poured in on Tommie Smith, and his life—along with the lives of Lee Evans, Ken Noel, and my own—were repeatedly threatened by anonymous letter writers and phone callers.

Cries of "It won't last" and "The Negro athlete loves to compete too much to become party to such an impossible rebellion" filled the press. They were totally wrong on the first count and almost totally wrong on the second. The first miscalculation by the press and the sports establishment stemmed from their failure to recognize that they were no longer dealing with the "Negro" athlete of the past. Confronting them now was the new black athlete and a new generation of Afro-Americans. Second, to make sure that the movement would last, the Olympic Committee set about devising a set of intermediate goals to maintain the momentum of the movement until the Olympics arrived in October 1968, a period covering almost a year. We were well aware that time alone might eclipse the start we had made in Los Angeles unless we could manage to keep news of our activities before the public. To this end, we sought outside help and advice.

We decided that the best person to turn to for advice and direction was Louis Lomax, a veteran civil rights activist and a personal friend of mine. On November 25, 1967, I flew to Los Angeles from San Jose to discuss with Lomax the possible alternative steps that could best serve the ends we sought. Over coffee in Lomax' kitchen we drew up a list of six demands on which we would focus until the following October. Next, we decided to bring as many recognized leaders as possible into the movement and by so doing to strengthen the forces behind the Olympic Project for Human Rights. The leaders contacted were the late Rev. Dr. Martin Luther King, Jr., President of the Southern Christian Leadership Conference, and Floyd McKissick, Director of the Congress of Racial Equality. An attempt was made to contact H. Rap Brown, but to no avail. Leaders of other organizations that we regarded as primarily "Negro oriented," such as the Urban League and National Association for the Advancement of Colored People, we purposely avoided. Arrangements were made to hold a meeting in New York City at which time the six demands would be presented to the public. The meeting was held on December 15, 1967, in the conference room of New York City's Americana Hotel. With me at the meeting were Lomax, McKissick, and Dr. King, as well as a host of other less prominent supporters. Each of the leaders present delivered a short statement of support for the movement. Perhaps the most noteworthy was

Dr. King's, in which he stated that perhaps the condition of race relations in the United States today demanded a total boycott of the Olympic games by black people for little else in the way of non-violent protest was left to them. I then presented the list of demands. They were:

1. Restoration of Muhammad Ali's title and right to box in this country.
2. Removal of the anti-semitic and anti-black personality Avery Brundage from his post as Chairman of the International Olympic Committee.
3. Curtailment of participation of all-white teams and individuals from the Union of South Africa and Southern Rhodesia in all United States and Olympic Athletic events.
4. The addition of at least two black coaches to the men's track and field coaching staff appointed to coach the 1968 United States Olympic team. (Stanley V. Wright is a member of the coaching team but he is a devout Negro and therefore is unacceptable.)
5. The appointment of at least two black people to policy making positions on the United States Olympic Committee.
6. The complete desegregation of the bigot dominated and racist New York Athletic Club.

Prior to this press conference, copies of the demands were sent to as many black athletes as could be located. How many actually knew of them prior to the press release, however, is unknown. After the press conference, we retired to Lomax' suite to discuss other possible strategies that might be employed to keep the ball rolling. Dr. King suggested that an information booklet be sent to all those athletes who allegedly were skeptical of the social or political relevance of the Olympic Project for Human Rights. Also, each person at the press conference agreed to act in an unofficial advisory capacity to the movement and Lomax, McKissick, and Dr. King agreed to become formal advisors. The booklet that Dr. King suggested be sent to the unconvinced or wavering black athletes explained why it had been put together, outlined the goals of the proposed boycott and set forth the justifications for such a step, and repeated and elaborated on the six demands. Major excerpts from the booklet are reprinted in Appendix E.

Because of the surprising momentum and support the movement had generated, the sports establishment and its chief ally, the press, stepped up their efforts to kill the project. Former Negro athletes, hitherto silent and obscure, suddenly became mainstays on the sports club and sports banquet circuits. Names such as Jesse Owens, Ralph Metcalf, and Rafer Johnson appeared daily in the sports pages of major newspapers throughout the country. Here is a prime example of how the establishment uses Negroes to hinder the liberation efforts of black people. These people were suddenly heroes to the white establishment. Their value to the establishment went up in direct proportion to the increasing success of our efforts. Jesse Owens' tax troubles were conveniently forgotten by the establishment. Granted a half hour of prime nationwide television time, Owens re-emphasized his ridiculously naïve belief in the sanctity of athletics and spoke warmly about the friendships and understanding brought about between blacks and whites through sports.

During all this time Owens seemed to feel that the boycotters were more interested in publicity than in human rights. But what really troubled him was the thought that anyone would dare launch a direct attack against such a hallowed institution as the Olympic games in particular and sports in general. All the fine young Negroes who would be competing in Mexico City, he believed, would help erase misunderstanding between the races. Sports was the one area where Negroes had been accepted on a par with whites and top-ranking Negro athletes had always been looked up to and respected by young and old of both races. A boycott, he feared, would tear down everything that had been accomplished and do irreparable damage to the cause of the Negro in America.

Nor was Owens about to tolerate any criticism of Avery Brundage. As far as he knew, Owens pointed out, Brundage always had been fair and cordial toward him. All questions had elicited frank, straight answers. Owens conceded that Brundage was not a warm, outgoing person, but the fact that he had held together the Olympics for so long set him apart and rendered him virtually immune from suspicion and criticism.

Owens claims no knowledge of Brundage's ownership of the Montecito Country Club in Santa Barbara, California. (Brundage has been accused by the O.C.H.R. of owning and running the racially exclusive club.) Owens explained that Brundage could not be charged with discrimination even if he did own the club and even if the club did exclude all Jews and Negroes from membership. His reasoning? Brundage probably had someone else run the club for him and thus was free of all blame.

It is hard to believe that Owens could have been so gullible and misinformed. His comments elicited rejoinders from a number of athletes supporting the Olympic Project for Human Rights. John Carlos, the present holder of the world record in the 200-meter dash, could not understand how Owens could say that athletic competition brought blacks and whites closer when Owens himself, the great hero of the 1936 Olympic games, was a victim of white racism in his own country. Furthermore, the German supposedly befriended by Owens during the 1936 games promptly became a member of the anti-semitic, white supremacy Nazi party in Germany and later was killed in Europe fighting for Hitler's dream of world domination.

Tommie Smith also questioned the value of sports as a disseminator of virtue and good will. Smith felt that if sports and the Olympic games in particular did so much to create good will between the races, then as the proportion of black people participating in the Olympic games for the U.S. rose, there should, by Owens' argument, be a commensurate rise in racial harmony in America. Such has not been the case. More and more black people have been participating in Olympic games for the United States, yet race relations in America are worse today than at any other time since slavery. If one were to act upon the contentions of the sports establishment and its Negro flunkies, then the logical thing to do in order to decrease conflict between the races would be for all blacks to withdraw from sports entirely. But of course, the whole argument is spurious. It was dragged out only because the authority and legitimacy of a thoroughly frightened and defensive sports establishment were being challenged.

Others also got into the act. Rafer Johnson, then working for a Los Angeles television station, tried to set up a group called the "Committee for the Perpetuation of Friendship Through Sports" as another means of short-stopping the revolt. It never got off the ground.

Johnson also made his feelings and position clear on a number of other occasions when discussing the proposed boycott. He contended that the question of participating in the games was an individual matter, just as anyone who won a place on the team had to win it on his individual efforts and merit. If someone wanted to pull out, that was his business. But he couldn't see a group withdrawing, no matter what they were protesting against, even if they were objecting to discrimination and other offenses against a minority group. The relevancy of the boycott escaped him. A boycott, he felt, would not bring better housing for the Negro nor assure his acceptance in society nor increase understanding between the races, so therefore it was not justified. He too, like Owens, parroted the old line about sports being the great equalizer and that Negroes, along with everyone else, should be proud to participate in the games and to give 100 per cent of themselves for team and country. At one point Johnson also questioned my motives and insinuated that my part in the boycott was merely the disgruntled response of an outsider who had failed to qualify for the team. Anyone who purported to speak for Negro Olympians should be an athlete who has competed in the games and knew first-hand what the situation was, he felt. If the boycott had been conceived and launched by a former Olympic athlete or group of Olympic athletes he might be inclined to take it more seriously, he once admitted. At one point he compared what I was trying to do with a hypothetical situation in which he depicted himself as trying to convince Dr. Martin Luther King to turn down the Nobel Prize in order to spotlight the plight of the Negro in America. Neither situation, Johnson affirmed, made much sense as far as he could see. Wait, he advised on one occasion, until we are sure that Negroes will make the team. He admitted that such an eventuality was extremely unlikely, but still maintained that the entire project should be held in abeyance until we were sure.

What Johnson failed to realize was that neither a Nobel Prize nor an Olympics medal elevates a black person to human status in America. Muhammad Ali was denied service in a restaurant in his home town of Louisville, Kentucky, right after the 1964 Olympic games—and at the time his gold medal actually was hanging around his neck. Dr. King, Nobel Peace Prize winner and world-renowned apostle of non-violence, was violently shot down in his own country. The only reason why Rafer Johnson has not been attacked is that he has taken no stand in support of liberation for black people.

Regardless of the opposition, notwithstanding its source, the demands had been issued and the activities geared toward enforcing those demands would continue. In order to justify the committee's position and their own support, each black athlete issued a personal statement explaining why he supported the demands and the Olympic Project for Human Rights. The statement issued by Tommie Smith was typical of these position papers:

> I have received many letters and phone calls about my decision to support the Olympic Project for Human Rights. I have tried to explain this at a number of speaking engagements. I will do this again here.
>
> It is true that I want to participate in the Olympics and also in all of the other track meets scheduled for next year. But I also recognize the political and social implication of some black people participating for a country in which the vast majority of black people suffer from unthinkable discrimination and racism. I therefore feel that it is my obligation as a black man to do whatever is necessary, by any means necessary, to aid my people in obtaining the freedom that we all seek. If I can open a single door that might lead in the direction of freedom for my people, then I feel that I must open that door. I am not only willing to give up an opportunity to participate in the Olympics, but I am also willing to give up my life if there is even a chance that it will serve to dramatize, much less solve, the problems faced by my people.
>
> TOMMIE SMITH
> San Jose State College

Smith's letter only sparked more derogatory comments from the white press. Jim Murray of the *Los Angeles Times* compared him to a "child who holds his breath to make his parents feel bad," and accused the author of being close to Hitler in his political and social philosophy. Of course, this kind of response was to be expected. For anytime a warrior is decorated or praised by his enemy, he is obviously not fighting the right enemy. Smith and the other athletes simply shrugged off the insults.

After the December 15 meeting in New York City, the Olympic Committee for Human Rights began to organize for the first test of its demands and resolutions. The New York Athletic Club's indoor track meet was scheduled for February. At the Black Youth Conference, a resolution had been passed to boycott this meet. Although many athletes had been contacted about the proposed boycott, the committee still had its work cut out for it. For facing the California-based committee was the task of mounting a boycott and demonstration to be held 3,000 miles away—and this with no available funds other than my salary and no means of communicating with the East coast other than by telephone. Offers of money usually were tied to requests for a degree of control over the movement. There was also the attraction of the new Madison Square Garden. This was to be the first big athletic event to be held in the new arena, and many athletes wanted to take part.

The New York Athletic Club Boycott

The central aim of the N.Y.A.C. boycott was not to force the club to integrate black people into its segregated organizational structure, but rather to regain some of the dignity that black athletes had compromised over several decades by participating for a club that would not even allow a black person to shower in its facilities. The philosophy underlying the move was simply this. If black athletes are acceptable enough to make the N.Y.A.C. track meet a success each year, then black athletes are also due the human respect and consideration granted other athletes competing in the meet. The onset of the New York Athletic Club boycott marked the end of an age when Afro-American athletes would compromise black dignity for a watch, a television set, a trophy, or merely the love of competition.

The organization of the N.Y.A.C. boycott formally began with a series of telephone contacts between the Olympic Committee for Human Rights and a number of New York City-based organizations and individuals. Some of the individuals contacted were Omar Ahmad, co-chairman of the 1966 Black Power Conference; H. Rap Brown, chairman of S.N.C.C.; Jay Cooper, chairman of the Columbia University Black American Law Students Association. It was these persons, working through their various organizations, who took on the major responsibility of mobilizing black people to demonstrate and picket the meet. Marshall Brown, a beautiful black man who also happened to be an A.A.U. official, took on the responsibility of contacting all the black athletes on the East coast. He also got in touch with many of the schools and clubs that had traditionally participated in the meet and enlightened them about the policies of the N.Y.A.C. and the goals of the boycott. It fell to the committee to ensure adequate publicity for the boycott, to contact West coast and Midwest based athletes, and to press the N.Y.A.C. board of directors to justify, explain, or clarify their policies. The committee set itself one last task—to attract international attention to the boycott. Our task was made easier by the fact that a number of foreign teams then were touring America's indoor track meet circuit. We decided to center our efforts on the Russian National track team. A telegram was sent to the Russian Embassy in Washington, D.C., to the effect that the N.Y.A.C. track meet would be picketed by black people protesting the racist exploitation of Afro-Americans by the sports establishment in America in general and the directors of the N.Y.A.C. in particular. The Russian Ambassador was informed that the Olympic Committee for Human Rights could not guarantee the safety of Russian athletes attempting to cross the N.Y.A.C. picketline. We also intimated that we hoped that the Russians would support our efforts.

The day before the meet was to be held, an unofficial tally of the schools and athletes that had withdrawn showed that the meet was headed for disaster. The club had had to cancel its entire high school division of competition because of mass withdrawals. Only nine Negro athletes were still on the roster of competitors. A representative of the U.S. Secretary of Defense had sent a telegram to the N.Y.A.C. advising its board of directors that none of the military academies would be permitted to compete. Many college teams that had traditionally competed in the meet had also pulled out. Later that evening, a press conference was held in the office of Jessie Gray, the leader of a New York City rent strike against slum lords. With me at the conference were H. Rap Brown, Ray Ennis of CORE, Omar Ahmad, and a host of other East coast organizers and 'supporters of the boycott.

The following press release was issued:

> We are here to finalize the first step in our drive to realize a boycott of the Olympic Games by Black Athletes.
> The intransigence of the N.Y.A.C. in its refusal to even admit the problem of racism in its ranks, much less take steps to rectify it, is, we believe, indica-

tive of the present demeanor of White America toward taking real steps to deal with racism in this society.

We see, through this protest, that it isn't just racist *individuals* we are up against. It's a racist conspiracy involving many of the would-be great institutions of the Society.

In this case, we are confronted not only with racism in the N.Y.A.C., but also a racist conspiracy involving the A.A.U. and the Directors and Supervisors of Madison Square Garden.

The A.A.U. has paid (partially or in total) for the transportation, aid, and other expenses of Foreign Athletes brought in by the N.Y.A.C. at the last minute in an effort to break this protest. The A.A.U. has given its approval of this meet, as it has given its approval to all past meets, even though it has been well known for years that the N.Y.A.C. was a White racist organization.

The supervisors of Madison Square Garden have allowed the N.Y.A.C. to hold its racist functions in the facility for years and thus has perpetuated a racist function in this society.

We are taking a number of steps of our own to rectify this situation.

(1) We are initiating a number of legal actions against the N.Y.A.C.

(2) We shall picket what remnants of a track meet the N.Y.A.C. may be able to put together.

(3) We shall white-list any and all universities and colleges taking part in the N.Y.A.C. function and we shall move on them accordingly.

On the night of February 15, 1968, the boycott went off as scheduled. Attendance was down by 50% over previous years. The times and distances registered in various events were mediocre at best. The college and club representation was minimal and, to top it all off, the Russian National Team canceled its scheduled participation in the meet at the last minute "in order to avoid interference in a conflict involving the internal integrity of the United States." Typical of the headlines following the boycott was the following from the *Palo Alto Times* (California):

"N.Y.A.C. MEET FLOPS: BOYCOTT DOESN'T"

Even *Time* magazine admitted that the boycott had been at least partially successful, although it added that its success could be traced to intimidation and coercion by the Olympic Committee for Human Rights and its associates. *Time* obviously was referring to reports attributed to white coaches that their athletes were not attending the meet because of threats they had received. However, upon checking with athletes who were supposedly threatened, such as John Thomas and others, the accusations were not confirmed.

Actually, many black athletes had already made up their minds not to attend the N.Y.A.C. meet even before mobilization for the boycott had begun. To get them to change their minds, N.Y.A.C. officials desperately resorted to a variety of measures to salvage what they could from the situation. But all their efforts could not shake the black boycotters' resolve. For black dignity was no longer for sale at any price. The auction block was down.

Many Caucasian athletes, to their everlasting credit, sided with the black athletes. Men like Dave Patrick of Villanova refused to compromise their principles and compete. But it is unlikely that the white athletes would have taken such a stand if Afro-American athletes had not initiated the action.

Many white athletes and some white-dominated schools did participate however. Those schools and those athletes who decided to enter did so ostensibly because they "didn't want to be portrayed as [supporters] of Rap Brown and Harry Edwards." White-dominated schools, such as the University of Texas at El Paso, reportedly made black athletes participate in the meet under penalty of losing their athletic grants-in-aid. Such coercion merely lent impetus to the strategy of using athletics as a power lever for bringing about political and social changes on the nation's campuses. The first step in this direction was taken by the Olympic Committee for Human Rights when it white-listed a group of universities and began to organize to help black students and athletes enrolled at white-dominated schools to gain a greater voice in determining the curriculum content and treatment of Afro-Americans on their various campuses.

The black athletes and the Olympic Committee for Human Rights had passed the first serious challenge to their goals and demands. The next challenge was to go to the white-listed colleges.

4

Feeding the Flame

Confrontation on the Campus

The successful boycott of the N.Y.A.C. fueled further attacks on the committee and its supporters. Questions such as the following were asked: "What was gained through the N.Y.A.C. boycott and what will be gained through boycotting the '68 Olympic Games?" "Have more black people been fed as a result of boycotting the N.Y.A.C.?" "Will a boycott of the Olympic Games result in better housing or fewer rats for black people?" In reply to these questions, I wrote the following article for the late *Saturday Evening Post*:

> John Carlos, of Harlem, a world-class sprinter, phoned me from East Texas State College a few weeks ago. "I'm quitting school," he said. "Can't take the heat here, man. Don't like the snubs, the restricted housing, the way they mistreat my wife, the whole phony deal." To my question, "John Carlos, what will you do now?"—he said: "Join a freedom movement somewhere, maybe." I told him, "Listen, Quick Cat, make your sociological break count. Come to San Jose State and work with the brothers to end all of this racist bull. Join us in this movement to liberate black people through the use of athletics."
>
> He joined. Top black athletes of the country are mobilizing . . ., risking their scholarships, school eligibility, and families' welfare, . . . to express what they should have stood for years ago: you cannot, and maintain a claim to manhood, run, hurdle, jump, throw punches, lift weights, or stuff balls into baskets in the name of the American nation when your people are headed for perdition. Grinning black faces atop an Olympic victory stand only mock kids smothering in slums, old women dying of malnutrition, bombed-out churches, the bodies strewn along the path of riot. "How can you strain and

sweat," I challenged Tommie Smith, . . . who is known as the world's fastest human, "for the ideological merchandisers who promote the Olympic Games? They tell the world that the Games are free of discrimination, a wonderful example of fair play to everyone. And they use big, box-office performers like you to make the U.S. a big part of that scene. Meanwhile, neglect kills off your people faster than you can sprint. Mothers, dads, brothers, relatives of the same black guys who compete in the Olympics get no anthems or medals—they're where they started, at the bottom, hopeless, with a gun or club waiting when they object."

Tommie Smith slept four in a straw bed as a boy; he often shared one school lunch with five other little Smiths. His parents, Jim and Dora, were shacktown migrants, picking California cotton for 90 cents an hour. Tom Smith joined the boycott.

Nothing on the human rights front has caused more high-level shock and arm-flapping than the proposed walk-out. . . . Mass refusal to understand [its] meaning has followed. The most spotlighted basketball player of the day, Lew Alcindor of UCLA, can say (as he recently did), "Knowing I live in a racist country, I must react in some way—and this boycott is my way, my obligation to all Afro-Americans." In taking his stand, Alcindor suffers the charge that he is a fool, ingrate, and non-patriot. Up front among the critics are California Governor Ronald Reagan, Roy Wilkins, the docile NAACP spokesman, and Olympic president Avery Brundage, who sized up the nonstarters as a weird lot who illogically attack an ancient, laurel-wreathed institution, nobly conceived in the principle of treating all comers alike. Self-defeatists, we are led by "black Hitlers" and "Muslim hate-mongers" who would sabotage an arena overrunning with the very good will and status-making opportunity we need most.

That's officialese for: "Sports and social chaos are strangers; they are so entirely separate that what you do for your country, on the public stage, has nothing to do with what your country does to your beloved and to you."

To accord a carnival of fun-and-games a sanctity setting it apart from the misery inflicted upon one U.S. segment—one which supplies the carnival with much of its manpower—is 200 per cent hypocritical. For a number of reasons. Of nearly 40 nationally-uniformed youths who will participate in the next Olympics, all are part of steaks-and-gravy America—all except approximately one-seventh of that number. No matter how many tapes they break, black Olympians will revert, after the cheering and as they move out in life, to their old, inherited status. Stop-watches, for them, do just that—they stop. And with the growth of understanding by these exploited cats that their good time lasts only as long as the juice flows in their legs and arms has come some soul-searching. The Olympic Project for Human Rights meetings are filled with testimonials by such old pros as Bill Russell, former Games gold-medal winner and coach of the Boston Celtics. "Except for a few hundred favored big stars," he tells us, "blacks lead sports leagues all over the country in everything except hotel accommodations and other equal rights. When they can't lead anymore, sports biz and employers generally don't know they even exist. He who voluntarily helps the political propaganda aims of a society calling itself 'free' is a chump."

But far more sweepingly, such a volunteer is a cop-out, a traitor to his race. I am a college sociology teacher, age 25. Before I gave up games and went academic, I set a national junior college discus throw record of nearly 180 feet and track coaches fell all over me, as a likely internationalist. One Western coach called me (I'm 6-feet-8, 250 pounds), "a terrific animal"—without a moment's concern that I overheard his description. But discus-tossing in no way dimmed my memory of the south side of East St. Louis, Illinois, where I grew up. Like everyone else, the Edwards family lived on beans and paste and watched neighbor kids freeze to death. We used an outhouse which finally collapsed in the hold and drank boiled drainage-ditch water. Young mothers just *flew out* of the place. My own mother abandoned us when I was eight years old, later showing up with 86 stitches in her body after a street brawl. Cops jailed me for juvenile offenses. They jailed me when I was innocent. A brother of mine, today, serves 25-years-to-life in the Iowa State Penitentiary. Intelligent hearthside conversation didn't exist—intergroup allegiance and family discipline died under the weight of poverty. I was the first boy from my area to graduate from high school. Until I was 17 I had never held a meaningful conversation with a white adult and until shortly before that I was unaware that one could vote in an election without first receiving pay—the $5 handed to a "block nigger" for his preempted ballot being a postulate of staying alive in East St. Louis.

One in tens of thousands of teen-agers has the muscle, speed, and coordination to "escape" such scenes—that is, physically leave the ghetto by signing with one of the universities which hotly recruit, buy, and ballyhoo Negro high school sport whizzes. And, once out of it and in a high-education environment, he's considered lucky. I was one of these. Yet no medals I've won nor the B.A. and M.A. degrees which follow my name [and the Ph.D that is coming] can balance the East St. Louis I saw upon returning there last year. Jobs in trade unions, in public utilities, behind downtown store counters, remained blocked to 35,000 of the city's 105,000 population. Rags plugged paneless windows of tin shacks, children had been incinerated in fire-traps, riot had come and gone. A dungheap comatoseness still ruled six square miles. "Are you still selling your vote for five bucks?" I asked the shot-to-hell young adults I grew up with. "What else is it good for?" they replied.

If the weapons at their command aren't used in behalf of those left behind—it begins to occur to many athletes—how do they go on living with themselves? We have an avenue of power open to us: the most interracially significant gathering of peoples short of the U.N. If the most mobile minority in the public eye—Afro-American dashmen, leapers, musclemen, etc.—can arouse continuing worldwide publicity by not moving at all, at least the ditch-water drinkers will be remembered. Possibly the gain will be larger. Until now, foreign interest in U.S. bigotry has been scattered and blurred, but when the Olympic Games walk-out first was announced, it rated Page One space in London, Paris, Tokyo, Rome. France's top sports periodical, *L'Equipe,* saw it as "the revolution incredible." The London *Daily Times'* Neil Allen wrote, "As we diagnose it, you are hitting at the middleclass America, the social force most perpetuating racism—telling it that no longer can sport be excluded from goals of assimilation." Japan's Sports Federation chief Tetsuo Ohba expressed surprise "at the depth of your racial problem," pointedly adding, "The Negro super-stars made the Games worth seeing." As the national boycott leader, I have received dozens of *why?*-type inquiries from Europe, Asia, and Africa.

Focus of attention in this direction, abroad, actually began nearly two years ago when Muhammad Ali's world heavyweight title was lifted. U.S. black fight champs have been castrated before—in 1913, for instance, when Jack Johnson was forced into exile by white supremacists. Johnson was the classic, tragic loser. But the modern spotlight has caused the plight of one who believes that war is evil and who stuck with his belief to be well-noted. Ali's treatment stunned black multitudes everywhere. To us, he was—is—a god. Demands that we appear in the Olympics, when placed alongside Ali's case, are revealed for what they are, especially when based on the pitch that our youngsters are missing the chance of a lifetime—the glory of being part of a world-championship show. Ali, as Cassius Clay, won an Olympic gold medal in 1960. Swell, baby. "Trust no Future, howe'er pleasant," as Longfellow said.

Another form of distortion of sportsmanship in which we are deeply involved is the class struggle heightened by Olympic medal-fever (outscore the Russians, show our superiority by use of complicated point tabulations). At the 1964 Tokyo-held games the U.S. won 20 gold medals in track-and-field, nine of them contributed by blacks. In Mexico City, without our help, vicarious patriotism no doubt will suffer. But what happens to the national point total concerns us not at all; we say, only, if Olympic zealots think white, then let them go to the starting line white. If all our past heroes of the Games, their medals jangling, paraded into Washington, Detroit, or Cleveland, and confronted riot squads, all their speed wouldn't enable them to outrun bayonets and bullets. The sole factor separating a Tommie Smith, Ralph Boston, or John Carlos from becoming an ambushed Rev. Reeb or Medgar Evers is that they've been on no firing lines. Beyond the win-or-lose motivation there exists another intimate—and overlooked—concern of our membership.

Since the time of Jesse Owens it has been presumed that any poor but rugged youngster who was able to jump racial fences into a college haven was happy all day long. He—the All-American, the subsidized, semiprofessional racer—was fortunate. Mostly, this is a myth. In 1960, for example, I was recruited by San Jose State College, a prominent "track school." Fine things were promised. "You'll be accepted here," the head coach and deans assured me. It developed that of 16 campus fraternities (as Greek in name as Plato, who revered the democracy of the Olympic Games) not one would pledge Harry Edwards (or anyone of color). The better restaurants were out of bounds and social activity was nil—I was invited nowhere outside "blood" circles. Leaving California, I spent two years acquiring a Master's degree at Cornell University. Returning to San Jose State as a teacher, I knocked on door after door bearing "vacancy" signs, but Mr. Charley was so sorry—the rental room suddenly wasn't available. The end-up: a cold cement-floor garage, costing $75 a month. Not long later I came to know Tommie Smith, whose 0:19.5 is the world 220-yard record and whom this same state college uses to impress and procure other speedsters and footballers of his race. "I have you beat," he said. "My wife's pregnant. We have no decent house. So far 13 lovely people have turned me down."

Much of the headbusting and police crackdowns at schools originate in Afro-American student frustration over housing, an area where valuable, "taken-care-of athletes" are thought to be uninvolved. Athletic Department p.r. men skillfully make this seem so. However, the great majority of black varsity men live, like Smith, in backstreet bed-in-the-wall pads located far from their classes, and overpriced. Existing as celebrity-pariahs, they go along with it because (1) they're dependent upon Charley's scholarship funding; (2) they're shy and tractable, taught early to "respect everyone, whether they respect you or not," or—"remember, as part of the Big Team you're safe from those Spookhunters outside"; (3) if they openly rebelled, back to pushing a poolhall broom they'd go. The answer was expressed' some weeks ago by Lee Evans, a collegian who ranks as the world's second-best quarter-miler of all time. "That bag," he says, "is rapidly changing. We're all through having our insides churned just when we think we're emancipated."

The examples are many and they vary little: in 1967, Southern California U's great footballer-trackman, O. J. Simpson, was worth at least $500,000 to

USC at the box-office. Many awards followed. Simpson, should he desire, could not become a member of more than 90 per cent of the groups which honored him with banquets and trophies. [Typical are the many restricted athletic clubs and country clubs throughout the nation.] Such organizations, however, feel quite justified in using Simpson's name to enhance their own identification with athletics.

At Southern Methodist University last year, "one-man-team" halfback Jerry Levias drew so many death threats and so much abuse by mail and phone that he was given a bodyguard and begged by his family to quit sports. Varsity Negroes at the University of Washington, excluded from organized dances, golf, and ski-trips, boycotted the school's sports program. At UCLA a public-relations gag was put on 7-ft-1 Lew Alcindor; he shook it off to reveal that he's been niggerblasted by fans, cold-shouldered by students, and told to get lost. In Kansas City, former Heisman Trophy-winner-turned-pro Mike Garrett found a bachelor apartment unobtainable and exploded in print. "Trouble-maker" the local community said of him. In sections of the Bible Belt and in Southern states where many Olympic point-winners are developed, trackmen routinely break records, but their friends must sit far from the finish line in segregated seats. At a recent Los Angeles Boycott Olympics Project confer-ence, word arrived that Dickie Howard had been found dead, not far away, of an overdose of drugs. Howard was a fairly good student and he won an Olympic 400 meter bronze medal at Rome in 1960. Finding too many doors shut, he disintegrated and at 29 took his own life. Post-Olympic careers for black grads in coaching, teaching, advertising, and business are so few (a Bob Hayes in pro football, a Rafer Johnson in radio, a Hayes Jones in recreation direction, are but tokens in the overall picture) that the following happened: a college alumnus famous for his accomplishments as an Olympic athlete approached a TV agency. As he well knew, the endorsement, testimonial, and product-pushing industry generally employs as many of his kind as you'll find swimming in pools in Southampton. However, he had a winning smile. To his suggestion that he could sell breakfast food or toothpaste, network executives said, "Use you on commercials? Not hardly. We'd lose 60 per cent of our audience. But we do have a job open." He promptly was handed a card to be held up before studio audiences, reading—"Laugh."

Not laughing himself, he held it up. No other work was open to him.

As much as Olympic officials denounce the profit motive and try to legislate it away, most athletes waste no time in cashing in on their reputations. The Games and commercialism are so closely tied that no longer is it arguable that they are not. One big goal is a job with a school. What major universities employ a black athletic director, head coach, assistant coach, or even a head scout? Answer: almost none. Equipment-man and bus-driving positions are open, always, in number.

Once upon a time, children, we inform men who are undecided about joining the boycott and come to us torn between their personal need and a larger need, there was Binga Dismond. He's forgotten now. Binga was the original Negro track sensation in America—a meteor who flared in Chicago in 1916–17, long before the Eddie Tolans, Ralph Metcalfes, and DeHart Hubbards. "Binga," wrote Charley Paddock, the Caucasian sprint champion of that time, "could beat any man alive at 440 yards. But he was required to run on the outside of the pack, all the way around, so as to avoid physical contact with any white. Eventually, discouraged, he disappeared." From "Long Way" Dismond we move to the subject of Jesse Owens: "immortal" Jesse, whose four gold medals won at the 1936 Olympics in Berlin left Hitler much discomfited. For 30 years Olympic Committee and Amateur Athletic Union officials have used Owens as the prime illustration of how pride and hope of a minority can be uplifted through the feats of a blood brother. The recorded facts—not mentioned—are:

The "Buckeye Bullet" finished his amazing Reich Sports-field appearances on a Sunday. Within 12 hours he was put aboard a train to Cologne and sent on a grueling European trip by his promoters, the AAU. In the next 10 days, Owens raced eight times and lost 14 pounds. Exhausted, he was ordered to Sweden for still more exhibitions. All gate receipts would accrue to the Swedes and the AAU. Owens refused to go. Within weeks, he was suspended by the AAU and thrown out of amateur sports, for life. When Owens next raced it was for money against horses and motorcycles in sleazy hippodromes in Mexico and Reno. Over ensuing years a modicum of advantages have come Jesse Owens' way; but to friends he says, "I've never been in the mainstream. They won't put me on any key Olympic committees, the policy groups. I've been used."

None of the organizers of Boycott Olympics was surprised when Owens, last November, expressed sympathy with our motives, but found boycott over-severe—a "wrong approach" to the problem. For he belongs to a controlled generation, the inheritors of Binga Dismond running on the outside. Does it occur to Jesse Owens that blacks are ineligible by color-line and by endless economic obstacles to compete in some 80 per cent of scheduled Olympic events? Rowing, skating, swimming, shooting, horsebacking, yachting, skiing, fencing, gymnastics, modern pentathlon, water polo, among others, are activities outside our cultural reach, although wasn't it Baron Pierre de Coubertin, the French scholar and humanist, who inspired the revival of the Olympics in 1896, who wrote, "The important thing in the Games is not winning, but taking part"? And who inscribed, "The foundation of human morality lies in mutual respect—and to respect one another, it is necessary to know one another." "Know" requires association, yes? Nineteen Olympiads later, no black ever has been a member of the American Olympic Committee's governing board, nor held a responsible post on any of the multiple individual sport federations. When we demand a place, back comes the disguised echo—of Maddox, Barnett, Wallace, Bull Connor.

Concededly, poor whites aren't yachtsmen, equestrians or badge-wearers, either. But as United States District Court Judge Wade H. McCree of Detroit remarked, "No one in this country is poor or outside because he's white." I'm sure Jesse Owens grasps the whole Olympic picture, agrees deep-down with us and would move to our support but for the bonds forged long ago.

Humble is out now. Action that is non-action is in. Quadrennially, the newspapers exclaim over feats of the Ralph Bostons, Bob Hayses, and Henry Carrs—record-breakers. Olympic symbols. Symbolically, they can only serve a wrong purpose. Overseas audiences hear little of bloodshed in the human-rights struggle. But when the Asian, Nordic, or Slav sees a white Richmond Flowers of Tennessee passing a relay baton to a Charles Greene or an O. J. Simpson they deduce, "Those boys, indeed, are equal." Greene or Simpson, of course, couldn't race on many southern U.S. tracks or join a fraternity or a downtown A.C. in the North, any more than Thurgood Marshall, of our highest courts, could be named a county attorney in Alabama. On the Olympic Committee for Human Rights, we think simply. We believe that the answer to why Afro-Americans are relegated to a subhuman sphere is one of two—either they want to be classed that way or society feels that they should be there. The first reason is obviously ludicrous. Application of the second of the two answers has led the Union to the edge of ultimate revolution. If the fastest among us can show that our sense of personal worth and obligation outweighs any rewards offered us and that we represent the many, something may be accomplished. The aim of Pierre de Coubertin may be recognized more than 70 years later.

All of the inquiries, questions, and criticisms notwithstanding, rebelling black athletes had scored their first substantial victory and the next arena of confrontation was to be the area of college athletics.

The Olympic Committee for Human Rights had white-listed three schools. These were the University of California at Berkeley, the University of Texas at El Paso, and the University of Washington. The first target was the University of California at Berkeley.

At the University of California a revolt of black athletes was already under-way. Because the athletic director at the school had gone out of his way to justify sending an all-white mile relay team to the N.Y.A.C. track meet, the O.C.H.R. felt that it should lend the indigenous revolt of U.C. black athletes some direct support. This revolt was led by Bob Presley, the Golden Bears' star basketball center and Bob Smith, an erstwhile defensive half-back. Ken Noel and I called a press conference on February 18, 1968, at which time we demanded the immediate resignation of Pete Newell, the athletic director at U.C., and Rene Hêrrerias, the head basketball coach. These resignations were demanded on the grounds that both had shown themselves to be either demonstrable racists or, at the very least, insensitive and unconcerned about the needs and problems faced by black athletes on the University of California campus. The support of the U.C. Black Student Union was enlisted and pressure was put on the administration of the university to abide by the demands of the athletes and the O.C.H.R. The penalty set by the committee and the black athletes for not abiding by the demands were, first of all, the disruption and picketing of all U.C. athletic events. Second, the black athletes at the university had threatened to boycott all athletic competition unless all demands were met. And finally, the O.C.H.R. released a statement to the effect that no prospective black athlete was to accept or even consider an athletic grant-in-aid to the University of California at Berkeley until such time as the aforementioned demands had been met.

Aside from the demands for the resignation of the head basketball coach and the athletic director, the black athletes had demanded better treatment of Afro-Americans on the Berkeley campus, the inclusion of courses of relevance to black people in the university curriculum, and the recruitment of more black students. They also demanded that a number of black coaches be hired by the university.

The end result of the confrontation was a victory for the rebelling Afro-Americans. Newell and Hêrrerias resigned. A plan was instituted to bring more black students to the U.C. campus. An entire curriculum of black studies was put on the drawing board and several courses in black history, philosophy, and literature were instituted immediately. Two black coaches were hired, one for the football and one for the basketball coaching staffs. And most of all, black people at the University of California—and athletes in particular—regained some of the black dignity that had been almost completely destroyed by three hundred and fifty years of unimaginable repression.

But the victory was not without its martyrs. Bob Smith, the football star and chief spokesman for the rebelling students and athletes on the D.C. campus, had been promised by one of the pro teams, as early as his junior year, that he would be a high pick in the 1967 professional football draft, no lower than the third round. After the D.C. athletic revolt, Smith was not drafted at all. The expected six-figure bonus that would have come his way was sacrificed on the altar of black dignity. It is also likely that other athletes who supported the U.C. revolt will, in one way or another, fall victim to similar conspiracies.

The next target was the University of Washington in Seattle. I was asked by black athletes and students to come to that campus to help organize a program aimed at ending the discrimination that constantly faced Afro-Americans at the 26,000-student university. The political lever to be used to bring about these changes—similar to those demanded and won at the University of California at Berkeley—again was to be athletics. The black athletes threatened to boycott all athletic events if their demands were not met and the Afro-American students, through their Black Student Union, supported that program.

Bigotry and racism have a long history at U.W. and so the idea of rebelling was not exactly new on the Seattle campus. The "word" had been out for some time that the university discriminated against black athletes.

The charges were hotly denied by U.W. football coach, Jim Owens, former Oklahoma All-American, but the feeling persisted in Seattle's heavily black central area that Afro-American players were not given a fair shake. Charlie Mitchell, a U.W. backfield star in the early sixties and now with the Denver Broncos of the AFL said: "It doesn't matter to Owens what happens to individual black players at U.W. It's what the people can be made to think is happening that counts as far as he is concerned." One player was pinpointed as the main target of discrimination. Junior Coffey, now a fullback with the Atlanta Falcons of the NFL and that club's leading ground gainer in 1967–68, seemed headed for sure All-American honors in his last year as a Husky. By the end of the season he was riding the bench. Why? Black people in Seattle felt it was because he dated a Caucasian girl. Owens and his staff maintain that Coffey was "dogging it" and pointed to another Husky black player who did make consensus All-America, played every game, and dated a Caucasian girl. Would Vince Lombardi, who first drafted Coffey for the Green Bay Packers before Coffey went to Atlanta as an expansion pick, have chosen a player with a reputation for "dogging" it? George Fleming, named one of the outstanding players in U.W.'s win over Wisconsin in the 1960 Rose Bowl, said the second case was "just an example."

Fleming, who played with Oakland of the A.F.L. and in the Canadian Pro League, is an executive with Pacific Northwest Bell Telephone and still keeps his hand in football—or rather his foot in football—by kicking for the Continental League Seattle Rangers. He said he has given Owens some suggestions to see "if he was sincere" about improving the Afro-Americans' lot on the U.W. campus. "So far," Fleming says, "Owens hasn't replied to any of my suggestions."

Joe Jones, another hero from the Rose Bowl days of '60 and '61, said Mike Garrett, Heisman Trophy Winner from U.S.C., now with the Kansas City Chiefs of the AFL, "was seriously considering going to Washington until he got the word."

What was the "word?" It was that ability is not the sole criterion for staying off the bench. Of the varsity complement of 90 players in 1968, only six were black. All were either first or second string. Out of the 48 frosh players for the Husky Pups, there were no Afro-Americans. The word, apparently, was "stay away from the University of Washington if you are interested in athletics." The black alumni have contributed to this attitude. In May, 1967 they boycotted the annual alumni game. Said Jones, "We just said, 'To hell with it.'"

The efforts at the University of Washington were only partially successful. Black coaches were hired, black studies were instituted as a regular part of the school's curriculum, and steps were taken to ensure fair and just treatment for Afro-Americans enrolled at the university in all areas, but most particularly in housing and on-campus employment. An athletic trainer who had been accused of racism was censured and suspended until such time as the exact nature of the charges against him could be clarified and the situation disposed of. Owens emerged relatively clean. But by and large, the black athletes and students had taken a long step toward gaining some degree of control of their own destinies at the predominantly white university.

The next college to be shaken by the revolt was the University of Texas at El Paso. The Olympic Committee for Human Rights had been contacted by a number of black athletes on the campus. The committee was particularly concerned over the condition of black athletes at U.T.E.P. because of past positions taken by the athletic department at that school on issues affecting primarily the interests and activities of the school's black students. The U.T.E.P. athletic staff had vigorously favored transferring the canceled San Jose State–U.T.E.P. football game to Texas in an effort to defeat the black student revolt on the San Jose campus. The head track coach at U.T.E.P. had reportedly forced black athletes, under penalty of losing their financial aid, to participate in the N.Y.A.C. track meet. Now, black athletes on U.T.E.P.'s track team were choosing not to compete against a Mormon school, Brigham Young University. Inflaming the situation even more was the tragic assassination of the Rev. Martin Luther King, Jr. This tragedy had seriously shaken most American black people, including the athletes at U.T.E.P. Seemingly, it affected the staff of that school's athletic department little, if at all. For it was business as usual for them. But for the black athletes at U.T.E.P., Dr. King's murder and the derogatory nature of Mormon ideology regarding black people were more than sufficient to justify a boycott.

I flew to Texas on April 8 from New Mexico, where I had lectured at Santa Fe College the day before. Speaking on the Texas campus at the time of my arrival was Dick Gregory. During the course of his lecture Gregory reaffirmed his endorsement and support of an Afro-American boycott of the Olympic games.

The athletic department had gone to great lengths to prevent the black athletes on the campus from hearing either Gregory's or my scheduled lectures. A night football practice session was called—which, just incidentally, coincided with the time scheduled for my talk. The scheme failed, because a second meeting was scheduled the next day. The U.T.E.P. Black Student Union had arranged for the meeting, and for it to be attended by many black non-athletes as well as athletes. It was during the course of this meeting that track meet boycott strategy was devised. The boycott was to be both a gesture of reverence to the slain Dr. King; a protest against Mormon ideology, that every black person is morally, intellectually and physically inferior; and retribution for the lack of concern displayed by the U.T.E.P. athletic department toward Afro-American athletes, toward the murder of Dr. King, and for its position on the N.Y.A.C. issue.

The U.T.E.P., in an effort to forestall the revolt, demanded that the athletes compete against B.Y.U. or face the loss of their financial aid. The athletes held a meeting among themselves and decided that black dignity was no longer for sale—at any price, that the loss of their athletic grants-in-aid and therefore their opportunity to gain an education—of sorts—was a small cost for regaining their pride and self-respect. In short, the boycott decision stood. Characteristically, the Department of Intercollegiate Athletics at U.T.E.P. cut off all financial aid to the Afro-Americans and suspended them from further competition, including world-record holder long jumper and Olympic champion, Bob Beamon. This was not the end of the confrontation, however. When the school attempted to hold a home track meet without the black athletes, Afro-American women on the campus interrupted the meet by invading the track, sitting down, and refusing to move. The university had to call out 50 city and state policemen to remove them.

The results of the confrontation at U.T.E.P. are not yet all in. As yet, the university has not conceded to a single demand justly made by the Afro-American students and athletes. The athletes who were suspended from athletic competition and dropped from the financial aid rolls have returned to school. Their expenses are being paid by a number of faculty members and students at the university. The war is not yet over, however. A number of confrontations have been planned on other college campuses in support of the black brothers and sisters at U.T.E.P. And the Afro-Americans at U.T.E.P. are committed to the fight for black dignity. For they have already had a taste of victory in the simple act of revolting. Victory for the slave depends not necessarily upon winning the battle. By the very act of revolting, he has cast doubt on the absolute authority of his oppressors. And this doubt is what determines whether the oppressors will perceive Afro-Americans as tools to be used or as men to be respected and contended with.

In the fall of 1968, black football players at San Jose State College followed the lead of the black athletes at U.T.E.P. regarding athletic competition against B.Y.U. with substantially the same results. The president of the college ruled that the athletes involved had forfeited their athletic grants-in-aid by their act of conscience. He softened his stand somewhat by setting funds aside to aid these athletes in finishing their education. But, as was stated by San Jose State football stars Frank Slaton, Dwight Tucker, and Don Jackson in a printed press release, "Even though educational funds were set aside for us, justice was still sacrificed in order to perpetuate the arbitrary and unjust exercise of authority." (President Clark later acknowledged the "shakiness" of his decision to me. He was assured at that time, however, that he would have, in the near future, ample opportunity to correct his errors, for B.Y.U. has been scheduled by San Jose State as an opponent in football, basketball, and track through the academic year 1974–75.)

The issue here is not religious freedom. The black athletes involved, by and large, feel that any person does in fact have the right to believe in anything he feels is in line with his moral and ethical standards. But these athletes, although they defend the right of religious choice for the Mormons, insist upon their right not to compete against teams that represent Mormon domi-nated and controlled institutions. By their actions, the authorities at San Jose State and of the University of Texas at El Paso lent tacit approval to the racism inherent in the Mormon creed. Rather than thwarting the revolt of the black athletes, they fed the athlete's determination to end not only racism but also the rule of those who either overtly or covertly perpetuate it in athletics.

Beyond the confines of the U.T.E.P. and S.J.S. campuses, many other schools saw the handwriting on the wall. These schools immediately instituted rules and regulations regarding the right of athletes to abstain from competition when the opposing team represents an institution or organization whose philosophies or practices violate the ethics and conscience of the athlete in question. Typical was the response of Stanford University. In the words of Chuck Taylor, athletic director, "We at Stanford recognize that there are organizations and institutions which are devotees of racist philosophies and practices . . . and we support and defend the right of any athlete to abstain from competition against the representatives of such bodies when such participation would, in all good conscience, violate the moral and ethical values of that athlete."

The slaves at U.T.E.P. are slaves no more, but black people who, inspired by a hunger for liberation, have contributed significantly to the establishment of freedom and dignity as realities in American athletics.

All in all, black athletes and students revolted on 37 major college campuses during the 1967–68 academic year. (A selected documentation of these revolts is included in Appendix B.) On all these campuses, athletics was the main lever used to pry overdue changes from white-oriented college administrators and athletic departments. On the surface, these revolts were aimed at abuses that ranged from the easily corrected—such as changing the nominal classification of black people from Negro to Afro-American, as was demanded by black athletes and students at Iowa State University—to the difficult to achieve—the demands for dismissals of tenured faculty members and coaches at such schools as the University of California at Berkeley and the University of Washington in Seattle. But the real motive behind the demonstrations was the regaining of black dignity, pride, and some degree of self-determination.

The O.C.H.R. directly advised athletes and students from over two-thirds of the campuses that were struck. We will continue our assaults against the forces of institutional racism and oppression, resolutely, concertedly, and—depending upon the response of the white athletic and academic establishments—perhaps more violently.

The Black Professional Athlete in Revolt

Following the Black Youth Conference in Los Angeles and the heroic stands taken by many black amateur athletes, the winds of revolt began blowing through the realm of professional athletics. Black athletes on the St. Louis Cardinals football club organized and rebelled against racist and discriminatory tactics on that team, openly naming offending coaches and white teammates in the process. And steps were taken by black athletes to ensure protection of Afro-American Cardinals against the harassments and acts of discrimination perpetrated against them by the Cardinals' staff, owners, and white players. The black Cleveland Browns, led by John Wooten, refused to stand by meekly and swallow the discrimination and racism handed out to them by the white Browns. The winds of revolt blow briskly through professional sports. Complaints are being voiced; an awareness is apparent; changes are being demanded.

Special mention is due Muhammad Ali. *For in a very real sense he is the saint of this revolution in sports.* He rebelled at a time when he, as an athlete, stood alone. He lost almost everything of value to any athlete—his prestige, his income, and his title. But he maintained and enhanced the most crucial factor in the minds of black people everywhere—black dignity. On his behalf, thousands of people turned out in freezing New York City weather for an O.C.H.R.-organized demonstration against a "heavyweight championship" fight at Madison Square Garden on March 4, 1968. Young blacks, and old, revere him as a black champion in the struggle for black liberation. In a real sense, Ali epitomizes the open, spirited, clean-living sports figure that the American sports industry supposedly loves to develop. And were it not for the fact that he is black and that he subscribes to a religion that meets his spiritual needs as a black man living in and confined to racist white America, he would more than likely be cast as the All-American boy. But he is black, and he is a Muslim. Even so, for a significant proportion of people—black people in particular—he is still champion and the warrior saint in the revolt of the black athlete in America.

5

Mexico City, 1968

The Olympic Project for Human Rights: Its Latter and Final Stages

During the spring months of 1968, the Olympic Committee for Human Rights, in addition to mobilizing and counseling black athletes and students on various campuses, had continued its drive to keep the Olympic Project for Human Rights in the forefront of public concern. It had largely succeeded. If public concern and impact can be measured by the responses of establishment officials to our efforts, one need only observe that Hubert H. Humphrey, then vice-president of the United States and a 1968 presidential candidate, took time out at several news conferences to criticize the Olympic Project for Human Rights. Also, several major magazines, usually conservative in their politics, came out with stories either neutral or sympathetic to the revolt of the black athletes.

This drive for the public eye was marked by several intermediate victories. Chief among these was the uniting of the O.C.H.R. and other non-white and anti-racist individuals, groups, organizations, and nations that were seeking to ban the Union of South Africa from the 1968 Olympic games. Following the example set by the O.C.H.R. and Afro-American athletes, the thirty-two nations of the Organization of African Unity declared that if South Africa—which had just recently been re-admitted to the International Olympic establishment after being banned from the 1964 games—were in fact allowed to participate, they would boycott the games in protest. Many communist and politically neutral nations soon joined the movement. In an effort to bring more unity into the drive, the O.C.H.R. issued a press release, excerpts of which follow:

> In accordance with our continuing drive toward a total black boycott of the 1968 Olympic Games we are issuing the following statement for immediate release:
>
> In conjunction with our demands made in November of 1967 concerning the United States Olympic Committee and Avery Brundage we issue the following based upon our investigations:
>
> The U.S. Olympic Committee, which, in line with its racist demeanor, does not seat any Black people, was a prime force in the political lobbying which enabled the White racist country of South Africa to be reinstated into the international Olympic movement under the sham integration that they've concocted. The basic motives underlying the activities of the U.S. Olympic Committee is the safeguarding of the present amicable state of U.S./South African political, economic, and military relations.
>
> Avery Brundage, . . . personally sought to solidify support behind the move to readmit South Africa even though, basically, there has been no change in White South Africa's demeanor toward its 14 million oppressed Black people either in the world of sports or in the general society.
>
> Last November we asked that Black people be seated on the U.S. Olympic Committee in order that the basic moral and ethical structure of amateur sport could be upheld and also so that the interest of Black athletes could be guaranteed against just such racist sell-outs as has been experienced in the South African Case. The committee ignored the pleas of the Black athletes and their supporters.
>
> Last November, we also demanded the ouster of Avery Brundage [claiming that] the man is a . . . racist. Now due to his personal lobbying activities on behalf of South Africa, everyone can see that he is. . . . But now it is too late—he has accomplished the very task that Black athletes in this country tried to prevent—the re-admission of South Africa and the eventual destruction of the International Olympic Movement.
>
> In light of the above intransigency of the white racist dominated Olympic movement in this country we shall move immediately to build upon our already established ground work in an effort to realize the following goals:
>
> We shall issue immediately to all nations which have pulled out of the Mexico City Games a statement to the effect that the Black Nation in this country

endorses fully their decisions to pull out and that it is our firm intention to follow suit. Based upon our initial inquiries, we feel assured that there will be no Black American in Mexico for the 1968 Games.

We shall work to establish a bond of communication between Black America and Black Africa based upon our mutual descent and the problems growing out of the genocidal policies of certain white racist societies (i.e., the United States of America, the Union of South Africa, Southern Rhodesia, etc.).

We shall initiate immediately a movement to establish a second set of games preferably to be held in an African Nation during the late summer so that Black people and students may participate without interrupting their educational careers. These games will be financed by a co-ordinated effort around the world to raise funds in order that 1968 will in fact be a year of athletic competition in the true Olympic spirit. We shall initiate a fund-raising drive here in the United States to support and maintain all athletes who qualify to participate in these African Games. We shall carry out trials, qualifying meets, etc. We shall enter into the negotiations and organizational preparations necessary immediately.

PROFESSOR HARRY EDWARDS
Chairman, Olympic Committee
for Human Rights

As a result, South Africa was banned from the Olympic community, thereby depriving at least one white-supremacist nation of the political advantages and prestige to be gained from international competition. The exclusion marked a victory of international significance for the Olympic Committee for Human Rights and the Afro-American athletes who it represented. For the first time Afro-Americans had united with other black nations to defeat forces in the world that were seeking to perpetuate racism and discrimination. Both the United States Olympic Committee and the Olympic Committee of the Union of South Africa described the action as illegal and as an unethical political use of the games. The simple fact of the matter is that the Olympic Games have been politically tinged at least since the 1936 games held in Nazi Germany. The real reason for the outcry was that the games were being used for the political interest of non-whites against the establishment. Permitting itself to become thus aligned with the Union of South Africa only demonstrated plainly that this country and the Union of South Africa had much more in common than merely the initials "U.S.A." And the entire world took note.

Of the letters the O.C.H.R. received from home and abroad, the following two are typical:

AFRICAN NATIONAL CONGRESS
(South Africa)

March 5, 1968

Professor Harry Edwards
San Jose State College
San Jose
California

DEAR PROFESSOR EDWARDS,

We refer to your statement of protest against the readmission of South Africa to the Olympic Games which you made at a Press Conference at the American Committee on Africa dated February 4, 1968.

Your views and support for our struggle against apartheid give us tremendous encouragement that all is not lost regarding public opinion in the U.S.A. We hope that your attitude to our struggle especially in the sphere of sports will gain the support of more and more Americans.

Accept, Sir, assurances of our highest esteem.

Yours faithfully,
ALFRED KGOKONG
Director of Publicity & Information

AMERICAN COMMITTEE ON AFRICA
(New York City)

February 16, 1968

DEAR PROFESSOR EDWARDS,

We would like to express our deep gratitude and admiration for your concern with the problem of South Africa's readmission to the Olympics, and for your signing and returning the statement of protest circulated by Jackie Robinson. Without this action on your part and that of other athletes, we would have been unable to hold a press conference in New York and publicize the issue in the press, and on radio and television. (See enclosed press clippings.)

But in spite of our efforts and those of other groups, you no doubt know that South Africa has been readmitted to the Olympics by a very narrow margin. According to Reuters (a British News Agency), the secret vote of the International Olympic Committee was so close that South Africa gained entrance by less than half a dozen votes. We will keep you informed on the latest developments on the part of African nations and others to boycott the Olympics and to protest the racist decision of the I.O.C.

In the meantime, we urge you very strongly to send a telegram or letter to the U.S. Olympic Committee, 57 Park Avenue, New York, N.Y. protesting the decision of the I.O.C. Last night we sent the following telegram to Mr. Avery Brundage, President, and Mr. J. W. Westerhoff, Secretary-General of the I.O.C. in Grenoble:

> I.O.C. decision readmitting South Africa to Olympics has destroyed the integrity and worth of the games. South Africa's policy does not change apartheid in sports in South Africa and still defies Olympic rules. Reaction in much of the world will confirm fact that I.O.C. accepts racism.

To Mr. Douglas Roby, President of the U.S. Olympic Committee, we sent this message:

Deeply shocked at I.O.C. decision readmitting South Africa to Olympics. U.S. Olympic Committee had obligation to make vote public. We hope all American athletes will boycott Olympics in solidarity with African nations against apartheid.

If you know any other athletes who are interested in preventing South Africa's presence in Mexico City this fall, please urge them to join in our protest by contacting the American Committee. In the continuing fight against racism and against South Africa's false return to "international respectability", we know that we can count on your continued support.

> Yours,
> GEORGE M. HOUSER
> Executive Director

Most of the parties backing the continuing ban against the Union of South Africa were keenly aware of the political overtones implicit in South Africa's being readmitted. The white establishment in South Africa has for years operated from the premise that eventually most of the stable countries of the world, particularly those in the Western Hemisphere, would one day accept the political ideology and implications of *apartheid*. Including a racially-mixed South African team in the 1968 games, clearly a sham form of integration, would have gone far to extend official blessings to it. Such an act would have seriously compounded the struggle of black Africans and black South Africans to break the back of the cruel, immoral, and oppressive South African political, social, and economic system.

From the significant victory in the international arena, the O.C.H.R. stepped up its drive to rally black athletes for a boycott of the 1968 Olympic games. In connection with these efforts, a press conference was called to make the following announcements:

OLYMPIC BOYCOTT
The Olympic Committee for Human Rights has undertaken to organize demonstrations of support for the Olympic Project for Human Rights at the following major track meets:

West Coast Relays
California Relays
United States Olympic Trials at Los Angeles

We also wish to announce that the efforts of the Olympic Committe for Human Rights and the goals of the Olympic Project for Human Rights are to be carried out as solemn memorials to the late Dr. Martin Luther King, Jr. in recognition of the unselfish sacrifices of him and his family toward the realization of freedom, justice, and equality for all mankind.

HARRY EDWARDS, Chairman
Olympic Committee for Human Rights

The demonstrations came off smoothly and without incident. Black people had been requested to pack the stadiums where the meets were held in order to furnish visible support for the athletes supporting the Olympic Project for Human Rights. So great was the turn-out of black people at the West Coast Relays that one sports reporter dubbed the day upon which the major portion of the meet was held "Black Saturday."

During the course of meetings held between O.C.H.R. representatives and black athletes, a new element began to emerge. Although there was a great deal of unity about the desirability and validity of the goals of the Olympic Project for Human Rights, this consensus did not extend to how best to achieve these goals. Some athletes felt that to boycott the games would be somewhat self-defeating. Others simply felt that to boycott the games would be futile because as they saw it, "No one really cared about the Olympics anyway." Despite the weaknesses of these arguments and others, they were persistent enough to suggest to us in O.C.H.R. that we should begin thinking in terms of an alternative course of action. Several meetings were scheduled at future track meets in order to clear up the differences among the black athletes on the issue of boycotting. At one of these meetings, held at the Annual Amateur Athletic Union Track and Field Meet, it was decided that if two-thirds of the black athletes agreed to boycott before the Olympic trials were held, then the boycott would be on and it would be carried out. The next significant meeting took place during the Olympic trials themselves. During the course of individual inquiries, we discovered that of the twenty-six athletes who were virtually certain of making the team, thirteen were against a total boycott and twelve favored it. One was undecided. The O.P.H.R. then had to make a decision: to release those who had committed themselves to the boycott, or to continue to press for the boycott and settle for a partial one. The decision was to release from their pledge all those persons who had earlier informed the O.C.H.R. that they would boycott. This was done for a number of reasons. First of all, those individuals voting not to boycott could have easily replaced the boycotters, thereby rendering the sacrifices of these men useless. Second, the sports establishment in this country could point to the Negro athletes who refused to boycott and thus undermine the entire revolt. Third, the growing unity among black athletes would have been seriously impaired by permitting the movement to split between boycotters and non-boycotters. So, for these reasons, an alternative plan of action was devised and unanimously accepted by the fifty black athletes present at the final meeting. The plan was to run at Mexico City; but no black athlete was to participate in any victory celebrations. In this way, the athletes could compete and, at the same time, demonstrate their solidarity with the black masses at home for whom the victories have been few and far between.

It was also decided that this plan of action would begin at the trials. No black athlete was to take the victory stand after placing in his event. The U.S. Olympic Committee had planned elaborate victory-stand ceremonies, and on the first day of competition, these ceremonies were carried out for place winners in the white-dominated shot-put event. But upon learning of the plans of the Afro-American athletes, the committee cancelled all further victory ceremonies rather than face the public embarrassment and humiliation of black athletes refusing to step forward to have their feats recognized, while "Old Glory" waved meaninglessly overhead.

It was further decided that all Afro-American athletes would wear black armbands to protest the violence and injustice handed out to black Americans and the government's seeming inability or unwillingness to ensure their fundamental rights.

All of the plans relative to the planned demonstrations at Mexico City were to be kept from the press until we decided on the final disposition of the Olympic Project for Human Rights. We did not really expect that such a widely known "secret" could in fact be kept. The O.C.H.R. had long since found that if there are more than three black people who know of the intended actions of a group of black people, it will not be long before the white establishment knows, too. For inevitably there is at least one Negro in any such group; and, among the prospective Olympians, there were several known Negroes. We on the committee therefore set about to fill the air with as many rumors as possible. No one, least of all the opposition, then would know what the true facts of the matter were.

Some athletes had to be convinced to compete. Typical of these were Tommie Smith and John Carlos. They had to be convinced that for them to boycott under the existing circumstances would be a vain sacrifice. For unlike Lew Alcindor, the great black basketball star, they could easily have been replaced by Negroes more than willing to compete for the United States. One simply does not replace a Lew Alcindor or a Mike Warren or a Lucius Allen. If men of this caliber do not compete, win or lose, they are missed.

Undoubtedly, there would be some defections in Mexico City. But if only one single black athlete staged a gesture of protest during the course of victory ceremonies in Mexico City, the millions of oppressed black people in America would have been remembered.

The first official public statement on the final status of the Olympic Project for Human Rights was issued during the course of the 1968 National Conference on Black Power held in Philadelphia. The statement, which is reprinted in full in the Appendix, reviewed the accomplishments of the movement thus far, explained why the majority of black athletes would compete in the games, set forth what form of protest would be mounted at the games, and offered several resolutions to be acted on during the four-year interval between the '68 and '72 games. This communiqué marked the final statement of the Olympic Project for Human Rights on the Olympic phase of the revolt of black athletes. One final press conference was held, however, to clear up any additional questions the press might have. Meanwhile, we had received a letter from a group of students at Mexico City University requesting a statement of support for a demonstration that they planned at the Olympic site in Mexico City. The O.C.H.R. issued the following statement:

August 15, 1968

BROTHERS AND SISTERS:

We, the colonialized and oppressed Black people of racist America, support one-thousand percent all and any efforts on your parts to obtain redress of your grievances against the Uncle Tom puppet government of Mexico. It seems ridiculous to us also to see a government spend 150 million dollars on an imperialistic spectacle while millions of its citizens live at sub-human levels of existence due to lack of sufficient programs to provide food, jobs, and shelter.

The anti-human governments of the world must be made to understand BY ANY MEANS NECESSARY, that the rising tide of youth will use any means necessary to stop the generation to generation flow of inhumanity.

Your valiant efforts to dramatize the plights of oppressed peoples through use of the highly political Olympic Games will serve as a model for coming student generations.

Viva la Revolución del Mundo!!
We Shall Conquer Without a Doubt
PROFESSOR HARRY EDWARDS
Chairman, Olympic Committee for Human Rights

With that final press conference, the control and direction of the Olympic Project for Human Rights by the O.C.H.R. officially came to an end. With no funds save those accruing from the author's salary and speaking engagements; with no staff save those persons who volunteered their skills and time; and, with no other resources except the courage and determination of our Afro-American supporters and a few sympathetic whites, we had nevertheless opened up an entirely new chapter in the gloomy saga of sports and athletics in white America. But the chapter ending had yet to be composed. The Olympic games were still to be held and questions of the extent of black support for our activities and positions still loomed large for many.

Because of the overawing of some black athletes by the Olympic men's track and field coaching staff and by Avery Brundage, it became necessary to make certain changes with regard to the forms of protest outlined in the Statement to the Black Power Conference. The center of the protest did not, however, move from the victory stand. It was decided that each athlete would determine and carry out his own "thing," preferably focusing around the victory stand ceremonies. In this way, potential repercussions from a so-called "Black Power" conspiracy could be avoided and, also, each athlete would be free to determine his own course of protest. The results of this new strategy, devised for the most part by the athletes themselves, were no less than revolutionary in impact.

As we have mentioned many times, the Olympic games are political, if nothing else. The fact that all participating nations do not compete under a single flag, the Olympic flag, but under their respective national flags, heightens their political flavor. The U.S. makes its own individual contribution to this political atmosphere by insisting, since 1908, upon being the only nation participating in the games not to dip its flag to the head dignitary of the host nation as the athletes parade by on opening day. The Star Spangled Banner, the national anthem of the United States of America, was to be the focal point of the victory stand protest. It has been felt for many years among the more determined segments of the black liberation movement that the Star Spangled Banner was a monument to the hypocrisy of America. For the black man in America, the national anthem has not progressed far beyond what it was before Francis Scott Key put his words to it—an old English drinking song. For in America, a black man would have to be either drunk, insane, or both, not to recognize the hollowness in the anthem's phrases. To expose this hypocrisy, we intended to inject a small bit of truth and honesty in the name of black dignity into the 1968 Olympic games.

The first test of support for the Olympic Project for Human Rights came when Jim Hines and Charles Greene took the victory stand after finishing a close 1–2 in the 100-meter dash. The two took the stand and stood stolidly, facing the flag. Neither made so much as an utterance in protest of black degradation in America. What motivated Charley Greene to stand silent and motionless is anyone's guess. He is an intelligent person—too intelligent, I believe, to compromise his principles for a bit of racist-tainted metal hung on a string. Hines was determined to win. To him, the gold medal was his entrée to professional sports. He quickly signed a professional football contract after the games were over.

Then came the victory ceremonies for the 200-meter dash. Tommie Smith, the gold medalist, and John Carlos, the bronze medalist, had made it crystal clear that they intended to go through with their planned protest at the victory stand. Subtle attempts at intimidating the two had been made by members of both the U.S. Olympic Committee and the U.S. track and field coaching staff. But Carlos and Smith would not bend. They climbed the victory stand shoeless, each wearing a black glove. Smith had a black scarf tied around his neck. They were joined on the victory stand by Peter Norman, the silver medalist from Australia, who wore the official badge of the Olympic Project for Human Rights to underscore his support of the black liberation struggle. The men were presented with their medals and then each turned toward the flag of the country represented by the gold medal winner. The U.S. National Anthem was played. Smith and Carlos immediately raised their gloved fists and bowed their heads. In a taped interview with Howard Cosell, Smith explained the pair's protest gestures. He stated, "I wore a black right-hand glove and Carlos wore the left-hand glove of the same pair. My raised right hand stood for the power in black America. Carlos' raised left hand stood for the unity of black America. Together they formed an arch of unity and power. The black scarf around my neck stood for black pride. The black socks with no shoes stood for black poverty in racist America. The totality of our effort was the regaining of black dignity." Smith later confided to me that the gesture of the bowed head was in remembrance of the fallen warriors in the black liberation struggle in America—Malcolm X, Martin Luther King, Jr., and others.

The impact of the protest was immediate. The U.S. Olympic Committee, acting hastily and rashly, warned all other U.S. athletes, black and white, that "severe" penalties would follow any further protests. Smith and Carlos were given 48 hours to get out of Mexico and were suspended from the Olympic team.

When the original decision to call off the proposed boycott was made, one thing that the O.C.H.R. had banked on was that the U.S. Olympic Committee and the track and field staff would respond in just such an asinine fashion. We had hoped that their reaction would create protesters where there had been none before. This is precisely what happened. In response to their overkill tactics, many whites—such as Ed Burke and Hal Connolly—rebelled and threatened to go home before the closing ceremonies. (Because of this threat, special arrangements were made for the closing ceremonies. Only six athletes from each country were allowed to march in the final parade, thereby averting more potential U.S. embarrassment and avoiding having to appear with a vastly reduced contingent.) And Bob Beamon and Ralph Boston, two black athletes not typically considered to be militants, took the victory stand during the ceremonies following the running broad jump shoeless and wearing long black socks to protest black degradation in America and, more immediately, to protest the treatment of Smith and Carlos.

Then came the 400-meter dash ceremonies. The U.S. had swept the event with Lee Evans, Larry James, and Ron Freeman finishing one, two, three, respectively. Evans, a schoolmate of Carlos and Smith and a participant in the revolt from its initial planning, was looked to by both black athletes at the games and black people in America to follow Smith's and Carlos' example despite the committee's punitive warning. The victors took the stand, waving and smiling. There was no sign of protest. Evans had disappointed his people. Many felt that he was only waiting for his second turn on the victory stand following the 1600-meter relay race. Evans obviously felt the pressure he was under. He finally made up his mind not to follow Smith's and Carlos' lead. He reportedly went to his wife, Linda, and told her, "If I don't do anything out there after the relay, it is for you." She replied, "Lee, if you want to do something for me, go out there and stand up [against] those repressive devils." Torn between his desire to capitalize on his Olympic victories and his need to maintain the respect of his wife and of black people at home, Evans tried to do the impossible—he attempted to stand up and be counted on both sides of the fence at once. And, because this is a struggle for black survival in which there is no middle ground, he failed on both accounts, or so some felt. It was disclosed later that Evans was going to play professional football. (Remarkably enough, after the Smith-Carlos protest, Negroes who had never once donned a piece of football gear were suddenly prime professional football candidates.)

Later, after the games were over, Evans was to address an overflow crowd and publicly acknowledge his mistakes and also admit that he would do it differently if he had another chance. But Lee already had forded his Rubicon.

In other areas of Olympic competition, areas more directly tied to professional sports and its financial rewards, there were no protests at Mexico City to speak of. Negro basketball players dutifully shuffled their way up and down the Olympic court. Twentieth-century Negro gladiators, under the tutelage of old-school Negroes, boxed their way to gold medals and then, on one occasion, marched around the ring carrying an American flag and calling for "United States Power." George Foreman, the boxer guilty of this particular act, never seemed to consider that the flag that he so proudly flaunted was the same flag under which four black girls were murdered in Alabama; the same flag under which Martin Luther King, the generation's chief advocate of non-violence and brotherhood, was violently shot down in cold blood; the same flag under which troops marched into the black communities of America and shot down men, women, and children in the streets and in their homes; the same symbol of hypocrisy and inhumanity under which black soldiers have died over the decades trying to keep George Wallace safe from communism. For his blatantly political performance Foreman was not criticized or ejected from the games. For his behavior was in the interest of the establishment and of white folks. On his return to the U.S., he was treated as a hero—by whites. He appeared on no less than three nationwide television shows—because he had pleased whites. But the event that really cast his performance in the proper perspective for black people was his appearance as guest of honor during the half-time show at the Cotton Bowl in racist Dallas, Texas. A *Negro* as guest of honor at an athletic event that more appropriately might be called the "Cracker Bowl," featuring the University of Texas, which doesn't ever recruit blacks, and the University of Tennessee, which has recruited just *one*. Anytime racists honor a Negro, that Negro must have done something offensive to his race. And many people—black and white—felt that Foreman and his coach had done just that. Foreman's act and the manner in which it was received, and the behavior of Smith and Carlos and the way it was received, proves that white racism dominates the United States athletic establishment. It once again pointed out that what is in the interest of whites is de facto acceptable, and what is in the interest of blacks is de facto condemned in white America. "Foreman is a good nigger," was the remark made by a southern graduate student during the course of a rerun of the Olympic highlights shown recently by the ABC television network. But then, too, so were many of us at one time or another.

But in spite of the defections, the protests had their impact, and the world acknowledged them. Smith, Carlos, Alcindor, Mike Warren, and Lucius Allen were heroes to black Americans. Receptions were thrown at the United Nations by black African nations honoring these athletes for the stand they had taken. Thousands of black people turned out to honor them in Washington, D.C. Many black leaders—H. Rap Brown, Stokeley Carmichael, Adam Clayton Powell, and Elijah Muhammad—paid their personal respects. Thousands of telegrams from all over the world flowed into the homes and Olympic quarters of Smith and Carlos, supporting their actions and condemning the U.S. Olympic officials and the U.S. Olympic coaching staff for its actions.

Many whites at home also supported the actions of these black warriors. Exemplary of these letters and telegrams of support was that sent and later made public by Robert Clark, President of San Jose State College. Clark stated that Smith and Carlos, ". . . would not be received as outcasts in America, but as honorable men."

To point up the international nature of the black liberation struggle and to establish their sincere identification with the plight of black Americans, the

Cuban men's 400-meter relay team presented their silver medals to Stokeley Carmichael in the name of black America, and the Cuban women's 400-meter relay team followed suit by presenting their medals, also silver, to me. We had come a long way since November 23, 1967. The movement had made it crystal clear that this was the new generation of black people that Malcolm X had spoken of so often—a generation to which black dignity meant more than individual Negro "gains."

The Results of the Revolt

The results of the revolt of Afro-American athletes have, to date, been nothing short of historic.

First of all, some of the principles supposedly espoused by the American sports industry have at long last been realized. One has only to review the actions of Dave Patrick of Villanova during the N.Y.A.C. boycott or the actions of Hal Connolly and Ed Burke during the Olympic games, or to read the following statement written on behalf of five Harvard University crew athletes by their captain, to see that one result of the movement has been to bring about a new solidarity between Afro-American and many white athletes:

> We—as individuals—have been concerned with the place of the black man in American society and his struggle for equal rights. As members of the United States Olympic Team, each of us has come to feel a moral commitment to support our black teammates in their efforts to dramatize the injustices and inequities which permeate our society. This commitment has led us to initiate conversations with the Olympic Project for Human Rights.
>
> Our initial contacts have reaffirmed our conviction that the white majority cannot afford to ignore the voices of oppressed minorities and that the struggle for racial justice is not simply a black struggle but one in which every man who counts himself free must be involved.
>
> The general goals of the Project are those which we hold for all Americans and for all men: the demise of bigotry and racism and the establishment of true equality of opportunity. The Project when established sought to achieve a non-violent dramatization of the plight of the masses of Negroes in this country that would exceed riots and bloodshed in its effectiveness. We feel that working to correct racial injustices is the undeniable task of all athletes and all men, black and white.
>
> In order to support the dramatization that was begun by the Olympic Project for Human Rights we wish, as individual athletes who have had the honor

of being selected for the Olympic Team, to form a group whose purpose will be three-fold:

1. To help the white athletes selected for the Olympic team obtain information about the reasons for and goals of the black demonstrations,

2. to stimulate an open-ended discussion of the issues between white and black athletes, and

3. to discuss means of voicing our support at the Olympic games.

Because we do not know what specific form the black athletes' demonstration will take, we do not consider ourselves tied to any specific action. It is their criticisms of society which we here support. What form our visible support might take remains to be decided by the discussions we hope to initiate.

We hope that any Olympic athlete who is interested in such discussions will contact us at Kirkland House, Cambridge, Massachusetts 02138. From this we truly hope there might grow a meaningful demonstration on the part of the entire U.S. Olympic Team of support for the just cause of the black man in America.

It is not our intention or desire to embarrass our country or to use athletics for ulterior purposes. But we feel strongly that the racial crisis is a total cultural crisis. The position of the black athlete cannot be, and is not in fact, separated from his position as a black man or woman in America. America can only acquire greater dignity and greater hope by facing its most grievous problem openly and before the world. Surely the spirit of the Olympic Games cannot thrive on a hypocrisy that fails to acknowledge that even the highest individual achievement does not save a black athlete from the injustices visited upon him as a man. Surely the spirit of the Olympic Games requires us, as white participants, to explore all the means at our disposal to further the cause of brotherhood and the claims to equality of our black colleagues.

> CURTIS R. CANNING, CAPTAIN
> PAUL HOFFMAN
> J. CLEVE LIVINGSTON
> SCOTT N. STEKETEE
> DAVE HIGGINS

Dr. Tom Waddell, who finished sixth in the decathlon at Mexico City, put it more succinctly—"I'm strongly in favor of civil rights. I don't think it should be discarded at a track meet."

Another result has been the hiring of numerous black people for jobs hitherto closed to them. One baseball team hired a black manager and assigned him to one of its farm clubs. Otis Davis, a former 400-meter Olympic champion, was hired by the United States Olympic Committee as Director of Housing. Many state and private agencies have placed former black athletes in executive positions for the first time. The list could go on and on.

Results also accrued that had to do with the perpetuation of the revolt itself. One of these was the formulation of a plan to create a Federation of Black Amateur Athletes. The idea of a Federation of Black Amateur Athletes arose first of all out of the determination that existing athletic unions, such as the National Collegiate Athletic Association and the Amateur Athletic Union, have demonstrated that they lack either the capacity or the desire to protect the interests and guarantee the rights of black athletes, or both. A second factor was the knowledge that whatever organization controls amateur athletics, to any significant degree, also commands a great deal of power in the area of professional athletics. A third factor was the political, economic, and social power inherent in the control of organized athletics at all levels.

The union is to have three primary aims: (1) to protect the rights of all black athletes and to guarantee that such abuses and maltreatment as has been their lot in the past would not continue; (2) to utilize the political leverage of athletics for the benefit of the masses of black people in America; and (3) to channel back into the black community some of the millions of dollars that are realized by the sports industry through its dependence on black athletes.

The organization is to be set up in such a manner that an athlete could be advised and counseled by the federation from the time that he entered amateur athletics at the college level, through his professional career, and after his professional career, when he may want to go into private business. The federation would not only counsel athletes on contracts and business deals, but also would provide loans to athletes for establishing businesses in black communities. The capital for these loans was to come from percentages taken from contracts negotiated on behalf of black athletes and also from some form of union dues to be established. (At this time, none of the funds derived from contract negotiations or from dues paid into various athletic unions benefit black athletes or the black community in any way.) The federation is to be two years in the development phase before full-scale operations are begun. It will be controlled completely by a board of directors composed of active and former black athletes and will be structured along lines as shown in the accompanying diagram.

To date, the federation is well on its way to becoming a reality. Potential officers have been contacted, a number of prominent athletes have been approached to serve as possible charter members of the federation, and existing organizations have been contacted about the possibility of taking on the

Organizational Structure
Federation of Black Athletes

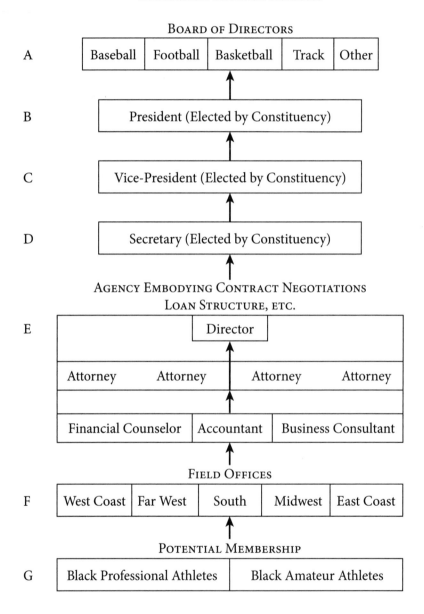

work of contract negotiations, business counseling, and so on. Under such a working relationship, the federation will funnel black athletes into such an organization which will then perform the services indicated or implied in Section "E" of the diagram. The federation will call strikes, boycotts, and demonstrations to correct injustices with the consent of three-fourths of its voting members. The organization in Section "E" will be responsible for negotiating *any* contracts-business, athletic, or otherwise, that the athletes may desire to make—and will grant business loans from the union's treasury at negligible rates of interest. (It is almost impossible for any black man to obtain a business loan today at any rate of interest.)

Before getting underway with the actual establishment of the planned federation, the O.C.H.R. checked out and approved or disapproved potential officers, investigated the feasibility of establishing field offices and decided the idea was sound, and selected sites for such offices. Our search for an agency to fill slot "E" of the diagram took one funny turn, although at the time we didn't exactly break up over it. Our investigations of one Washington, D.C.- based organization disclosed certain information which indicated that the organization in question was not really all it claimed to be. In the process of trying to get one of his lieutenants out of a Louisiana jail, the agency head wrote to the judge in charge of the case verifying that the man was indeed a member of his organization and then went on to add that the job and mis- sion of (the employee) was to attempt to maintain peace and order in the civil rights movement in the country today and to quell civil rights agitation brought about by the active factions of the movement called at times the black activists or militants. We carried the investigation no further.

If the federation does nothing more than preserve the dignity of one black athlete, if it adds but one more link to the chain that binds Afro-American athletes and the black masses, it will have been worthwhile. The days of the Negro Uncle Tom athlete are numbered. For from this point on, their kind shall be harder and harder to come by.

6

The Future Direction of the Revolt

In the future we will continue to exploit the inherent political nature of athletics. For the United States government has taught us well. In the ideological wars with other world powers, the U.S. State Department has time and time again used athletics—both professional and amateur—as political adjuncts. Yearly the U.S. State Department sends teams of athletes all over the world to conduct clinics and to compete against native teams. Why? Because State Department officials are sports buffs, rabid fans? No, these tours are scheduled and paid for by the State Department because the United States government knows full well that a person in another part of the world who may not understand how a Negro may sit on the U.S. Supreme Court while the majority of black people suffer unspeakable indignities may quite easily become convinced that such contradictions in American life are meaningless when an "integrated" team sets up a basketball clinic in his country. The political aspects of athletics are so important to the United States State Department that in 1968, as it has in the past, the department underwrote a program to help athletes from Africa, Asia, and Latin America in preparation for the 1968 Olympic games. American coaches and athletes were working in such far-flung places as South Korea, Mexico, and Australia under U.S. State Department sponsorship.

The political nature of athletics is further demonstrated by the uproar over the move to have South Africa and Southern Rhodesia banned from the 1968 Olympic games. The games also are politically important because there is great national prestige involved in "winning." The number of gold, silver, and bronze medals won by the U.S. and Soviet Russia, respectively, and by Kenya, or Jamaica, for that matter, are as important to the people and governments of these countries as to their respective press and sports establishments. In the future, black people too shall exploit, at every opportunity, these politically relevant athletic factors to their own advantage.

On the national and state levels, athletics also are a source of potential power for black people. Changes and programs that have been thwarted by the vagaries of national and state politics have yielded before campaigns using athletics as a political lever. Curriculum changes in colleges and universities, non-discriminatory codes in housing and jobs, and other long-delayed social and economic goals have been won where black students have used athletics as a political lever. Because of the growing national political significance of Afro-Americans in general, black athletes have become almost as familiar as loudspeaker trucks in the campaigns of candidates seeking high national and state offices.

Another factor that will govern the future direction of the revolt of the black athlete will be the increasing efforts of black people to control a greater percentage of the athletic industry in America. Today, the whole athletic industry in America—amateur and professional—is controlled by whites for the benefit of whites. Every time a dollar gained from athletics goes into another white-owned, white-controlled project, that dollar is denied the black community. And the real tragedy lies in the fact that so many of the athletic industry's dollars result from the efforts of black people. One has only to read the partial list of achievements by black athletes listed in Appendix C to understand the tremendous contribution that they have made to the economic development of the athletic industry. And then study the section that details how many of them have been given positions in the industry and judge for yourself whether the accomplishments have justified the return.

As the listings in Appendix C indicate, black people have been excluded from virtually all responsible positions in American sports. Not even the long-time ally of the white establishment—the shuffling, boot-licking Negro—has been allowed to move up in the power hierarchy. But then this is not his role. Under no circumstances can this situation be permitted to endure. The day of the black twentieth-century gladiator must be ended. Some control must be handed over to blacks-or be taken by them. Athletics represent one of the few areas where black people can compete against whites equally. Control of the industry also must be equal. This goal is a future must for the black athletic rebellion.

A third area of expansion during the future course of the athletic revolt shall be the educational milieu. We shall endeavor, wherever possible, to utilize athletics as a tool to bring about changes in the educational system of America so as to render it more amenable to the needs of black people. At this point, the American educational system fails to perform this role. White students complain of the irrelevancy of the white, middle-class bourgeois-oriented indoctrination offered by most of America's high schools and colleges. To black students, such training is worse than irrelevant; it is misleading, humiliating, and degrading, particularly as a great deal of it is infected with white racism. Athletics is an opening that blacks can exploit to trigger educational reforms that will benefit the entire black community in America. If boycotts and demonstrations are the only way we can get black professors and black studies programs, then boycotts and demonstrations there will be.

The Ramifications of the Revolt for the Sports Industry

The revolt of the black athlete already has shaken the sports establishment in this country. Many positive changes have resulted. Many more concessions must be forthcoming. Every trace of discrimination must be wiped out. This does not mean the institutionalized practice of setting up a token Negro as an example of what the whole of black youth should strive to become. It means instead according to black athletes the same opportunities that whites enjoy to profit from commercial endorsements, professional franchise ownerships, coaching and managerial jobs, relevant and valuable educational experiences, and positions of power on policy-making boards in both professional and amateur athletics. These changes are obviously intertwined with the potential for positive change in the social, political, and economic spheres in America today. But on paper, at any rate, the sports industry has both the capacity and avows the ethical principles whose implementation will lead the way to better relations among all black and white Americans through the establishment of true equality, opportunity, and justice. All that is needed now is the desire.

Undoubtedly, we will encounter setbacks. Some colleges already have cut their recruitment of black athletes—the University of Washington, for instance. Some professional football teams, too, have retaliated by ignoring promised draft choices and by white-listing "troublesome" black athletes. In the future, we will meet fire with fire. The owners and the other controllers of the sports purse can discriminate, retaliate, and punish and then run off to the suburbs, but they can't take their stadiums and other facilities with them. Many of these arenas are located in inner-city areas, localities overflowing with black people. And public attendance is a significant element in their financial master plans. The sports fan hasn't yet been born who will willingly attend an athletic event all the while knowing that he may be risking physical harm. As in other areas of the black liberation struggle, then, as efforts to advance in the area of athletics are repressed more and more ruthlessly, the revolt will undoubtedly become more violent. To date, a great deal has been accomplished without a single drop of blood being shed and without a single athletic facility being bombed or burned. How long this trend can continue depends—as it has in other areas—upon the white power structure and its supporters. At stake no longer are the profits to be made by the white controllers of sports, but the very survival of the industry itself. For should conditions deteriorate further, the time will have passed for demonstrations, rallies, pickets, and boycotts. As James Baldwin predicted years before Watts in the broad society, in the realm of athletics, it will be the fire next time.

The achievement of dignity or of a decent, human level of survival are not easily obtained by black people living in a white racist society, and almost impossible to achieve simultaneously. But we shall conquer without a doubt—through determination, sacrifice, and the courage to do whatever is necessary to remove oppression from our backs.

I have tried within the pages of this short book to say those things that Jackie Robinson wanted to say in 1947 but couldn't; that Bill Russell tried to say in 1957 but was not heard; and that Jesse Owens should have said in 1967, but didn't. Listen, America. Listen and understand. For, as is so true of Afro-Americans confronting racism and exploitation in other areas of your society, your "colored boy" in athletics is rapidly becoming a man, and he is determined to be respected and treated as such—by any means necessary.

Epilogue

The establishment in America, like other hypocritical and oppressive political and social entities both past and present, has a tremendous capacity to co-opt or coerce dissident and deviant movements into accepting its corrupt philosophies and values. The athletic phase of the black liberation struggle has been no less subject to those efforts than have those activities that have struck more centrally at the domestic, economic, political, and social pillars upon which American racism stands. During the initial phases of the revolt of the black athletes, I was offered no less than one-hundred and twenty-five thousand dollars if I would publicly reverse my stand toward athletics in general in America and on Afro-American participation in the Olympics in particular. Tin-horn politicians offered political favors to some of the athletes who had publicly endorsed the revolt and to those persons involved in organizing the movement in exchange for anti-black statements and acts. California State Senator Alquist actually approached a number of persons active in the revolt (including me) in an effort to gain support for himself and for Hubert Humphrey, who earlier had opposed the entire idea of an athletic revolt. (But this was early in the campaign, when Humphrey was trailing badly in many polls and it seemed that he, rather than George Wallace, might be the one to throw the 1968 presidential race into the House of Representatives.) Black athletes all over America were constantly warned that any undergraduate activities they were involved in that would brand them as "trouble-makers, bad niggers, or Negroes with chips on their shoulders, or with bad attitudes" would ruin their professional chances. Now the National Collegiate Athletic Association—an organization that has never overly concerned itself with justice for black athletes—has reaffirmed its allegiance to the pack. The N.C.A.A., apparently feeling that the student unrest may soon erupt more violently in athletics, adopted a proposal to halt ". . . the financial aid of a student-athlete if he is adjudged to have been guilty of manifest disobedience."

The action was taken at a general session as the N.C.A.A. ended its 63rd annual convention. The vote was 167–79 on the proposal offered by the N.C.A.A. Council. It stated:

> A member institution may terminate the financial aid of a student-athlete if he is adjudged to have been guilty of manifest disobedience through violation of institutional regulations or established athletic department policies and rules applicable to all student-athletes. Construed to be manifest disobedience are disruptive actions which interfere with the normal and orderly conduct of an institution's athletic program, refusal to meet the normal good conduct obligations required of all team members and defiance of the normal and necessary directions of the departmental staff members.

Edwin H. Cady, Indiana University faculty athletic representative, reflected the members' general feeling on the question. He called student unrest a threat to college athletic programs.

Speaking at a panel discussion, Cady said it was being "widely rumored" that student rebellion could move into college athletics soon on a wide scale. Some athletic departments in the nation have been criticized for their handling of Negro athletes. A racial storm even erupted at the convention over the question of whether an athlete can be stripped of his scholarship because of his haircut.

So obviously biased were the rulings of the N.C.A.A. that some individuals who had not heretofore backed the rebelling athletes reacted negatively to the new rule. "This looks like a throwback to the past hot summer and some of the things that happened then," said C. D. Henry of Louisiana's famed Grambling College, producer of Negro pro football stars. "Does it mean a boy can be kicked out for failing to get a haircut or for wearing an Afro haircut?" "This looks like a slap in the face to the black athlete," charged another black delegate.

The issue that struck a match to the fire was the elimination of grants-in-aid for "manifest disobedience." "What constitutes manifest disobedience?" Henry asked. "When I went to school in the Midwest there was only one Negro barber in town and the barber was inclined to get intoxicated. A teammate of mine had an idiosyncrasy. He didn't want a drunk man putting a razor to his head. So he would go home to Chicago—four hours and $10.69 by the Rocket [a train]. If he missed practice, would that be disobedience?"

Cited as the kind of cases in point were the revolts and protests at U.T.E.P., San Jose State, and at the Olympics. According to one member of the governing board of the N.C.A.A., ". . . seven San Jose State athletes lay down on the football field and refused to play a football game against Brigham Young. They had their scholarships taken away and the court upheld the action." (Actually, the seven athletes never put in an appearance on the field. They watched the game from the stands. In the matter of the scholarships, the court held only that the plaintiffs, the Associated Students of San Jose State, were not the proper party to sue on behalf of the seven students.) Others also cited this case plus those involving the U.T.E.P. track team's refusal to compete against Brigham Young and the black power demonstration of Tommie Smith and John Carlos during the Olympic games at Mexico City.

Some coaches in attendance expressed concern over the new dignity and identity of black athletes as manifest in their hair styles and beards. But others—some of whom were white—couldn't quite see why beards or the style of a man's hair should cause any anxiety. "I don't know what we can do about it if the fellows want to effect those Fu Manchu beards, like Joe Namath of the Jets," said Bob Devaney, the Nebraska football coach. "Joe seemed to pass all right."

These actions by the N.C.A.A.—and similar responses by the A.A.U. during the 1968 indoor and outdoor track and field seasons—reinforce the contention that there exists an urgent need for black athletes to organize a federation to protect themselves and their interests. Obviously no one else is looking out for them.

Undoubtedly, in the future some athletes will accept the bribes and the token jobs in exchange for their promises to endorse the status quo or to stand silent as humiliation and injustice continue to be heaped upon black people. Other athletes will be frightened off or bow to threats. But for every backslider there will be born hordes of new fighters for human dignity and justice in athletics. For as was demonstrated at the 1968 Olympic games, repression serves only to create more battles and the rebels to fight them. The revolt of the black athlete can no more be thwarted or reversed than the rivers of the world can be made to flow away from the oceans. For as Victor Hugo so eloquently stated long ago—

"Greater than the tread of mighty armies is an idea whose time has arrived."

The author with Captain Curt Canning of the Harvard Crew during a press conference in which five members of the crew announced their support of the Olympic Project for Human Rights. [United Press International Photo.]

Flanked by athletes who were supporting a boycott of the 1968 Olympic Games, George M. Houser (3rd left), executive director of the American Committee on Africa calls for the International Olympic Committee to reverse its decision readmitting South Africa to the games. (Left-right): Heyward Dotson, Staten Island, N.Y., Columbia University; Kwaku Ohene-Frempong, Ghana, Yale University; Houser; Steve Mokone, South Africa, University of Rochester; N.Y. Yankee infielder Ruben Amaro; and Yankee pitcher Jim Bouton. [United Press International Photo.]

The author (left) and H. Rap Brown (center) address meeting in Harlem prior to the boycott of the New York Athletic Club meet. [United Press International Photo.]

The U.S. 1,600-meter relay team gives the clenched fist salute in Olympic Stadium after receiving gold medals. The relatively mild demonstration drew little attention. (Left–right): Lee Evans, Ron Freeman (partly hidden), Larry James, and Vince Matthews. [United Press International Photo.]

George Foreman parades around the ring in Mexico City, waving a small American flag, minutes after winning the gold medal in the heavyweight division. [AP Photo/Kurt Strumpf.]

Assistant coach Stan V. Wright attempts to justify expulsion of Smith and Carlos from Olympic Village to Mel Pender (center) and Jim Hines. [United Press International Photo.]

The Olympic medallion commemorating Tommie Smith's and John Carlos' Victory stand protest in Mexico City.

Vince Matthews, member of the record-breaking 1,600 meter relay team, lets an interviewer know how he feels about the suspension of Smith and Carlos.

Black women attending the University of Texas at El Paso blocked the progress of a track meet at the university after several black U.T.E.P. track stars were suspended following their refusal to compete against Mormon-controlled Brigham Young University. [United Press International Photo.]

Lew Alcindor, U.C.L.A. superstar and militant defender of black dignity and freedom.

Some college and university administrators did not wait for black athletes to force the correction of long-standing injustices. The University of Southern California named Willie Brown, one of its former baseball and football stars, to assistant coaching positions in both sports. [U.S.C. Athletic News Service.]

In response to a demand by black athletes and students that San Jose State College hire a black football coach, the school hired Johnny Johnson, a former star fullback at San Jose State from 1960 through 1962, as an assistant mentor for the varsity football team. [San Jose State Athletic Department.]

Two "saints" of the black athletes' revolt, Malcolm X (peering at camera) and Muhammad Ali (signing autographs) in New York City in March, 1964. [AP Photo/Jack Kanthal.]

Bill Russell was one of the first world-renowned black athletes to address himself publicly to the realities of life for black athletes in America. [AP Photo/Frank Curtin.]

Muhammad Ali listens as Jim Brown explains his support of Ali's refusal to accept military induction.

Jackie Robinson (right) and Floyd Patterson flank the Rev. Martin Luther King, Jr., and the Reverend Ralph Abernathy. Robinson was one of the main actors in the successful move to keep South Africa out of the Olympics and in the boycott of the New York Athletic Club. [AP Photo.]

Arthur Ashe tells a panel on the television program "Face the Nation" that "prominent black athletes have a responsibility to champion the causes of their race."

Former Vice President Hubert Humphrey actively sought the support of many black athletes in 1968. Pictured with Humphrey are (left to right) Ray Scott of the Baltimore Bullets, John Mackey of the Baltimore Colts, Chris Hanburger of the Washington Redskins, Willie Wood of the Green Bay Packers, Steve Thurlow of the Redskins, and Thurlow's Washington teammate Bobby Mitchell. [United Press International Photo.]

Professional football players from the Chicago Bears and the Los Angeles Rams huddle with the late Senator Robert Kennedy during a Kennedy tour of shopping centers in Indiana's ghetto areas. [United Press International Photo.]

Appendices:
Brief Selected Documentaries

The following appendices are included in order to present in a more detailed fashion some of the issues, tactics, and goals characteristic of this initial phase of the revolt of the black athlete in America. There are some who may feel that the goals sought by the present generation of black athletes are far too insignificant and petty and the prices paid by so many athletes are far too harsh to justify some of the tactics used. But one should never underestimate the awesome motivating factors inherent in any man's desires for human dignity and freedom. For those involved, the costs are never too high and the rewards are never too petty. This is a new generation of black athletes. Their sacrifices in their own behalf and in behalf of their people and the gains already made are noble and grand indeed when contrasted with the shuffling, accommodating past generations of Negro athletes. Because of activities such as those documented in the following pages, the decade of the 1960's—and the years beyond—will be remembered as that period of time wherein the black athlete shed his cocoon of trophies, medals, newspaper clippings, and photographs and became a major frontline combatant in the war for justice, freedom, and human dignity. And no more honorable station has ever been achieved by any man, regardless of his calling.

Appendix A:
Olympic Project for Human Rights

Los Angeles (*United Press International*). The man who is heading a campaign to persuade Negro athletes to boycott the 1968 Olympic Games has called for the reinstatement of Cassius Clay as the Heavyweight Champion.

Harry Edwards, a Negro faculty member at San Jose State College, told the greater Los Angeles Press Club Wednesday that his group had added Clay's reinstatement to its goals.

The group's goals also have been expanded to include a ban on New York Athletic Club events, he said.

Edwards, who predicted he eventually will win the support of nearly all Negroes as well as many whites, planned to meet at New York today with Black Civil Rights Leader Dr. Martin Luther King, Jr. and Floyd McKissick.

He said his boycott campaign now included five steps and the threatened moves would be withdrawn only if "the whole package were accepted by various persons in authority."

He outlined the steps as follows:

—A boycott by Negro athletes of the Olympic Games.

—A boycott of all New York Athletic Club events because, he said, the Club has not had a Negro or Jewish athlete on its teams in this century.

—A demand that all-white teams from Southern Rhodesia and South Africa be banned from competing in the U.S., because American Negroes have not been permitted to run in those nations.

—Reinstatement of Cassius Clay as heavyweight champion, a position from which he was deposed because of his conviction for draft evasion.

—Desegregation of the United States Olympic Games Committee and assignment of more Negro coaches to the U.S. Olympic teams.

Edwards said about a dozen Negro athletes have joined his boycott campaign. He said the list included UCLA Basketball star Lew Alcindor, San Jose State Track standouts Tommie Smith and Lee Evans, long jumper Ralph Boston, high jumper Otis Burrell and sprinter John Carlos.

Two Statements: Pro and Con   *Letter from Gene Johnson—7 foot high jumper and member of 1963 U.S. Pan American Games Track Team*

Many things have been said regarding the proposed Olympic Boycott by the Negro athletes. Apparently the real issue is being obscured. The athletes who have come up with the proposed boycott have to be commended from my point of view. In essence what they are saying is this: There is a tremendous credibility gap between the treatment accorded our Negro "stars," and the black masses in general. The United States exalts its Olympic star athletes as representatives of a democratic and free society, when millions of Negro and other minority citizens are excluded from decent housing and meaningful employment. This is where the credibility factor enters. I would like to pose this as a question. What would be the fate of a Ralph Boston, if he was not a 27 foot broadjumper, of a Charlie Green, if he was not a 9.2 sprinter? They would be "faceless" black men caught in the same system of racial discrimination as many other black citizens.

I am extremely proud to see that those proposing the boycott have enough social awareness to realize that this struggle of the man in Fillmore, Watts, and in Harlem is their struggle also. The efforts of Negroes in athletics have benefited only the athlete involved.

The Civil Rights movement or struggle requires the aid and contributions of *all* black men regardless of their "station in life." Negro athletes should not be exempt from nor should they divorce themselves from this struggle. The mere fact that a great sacrifice, such as forgoing an opportunity to participate in the Olympics, is involved points to the urgency surrounding the issue. Undoubtedly, many Negro athletes will not agree to the proposed move. This is their opinion and it should be respected. However, my hat is off to Tommie Smith, Lee Evans, Otis Burrell, and Lew Alcindor. I am also certain that millions of American Negroes will take heart from the fact that their plight has not been overlooked by those of us "who have it made within the system."

> Sincerely,
> GENE JOHNSON
> Field Representative

Jesse Owens—Olympic Hero of 1936 Games

New York, New York (Dave Eisenberg, Conversations in Sports, Hearst Headline Special Service). I am not in accord with those who advocate a boycott of the Olympic Games. The Olympic Games and the athletic programs that we have in this country have helped people to bridge the big gap of misunderstanding in that particular area. Athletics helps youngsters who do not have the money to go on to colleges of their choice because their athletic abilities get them scholarships. They come out and become successes in the communities in which they live.

South Africa and the International Thrust Toward Dignity and Justice

Johannesburg, South Africa (Associated Press). South Africans Thursday night acclaimed the news that their country had been readmitted to the Olympic Games.

Matt Mare, president of the South African Amateur Athletic Union, commented: "I can only say that we are very pleased we have been readmitted to the Olympic Games. We are also pleased that the International Olympic Committee had the courage to send a committee to see conditions here for themselves and found the true facts." Mare added: "Now we hope that the IOC will not allow the opposition countries opposing South Africa's readmission to use their blocs to try to boycott the Olympic Games. As far as we are concerned, we accept the invitation with great pleasure and will send our best team—white and non-white."

Bill Stenhouse, president of the South African Bantu African Athletic and Cycling Federation, said he felt the support of African officials and sportsmen interviewed by the IOC delegation made no small contribution to the favorable report placed before the IOC by its fact-finding delegation. "I am quite sure that the Bantu athletes will be tickled pink by the decision in favor of South Africa's readmittance," he said.

Radio South Africa broke into programs to announce the news to the nation. The announcement came as a surprise to many who felt that prejudices against South Africa because of its race policies would keep the country out of the Games. South Africa was barred from the 1964 Olympics because of race discrimination in sport. Braun [Frank Braun, South African Olympic Games Committee President] said the South African Olympic Council will meet next Tuesday to discuss in detail the country's readmission to the

Olympics. South Africa will go to the games with one of the hottest favorites for a gold medal in swimming sensation Karen Muir. Miss Muir, 15, last month shattered the women's world records for the 200 meters, 220 yards, 100 meters and 110 yards backstroke.

Track sprinter Paul Nash is probably South Africa's strongest other chance for a medal. The country's non-white athletes, who will go to Mexico City with the white athletes as a mixed team, do not appear likely at this stage to produce any medalists.

Grenoble, France (*Associated Press*). Arthur G. Lentz, executive director of the United States Olympic Committee, Thursday night said that his group had always insisted on "integrated trials and an integrated team" as a condition for South African re-admittance to the Olympic Games.

Lentz said that the U.S. Olympic Committee had pressed for the South Africans "to select their team on the same basis as the United States—with the trials open to all comers." He added that if the "integrated trials and integrated team" condition was met, then "we would be in favor of it and we would submit to the IOC decision."

Lusaka, Zambia (*Associated Press*). President Kenneth Kaunda said Friday Zambia is studying the International Olympic Committee's decision to readmit South Africa.

Kampala, Uganda (*Associated Press*). Uganda's National Council of Sports issued a statement Friday announcing Uganda will reserve its decision on participation in the Mexico Olympics if South Africa is allowed to compete without complying fully with the Olympic Charter.

Grenoble, France (*Associated Press*). Ethiopia announced its withdrawal Friday from the 1968 Olympics about the same time Avery Brundage said he hoped no nation would pull out of the Mexico City Games this October because of South Africa's readmission.

While Brundage, the American president of the International Olympic Committee, was making his statement here, an official of the Ethiopian Sports Confederation announced in Addis Ababa that his country would not participate.

He said he was greatly shocked by the IOC's decision Thursday to readmit South Africa, which had been banned in 1963 for its racial policies. "This was a victory for the policy of apartheid and not for the South African Olympic Committee."

Kampala, Uganda (Associated Press). Uganda decided today to withdraw from the Mexico Olympics in protest against South Africa's readmission. The decision was announced by the National Council of Sports here.

Dar Es Salaam, Tanzania (Associated Press). Tanzania became the fourth African country to announce it will not take part in the Mexico City Olympic Games in October because South Africa has been re-admitted. Earlier, Algeria, Uganda and Ethiopia declared they would boycott the games.

Damascus, Syria (Associated Press). Syria announced Monday it would boycott the Olympic Games in Mexico this year in protest against South Africa's admission to the Games.

Cairo, United Arab Republic (Associated Press). The United Arab Republic has decided to boycott the summer Olympics in Mexico because of the readmission of South Africa to the Olympic movement, the semi-official Egyptian Middle East News Agency announced Saturday.

Port of Spain, Trinidad (Associated Press). The chairman of the Trinidad Olympic Association said Sunday he will ask the association to keep Trinidad out of the Summer Olympics in Mexico in protest to the readmission of South Africa to the Games.

Nairobi, Kenya (Associated Press). The Kenya Government announced today it would boycott the Mexico Summer Olympics because of South Africa's readmission to the Games.

Johannesburg, South Africa (Associated Press). South African Olympic Games Committee President Frank Braun expressed regret Tuesday night at the decision of 12 Afro-Asian nations to boycott the 1968 Olympics because South Africa will take part.

Grenoble, France (Associated Press). A boycott of the Summer Olympic Games in Mexico City built up Saturday when six more African countries pulled out and the Soviet Union considered withdrawing in protest to the readmission of South Africa.

Mexico City, Mexico (Associated Press). With growing frustration, Mexico received scattered reports Tuesday of a growing boycott against the 1968 Summer Olympics.

Johannesburg, South Africa (Associated Press). The president of the South African Olympic Games Committee will personally ask all the countries boycotting the summer Olympics because of his country's participation to reconsider.

Oslo, Norway (Associated Press). Three prominent Scandinavian Liberal politicians sharply criticized Tuesday the decision of the International Olympic Committee to readmit South Africa to the Olympic family of nations. In a joint communiqué the three—municipal minister Helge Seip of Norway, education minister Helge Larsen of Denmark, and leader of the people's party in Sweden, Sven Weden—urged the Olympic committees in the Scandinavian countries to reconsider. They called for the reversal of the IOC decision last week and the banning of South Africa from participating as long as racial discrimination continues in that country. The three politicians met in Oslo in connection with the meeting of the Nordic council.

Lusaka, Zambia (Associated Press). Zambia became the 15th country Wednesday to declare it will boycott the Olympics in Mexico City this October because of the reinstatement of South Africa by the International Olympic Committee.

Moscow, U.S.S.R. (Associated Press). Tass reported Sunday without much emphasis Saturday's call by African foreign ministers for a boycott of the Olympics by African and other states to protest the readmission of South Africa.

Havana, Cuba (Associated Press). Cuba criticized the International Olympic Committee Saturday for the IOC's decision 10 days ago to allow South Africa to participate.

London, England (Associated Press, John Farrow). Thirty-two African countries have pulled out of the Summer Olympics in Mexico City next fall and the big question now is whether the Russians will withdraw as well.

Moscow, U.S.S.R. (Associated Press, Michael Johnson). The Soviet Olympic Committee said Monday Soviet participation in the Mexico City Summer Olympics is still an open question. Readmission of South Africa to the Games has cast doubt on Soviet plans for the Olympics starting October 12, the spokesman said.

Johannesburg, South Africa (Associated Press). Frank Braun, president of the South African Olympic Committee, appealed Saturday to the Supreme African Sports Council not to boycott the 1968 Olympics because South Africa will be taking part.

Paris, France (Associated Press). Two of the world's top amateur athletic bodies have set out to justify South Africa's participation in the Olympics this fall, but the move to boycott the games continues to grow.

Avery Brundage, president of the International Olympic Committee, said here Sunday that South Africa will allow its "underprivileged nonwhites an opportunity to appear on the same basis as anyone else." Brundage said, "South African nonwhites long have sought the opportunity to participate in the games and it is unfortunate that some who pretend to be their friends would deprive them of it."

In Frankfurt, Germany, the International Amateur Athletic Federation supported the decision to allow South Africa into the games—a move that has led 16 countries to say they will pull out.

South Africa Barred From Games

Chicago, Illinois (Associated Press). South Africa was barred from the 1968 Olympics at Mexico City as a protective measure against possible violence at the Games.

That was the explanation of Avery Brundage, International Olympic Committee President, on his return to Chicago Thursday from Lausanne, Switzerland. It was in Lausanne that Brundage said he recommended to the IOC Executive Board a quick mail vote which knocked South Africa from the Games.

"The action by the Executive Board recommending a full committee vote against South Africa's participation was done at my suggestion," said the 80-year-old millionaire.

"The protesters seem to think we took this action just against South Africa. We did it, in effect, to protect their boys and girls who would be exposed to violence or unpleasantness in Mexico City.

"Some people thought we gave up to threats of boycott by some countries," Brundage continued. "That didn't come into the discussion at all. We were disturbed because it appeared actually dangerous for these people of South Africa to appear in Mexico."

Black Athletes Protest at Games in Name of Dignity, Justice and Humanity

Mexico City, Mexico (Associated Press, Will Grimsley). [Tommie] Smith, world record holder in the 200 meters, won the race in 19.8 seconds, setting a new mark. His teammate Carlos, from San Jose, Calif., a militant spokesman in the Negro athletes' civil rights movement, finished third behind Peter Norman of Australia. At the medal presentation ceremonies, conducted by Britain's Lord Burghley, Smith wore a black glove on his right hand and Carlos a black glove on his left. Smith had a black scarf around his neck. Carlos wore beads. Both held a single shoe, symbolizing another protest against a ban on a certain manufacturer's product.

As the band played the Star Spangled Banner, Smith thrust his gloved right hand and Carlos his black-sheathed left toward the sky in a Nazi-like salute. Both glued their eyes on the ground and refused to look at the American flag as it was being hoisted to the top of the mast at one end of the huge saucer, holding some 60,000 fans. The stadium rocked with boos and cat-calls and some of the spectators made thumbs-down gestures as they would to Mexican matadors preparing for the kill.

Over in the stands, the wives of the two athletes laughed heartily with friends. "Wait until Avery sees this," said Mrs. Smith. "He'll die." Moments later in the stadium press interview room, packed with reporters from many nations, Carlos, who acted as spokesman, cut loose a bitter tirade at the white social structure and the many Mexican fans who had jeered him. "They look upon us as nothing but animals," he said. "Low animals, roaches and ants. I want you to print this and print it right. If white people don't care to see black men perform they should not come out to the stadium." Then he added: "We are sort of show horses out there for the white people. They give us peanuts, pat us on the back and say, 'Boy, you did fine.' What do they think? It's U.S. Black athletes who threatened to boycott and the Black athletes of Africa, who are winning the medals." At the hectic interview sessions, the tall, bearded Carlos took his bronze medal from around his neck and tossed it to his wife, standing in a yellow dress at the fringe of the crowd of reporters. "Here, honey, this is yours," he said. "I don't want it." Then he added: "The next time I go to an Olympics, I will pay my way and go as a spectator." Smith left most of the talking to his teammate, but he never indicated he disagreed with a word. He nodded his head repeatedly.

As they prepared to leave the interview room, the two American athletes were asked what they would have done had Brundage attempted to present them their medals. "We will cross that bridge when we get to it," said Smith.

Long after dark and into the evening Wednesday night, athletes of various nations talked of the incident over dinner and in the Village recreation rooms. . . . "I think it's too bad," said Gary Knoke, an Australian track man who attends the University of Oregon. "Really, politics should not be injected into these games." A U.S. fencer, strolling through the Village, said: "Gee, I thought it was terrible. It's too bad. I sympathize with what some of those guys are trying to do, but this is not the time or place." He is white. A white American coach of another team, who asked that his name not be used, commented: "I'd send them home. That's what I'd do. I'd send those guys packing. It's a disgrace."

Neither Payton Jordan of Stanford University, the head track and field coach, or Stan Wright, a Negro assistant coach in charge of the sprinters, was available for comment after the incident. . . . Assistant coach Edward Haydon, a professor at the University of Chicago, said: "It was really a small protest considering the size of the problem. We are fortunate it was as restrained as it was. Remember some of these kids have a message they want to get across and this is their way of doing it. We can't feel too harsh toward them. They have worked and trained hard. Otherwise, we would not have such terrific performances. I haven't talked with Payton but I doubt there will be any wrist-slapping. It's a bigger matter than just a foot race."

Mexico City, Mexico (Associated Press, Will Grimsley). The U.S. Olympic committee's executive board issued a broad apology Thursday for the Black power display by sprinters Tommie Smith and John Carlos at Wednesday's victory ceremony in Olympic Stadium.

Mexico City, Mexico (United Press International). The U.S. Olympic committee met again today and decided that Tommie Smith and John Carlos would be suspended from the team because of their Black power display at Wednesday's victory ceremony. The two Black sprinters would be asked to leave the Village immediately.

Trenton, New Jersey (Trenton Times-Advertiser). W. Oliver Leggett, Assistant to Mayor Armenti of this city, [Trenton, New Jersey] has registered a strong protest against action taken by the U.S. Olympic Committee in the dismissal of Tommie Smith and John Carlos, two Black members of the 1968 Olympic Team.

"*It was not* Tommie Smith and John Carlos who introduced social protest or politics to the Olympic stadium," states a press release from Leggett. "It was demonstrated first by the prolonged and sustained applause the Czechoslovakian Olympic Team received when they entered the Olympic procession, even before the start of the games. This applause was obviously based on the sentiments of the recent confrontation of the Czechoslovakian and Soviet governments." Leggett states politics was further demonstrated by the U.S. in its 60-year-old tradition of failing to lower the American flag in respect to the reviewing stand of the host nation.

"Tommie Smith and John Carlos were dismissed on the obvious premise that injustice and inequities can be confined to orderly and comfortable areas of expression," Leggett goes on. "I suggest . . . that protest must be registered in every area of a people's participation."

Los Angeles, California (Muhammad Speaks, Captain Edward 2x). The heroic Black Power posture assumed by Olympic heroes Tommie Smith and John Carlos was immortalized in an engraved medallion produced by Power Inc., a metal manufacturing company. Production of the memorial piece, known as the "Universal Medallion," was initiated by the Black Industrial and Economic Union spearheaded by Black film star Jim Brown.

San Francisco, California (San Francisco Chronicle). Students here sponsored a large rally in honor of Tommie Smith and John Carlos. Between 800 and 1,000 students gathered for the rally where the two Black sprinters were the main speakers. Robert Clark, president of San Jose State, stated earlier shortly after the U.S. Olympic Committee had taken action against Smith and Carlos, that "they do not return in disgrace but as Olympic heroes."

San Francisco, California (Sam Skinner Sports, KDIA Radio). Blacks from communities throughout the United States responded to the protest demonstration staged by Tommie Smith and John Carlos at the victory ceremonies after the 200 meters, by sending letters and telegrams to the Village and their residences. Welcoming ceremonies were staged and carried out in New York City, Washington, D.C., and San Jose, California.

Appendix B:
The Revolt on the Campus

University of California at Berkeley

Ray Willsey, Head Coach
Varsity Football
Athletic Department
Eshleman Hall
University of California
Berkeley, California

COACH RAY WILLSEY:

It has become unmistakenly obvious that in some areas of coaching the practice of favoritism and inequity, which permeated last year's team, STILL EXISTS. It is no secret to anyone, especially those that know football, that last year's *victim* of favoritism and inequity was Wayne Brooks, who was completely black-balled as an offensive player and possibly this year as a defensive player. We have also painfully watched, in utter disgust, such great competitors as Bernie Keeles, McKinley Parker, Clyde Flowers, and George Harris become similar victims.

In reference to Bernie Keeles, in particular, we feel that he should be in contention for the starting position and not relegated to third and fourth string. This nation has shown that it is ready to accept Blacks as quarterbacks and the University of California must also.

We, the Black athletes, want a winning team. We want the best twenty-two players on the field. We want the best player in each position. *THIS HAS NOT BEEN DONE.* As stated on our first set of demands (of Black athletes), we will not tolerate the forestated situations and practices. WE WILL NOT PLAY ON ANY TEAM THAT PERPETRATES THESE PRACTICES.

We demand *significant* changes in the Fall. We know the community is behind us. As a show of good faith and because a *few* noticeable steps have been made in the athletic department in meeting our past demands, we will attempt to keep our grievances out of the mass media and the public eye.

Respectfully,
THE BLACK ATHLETES
THE AFRO-AMERICAN STUDENT UNION
THE MEXICAN-AMERICAN STUDENT CONFEDERATION
KAPPA ALPHA PSI FRATERNITY

Berkeley, California (Associated Press). Negro football candidates at the University of California are boycotting spring practice, demanding the right to say who should play which position, and when.

Coach Ray Willsey silently read their demands, presented by one athlete and one student non-athlete, declined them, and handed back the paper.

"I do not believe these prerogatives of a coach are negotiable," he said. "I cannot ignore my responsibilities. "

He refused to give any details of the demands.

He also refused to name any of the athletes.

"I will not initiate any name calling," he said today. "I don't want to appear to the public to be exposing them to criticism." He said in a statement: "It will be a tragedy that competition will be denied to some outstanding young men because of their actions. These men, by not reporting for practice, are, in effect, removing themselves from the California Football Team."

Berkeley, California (United Press International). Head Coach Ray Willsey refused today to bow to demands of Negro varsity football players at the University of California who are boycotting spring practice. A representative of the 12 Negro players and a member of Cal's Afro-American Student Union presented a list of demands Wednesday to Willsey. Later none of the Negro football players showed up for practice. Only two had showed up Tuesday.

Berkeley, California (United Press International). Hope rose today that football players and head football coach Ray Willsey of the University of California can resolve their current differences. The players presented Willsey with a list of demands Wednesday urging more equitable treatment for Negroes on the squad. They alleged some Negro players were not being given a full chance to prove themselves and Negro was pitted against Negro at the same position to eliminate one of them.

When Willsey handed back the list of demands without taking any action, all 14 Negroes on the varsity stayed away from practice Wednesday and Thursday. Willsey, who stated firmly he would be the sole judge of "who will play, where and when," dropped all of them from the team Thursday and ordered their uniforms be removed from lockers. "Football's not like an all-night movie where you can come and go," said the coach. "They're off the team and that's it."

Berkeley, California (*Associated Press*). Negro athletes at the University of California demanded Tuesday the replacement of three major sports coaches and improved conditions for themselves under threat of boycotting sports. About 25 of the 40 Negro athletes on the Berkeley campus called a news conference and presented eight complaints and their boycott threat.

Bobby Smith, defensive half-back who was on the All-Pacific-8 Conference team and chosen for the Shrine East-West and Hula Bowl games, was spokesman for the group. Their protest was labeled "Revolution of Black Athletes of the University of California." Those they said "must be replaced for reasons of their inability or unwillingness to relate to black athletes and their general incompetence" are Rene Hêrrerias, head basketball coach; William Dutton, defensive football line coach; and Joe Marvin, offensive backfield coach.

Berkeley, California (*Associated Press*). Rene Hêrrerias, who quit as basketball coach at the University of California Thursday, says, "The Negro situation was a factor but not the sole factor." Although plagued by racial friction during his eight seasons as coach, Hêrrerias, 42, said only a few days ago he would serve out his contract, which had a year to go.

Berkeley, California (*United Press International*). Now both Pete Newell and his protégé, Rene Hêrrerias, are out of work, . . .

Newell quit as the University of California Athletic Director on March 12, claiming personal reasons, and Hêrrerias followed suit Thursday by announcing he was resigning as head basketball coach, practically for the same reasons.

Berkeley, California (*Associated Press, Charles McMurtry*). [Jim] Padgett, at 35 a highly successful recruiter and junior college and freshman basketball coach, may succeed Rene Hêrrerias as head basketball coach at the University of California. . . .

Padgett is highly regarded by Negro athletes, many of whom he personally recruited from as far away as the Deep South. His freshman team was 17—1 last season and 38—11 in his three years here.

Western Michigan University

Kalamazoo, Michigan (United Press International). The athletic director of Western Michigan University plans to meet with Negro athletes Monday to discuss their charges that the University "is incapable of equitable relationships with Black athletes," and their demand for the dismissal of the basketball coach.

Sixteen of 19 Negro athletes at the University sent a letter to Athletic Director Dr. Joseph T. Hoy Wednesday, outlining the charges. They said, however, this is not to be construed as "a Negro boycott of university sports."

The group, headed by track star Tom Randall, charged basketball coach Sonny Means "is unwilling to work with Black athletes and the atmosphere promoted by coaches and some white athletes is not conducive to team spirit and competition by Black athletes."

In the letter, they asked that Means be dismissed or a Negro assistant basketball coach be appointed. They demanded also more Negroes on the coaching staff, and more scholarships for Negro athletes. "Further action on our part will depend on the replies of the administration," the letter said.

Kalamazoo, Michigan (Associated Press). Three new athletic assistants including the first fulltime Negro coaches in the school's history were recommended Tuesday for assignment at Western Michigan University this fall.

Recommendation of assistantships for Charles Comer, 30, in football, Fred Decker in baseball and Fletcher Lewis, 32, in track will be submitted formally by Dr. Joseph T. Hoy, Athletic Director, to the board of trustees on Friday for approval. Comer and Lewis are Negroes.

Princeton University

Princeton, New Jersey (United Press International). Four of Princeton's five black football players have indicated they will not play this year in opposition to "exploitation" of black athletes and "racist tendencies" in Princeton's varsity and freshman coaches.

In a letter made public yesterday by the student newspaper, the Negroes charged that varsity coach Dick Colman and freshman coach Ted McCarthy had not given starting assignments to deserving blacks and had avoided using blacks in the offensive backfield. The letter, sent in December to Colman, director of athletics R. Kenneth Fairman and college president Robert Goheen, alleged that of the last seven Negroes who played football at Princeton, six quit before their senior years because of racial discrimination.

Michigan State University

East Lansing, Michigan (Associated Press, Bob Voges and Jacqueline Korona). A group of Negro athletes, led by star football halfback Lamarr Thomas, threatened to boycott all sports at Michigan State Thursday unless their demands are met.

A list of seven grievances, including a lack of Negro coaches and academic counseling designed "for Blacks to place them in courses where they will maintain eligibility," were presented to the administration. Thomas, second leading ground-gainer for the Spartans last year, led a delegation that met Thursday with athletic director Biggie Munn and John Fuzak, MSU faculty representative to the Big Ten.

Thomas gained 311 yards last season and was topped only by Dwight Lee, lost through graduation. Thomas said he was the spokesman for some 30 to 40 Negro athletes on the campus. The group presented a long list of grievances and said: "We intend to abstain from practice until they (the administration) give us some indication that they will attend to our grievances in a satisfactory manner."

Among the grievances listed by the group were:

1. The college is not hiring enough Negro coaches.

2. MSU is discouraging Black students from participating in certain sports—especially baseball.

3. MSU does not employ enough Blacks in jobs in Jenison fieldhouse, the intramural building, the ticket office and the ice arena.

4. There are no Black trainers or doctors to treat all athletes.

5. The athletic counselor is "under undue pressure" assisting all athletes and should have a Black assistant.

6. Academic counseling for Blacks is designed to place them in courses where they will maintain eligibility. They are forced to take nonacademic courses rather than academic courses that will enable them to graduate in four years.

7. Michigan State never has elected a Negro cheer leader.

The group also said it supports a boycott of the 1968 Olympics by Negroes.

East Lansing, Michigan (Associated Press, Bob Voges). Michigan State University officials today sought to answer demands by a group of Negro athletes who are threatening to boycott all sports at the University.

The athletes, led by star football halfback Lamarr Thomas, presented a list of seven grievances Thursday and said they would stay away from football practice until administration officials indicate "that they will attend to our grievances in a satisfactory manner."

Thomas, saying he is spokesman for some 30 or 40 Negro athletes at MSU, led a delegation that met with athletic director Biggie Munn and John Fuzak, MSU faculty representative to the Big Ten conference.

Oklahoma City University

Oklahoma City, Oklahoma (United Press International, Mike Wester). Abe Lemons, athletic director and head basketball coach at Oklahoma City University, Sunday received administration backing in an "apologize or else" ultimatum he issued six Negro athletes over the weekend. Dr. John Olson, president of the university, said the administration would stand behind Lemons all the way. "I personally feel the list of grievances presented Lemons are unfounded, and we will stand behind coach Lemons all the way," Olson said.

Lemons received a list of 14 grievances from the six athletes Thursday and immediately said he did not intend to let "part of the team dictate the policies to affect the whole squad." "I believe it's a personality conflict, and has nothing to do with a racial problem," Lemons said. "In fact, I wish the news media hadn't even played up the fact that the six athletes were Negroes. It just so happens they are, but it has nothing to do with their grievances."

Saturday Lemons said he would demand an apology from the athletes before reinstating them on the team. He said he felt the athletes owed that much to the University. "I have not kicked them off the team," Lemons said. "I have given them an ultimatum, and the next step is up to them." Lemons said his "ultimatum" told the athletes to either get him fired as coach, transfer to another school to play under a "nice" coach, apologize to the University and other players or return to OCU next year on scholarship but not compete in basketball.

Lemons said a full squad meeting was planned Monday to see just how deep-rooted some of the grievances were. The six athletes presenting the grievances included Floyd Bridges, Ardell England, Willie Watson, Joe Hayes, Art Yancey and Charles Wallace.

Oklahoma City, Oklahoma (Associated Press). Oklahoma City University basketball coach Abe Lemons said yesterday the six Negro players who presented him a list of grievances Friday will not be members of the OCU team next year.

"I have no intention of trying to coach that group next year," Lemons said. The Negro players presented Lemons with a list of 14 grievances mainly against his coaching methods. "I told them they could do one of two things—get me fired or transfer," Lemons said.

Five of the six players involved still have eligibility remaining, and Lemons said their athletic scholarships would be honored next year, "if they wish to continue their education at OCU." Lemons announced his decision Saturday morning shortly before a meeting called by the six Negro athletes.

University of Texas at El Paso

El Paso, Texas (Associated Press). Seven Negro track and field athletes at the University of Texas at El Paso said in a statement Thursday they will boycott UTEP's track meet Saturday against Brigham Young.

The statement said the boycott was due to what the athletes called a belief at BYU "that the blacks are inferior and that we are disciples of the devil."

UTEP issued its own statement saying it will participate at the Provo, Utah, meet and "any member of the team who fails to do so will be considered by the athletic department as having voluntarily disassociated himself with the track team." Track coach Wayne Vandenburg said Wednesday night before the athletes' statement was made public, "There's not going to be a boycott of my team. If there is, they are not going to be members of my team."

The seven athletes include Bob Beamon, world's indoor long jump record holder. They also said Vandenburg should "have been more sympathetic toward us, the black athletes, concerning our feelings toward the assassination of Dr. Martin Luther King."

El Paso, Texas (United Press International). Wayne Vandenburg, track coach at the University of Texas at El Paso, said Thursday if world long jump record holder Bob Beamon and six Negro teammates do not compete in a Utah track meet this weekend they will be considered off the team. The seven athletes announced Thursday they might not compete in a triangular meet between UTEP, Brigham Young and Utah State at Provo, Utah, because this was a week of "holy cause for all Blacks." But Vandenburg said the Miners would compete in the meet Saturday, "if I have to run all the events myself."

El Paso, Texas (Associated Press). Eight Negro trackmen from the University of El Paso stayed home today and faced expulsion from the El Paso team after saying they would boycott a Saturday triangular meet at Brigham Young University in Provo, Utah. Coach Wayne Vandenburg and 14 of his athletes, including two Negroes, left for Utah by airplane. Vandenburg said earlier that team members missing the plane because of the boycott would be disassociating themselves from the team.

Provo, Utah (Associated Press). Members of the University of Texas at El Paso track team, minus champion long jumper Bob Beamon and seven others, worked out under cloudy skies Friday in preparation for a meet with Brigham Young University. Beamon, who holds the world record mark for the long jump in indoor competition, and seven other Negro athletes, remained in El Paso, Texas, in a self-imposed boycott over participation in the meet Saturday afternoon.

El Paso, Texas (Associated Press). A demonstration on behalf of 10 Negro track and field athletes had not achieved its goal Thursday as University officials stood firm on their removal of the Negroes from the team. University of Texas at El Paso officials also said there would be no change in plans for UTEP to hold a dual meet Saturday against Wisconsin.

Wisconsin and Texas-El Paso were two of the four teams in a meet Wednesday night when a demonstration by about 25 young persons disrupted competition. There were no reports of arrests, but more than 50 policemen stood guard at the field as the demonstrators chanted, "Reinstatement, Reinstatement."

Eleven Negro women, with arms interlocked, blocked the track for the 440-yard relay and 120-yard hurdles races. The demonstrators were seeking reinstatement of Negro athletes who boycotted a track and field meet at Provo, Utah, last week. University officials said the athletes thus were dissociating themselves from the team.

Wayne Vandenburg, coach of the UTEP Track Team, said 10 Negroes had left the team, the latest being half-mile runner John Nichols. Vandenburg said two Negroes from the Bahamas still were on the team. Vandenburg called the demonstration "ridiculous and showed a great deal of immaturity." He said none of the Negro athletes participated overtly.

Vandenburg said the Negro athletes would not be eligible for competition in NCAA track and field events because they would not be representing a school. He said their competition in U.S. Olympic tryouts would not be affected.

San Francisco State College

SAN FRANCISCO STATE COLLEGE

A Statement

We, the Black athletes of San Francisco State College are convinced that racism exists in the school's department of athletics. Moreover, we have been equally convinced by Black athletes who have played here in the past, that this practice has been subtly carried on for a number of years.

We believe the coaches of this college have exploited Black athletes and are, in fact, continuing to do so by failing to keep promises of job security and assistance in finding adequate housing; by excluding or overlooking Black players for positions as graduate assistant coaches; by showing an acute lack of interest, or knowledge, or whatever of Black athletes' special problems; by showing indifference to whether Black players ever finish their college education, interested only in whether or not Black athletes are eligible for competition, and by flagrantly lying to Black athletes in order to get them to enroll here. We offer these examples of how Black athletes have been exploited and lied to by the coaches and athletic department of this college:

(1) Euarl Smothers is an all-state football player from Texas; he was promised a football scholarship by the head football coach if he entered San Francisco State. *San Francisco State does not award athletic scholarships of any kind. It has never done so in the past.* Victor Rowen, the head football coach, has held his position for over ten (10) years. He is fully aware that he cannot give athletic scholarships. His offer to Euarl Smothers was nothing more than a *bold-faced lie* to dupe this athlete into coming to the West Coast and playing for him. This man is still making overtures to Smothers to enroll in SF State, though he has not made even the slightest mention of an adequate job to this Black athlete.

(2) Everett Adams is a Black athlete who virtually rewrote basketball record books during his career at San Francisco State (1964—66). During that time, he was promised all kinds of jobs. He received a job paying $1.50 per hour working only on weekends. His efforts to find better employment were put off with vague answers by the basketball coach. He never received a worthwhile job here, though white players of less than half of his ability received good jobs, during the school year and over the summer.

(3) Tom Crowder is a Black athlete who was recruited from Riverside Junior College by the basketball coach. Like Adams, he was prom-

ised a job that would take care of his school expenses. Like Adams, he never received it. The housing he was promised "fell through," and he was forced to move into a dilapidated building in the Fillmore District. During this time, Crowder relates, he and his roommate, a Black football player, alternated between sleeping on a broken down couch and the floor! The job he received paid $1.25 an hour, but was "raised" to $1.50 after a couple of months. Crowder almost starved. His second semester tuition was paid by money he had won in a card game during the team's annual trip to the East. He could not have continued in school without this unexpected windfall.

There are any number of like examples of how Black athletes have fared at this college, but we offer these as proof. We believe at this time, when the school will field more Black players than at any other time in its history, that we can no longer stand idly by and have this happen to us. No less than eight (8) Blacks will be participating in basketball next season, four of whom are probable starters. Two times this number have been recruited for football, and a number of Black athletes make up the track team. We will no longer be exploited. We have a list of demands we will present to the athletic department and its various coaches with hope that they will act on them immediately.

BLACK ATHLETES' DEMANDS

Housing

We demand that the same amount of effort be put forth in finding adequate housing for Black athletes as that effort which is put forth in finding places for white players. Few Black athletes have had housing found for them by the athletic department, although countless promises have been made by the coaches to do so. Consequently, Black players have had to go entire semesters with no place to live. Some players have had to commute as many as 25 miles a day to the campus while participating in sports. No Black player has ever had housing close to the SF State campus. We demand that Black personnel be hired to work with those landlords who are willing to take on Black athletes as tenants, since housing in the area of the college is unavailable to us, and the athletic department has shown a reluctance to look elsewhere for places for Black players.

Jobs

The Black athlete at San Francisco State is uniquely different from the average college player. He is often an older athlete, sometimes with a family to support, and has entered this college mostly because he desires to stay in this area close to that family. These athletes, along with the younger players, cannot draw upon family resources to help finance their education like white players. The jobs they receive are too often the only means they have to support themselves and their families. We demand that the athletic department adapt a more equal distribution of the better jobs among all of the athletes, and halt the practices of "saving" the best jobs for white players and the menial, inferior ones for Blacks.

We demand that the department and its coaches follow through on their commitments at recruiting time to Black players of adequate jobs. Few of the Black players who were promised employment by coaches were given it. Black athletes are forced to "fend for themselves" in seeking adequate jobs, while white players receive the employment promised to them. This has apparently been the practice at San Francisco State for a number of years, and we demand an immediate end to it. We also demand that a minimum wage of $2.25 per hour be instituted for athletes who are promised jobs by the coaches, and that we receive an equal number of the summer jobs that we know exist.

Black Coaches

At San Francisco State, no Black athlete has ever been named to move up to the ranks of graduate assistant coach for any of the college's various athletic teams after his playing days are over. *We believe that it is vital for Black athletes who are planning to enter the coaching field to receive some of these positions.* [What follows is a lengthy description of current and past hiring tactics at San Francisco State College and how these tactics have allegedly operated to exclude qualified black athletes from all the important coaching positions at the college. Specific complaints are outlined and the recent hiring of candidates for coaching positions are used to illustrate and to justify these complaints. Demands are made for an immediate end to the practices in the San Francisco state athletic department.]

In addition to our demands that Black athletes be chosen to fill some of the grad-coaching positions, we also demand that the department actively recruit and hire Black coaches, who can relate to and offer solutions to the special problems of Black players. Current coaches have shown an acute lack of interest, or knowledge, or whatever, to these problems.

We also demand that the same interest be taken in the care of injured Black players as that which is taken in the care of whites. Coaches have fawned over injured white players, but have shown a marked indifference over hurt Black athletes.

If our demands are not met, or no sufficient efforts are made by the athletic department to alleviate the discriminatory practices in athletics at San Francisco State, all Black athletes will withdraw from competition and discourage other Black players from enrolling at this college.

Signed,
BLACK ATHLETES OF SAN FRANCISCO STATE COLLEGE

San Francisco, California (Associated Press). "If the school does not make an effort to correct conditions, Black athletes will not participate in sports and will encourage prospective students not to enroll," basketball player Verne Smith told a news conference Thursday.

Athletic Director Jerry Wyness declared, "This was stirred up outside [meaning Professor Harry Edwards of San Jose State]. If it is legitimate, okay, if not, it's wasting my time. Our goal is to upgrade Negro students, and always has been. I never count the races or color. A number of Negroes were considered recently before the school hired three new coaches," Wyness said. "We hired the best men and will continue to do so regardless of color."

San Francisco, California (United Press International). Negro athletes at San Francisco State College, charging racism exists in the school's department of athletics, have threatened to quit all teams. Eight members of the varsity basketball squad and five on the football team are Negroes. At a news conference Thursday, the newly formed Black athletes at San Francisco State said they are convinced racist policies have been "subtly carried on for a number of years" at the college.

[*Author's note*] San Francisco State College's Associated Student Body government unanimously voted to cut off all athletic funds until the racist situation at that school was rectified.

Marquette

Milwaukee, Wisconsin (Associated Press, Ken Hartnett). Marquette, believed near a breakthrough into the national basketball rankings, is now on the verge of a breakup over the racial issue.

Six Marquette [basketball] players, including the sensational junior George Thompson, withdrew from the university Thursday. They said they were "disgusted and disappointed at the failure of Marquette to take a direct stand" on a student demand for a commitment to hire a Negro administrator. If the Roman Catholic institution relents in time, the players, all Negroes, may reconsider. But, it was apparent that their withdrawal was not just a ploy. "I've thought about it a long time," said Dean Meminger, a freshman who was regarded by coach Al McGuire as a player with the potential of a Bob Cousy. Meminger was expected to team with Thompson, junior Pat Smith and sophomore Joe Thomas next season on a squad potentially far stronger than the one that reached the NCAA Regionals last season and the National Invitational Tournament finals two seasons ago. But Thomas and Smith as well as Frank Edwards, a 1967—68 Red Shirt, joined Thompson and Meminger in the withdrawal. So did Blanton Simmons, a senior who was to have been graduated in June. The six were among 20 of Marquette's 49 Negro undergraduates to withdraw from the school in protest against what protestors call "institutional racism."

Hundreds of Marquette's more than 6,000 undergraduates have been demanding a "Christian commitment" from the Roman Catholic institution on the race question. The symbol of their demand was the hiring of a Negro who would administer a Negro scholarship program and coordinate other services for Negro students. The protesters asked for the commitment now but gave the university until August 1969 to hire the administrator. Marquette, which has defended its record on the racial question, has said it will not be coerced into action.

The loss of Thompson, the school's highest single season varsity scorer in history, and Meminger, highest scoring freshman player ever at Marquette, would tear the heart out of what McGuire hopes would be one of his best teams. Since Meminger enrolled at Marquette, Warrior fans have waited for the day when he and Thompson would be paired on the varsity. Thompson was the highest scorer for the varsity last year, and Meminger the top scorer for the freshmen, shattering Thompson's freshman marks. Thompson set five school records last year, including most points for one season, 664; highest season average, 22.8; most field goals, 252; most free throws, 160; and most points during two varsity years, 1,187. Athletic Director Stan Lowe admitted the six "are certainly key players. There's no question about it."

Augustus Moye, a student, announced at a news conference at the jammed Marquette Union that the 20 students were "disgusted and disappointed" at Marquette's alleged failure to take a positive action toward elimination of "institutional racism." The 20 said they would return to the University if demands made by the protesters were met.

The protest began May 8 when about 200 students held a sit-in in front of the union and briefly prevented guests at a university dinner from leaving the building. Police dispersed that demonstration and two students were arrested.

The demonstrations have continued since, calling on the university to take a greater involvement in the civil rights movement. Demands by the protesters include 100 scholarships for disadvantaged students, more Negroes on the administration and faculty and an open speakers policy. Moye's announcement came after protest leaders and university officials had met earlier in the day in an attempt to iron out the disputes.

After the news conference, protest leaders urged students to remain in the union until after the 10 p.m. scheduled closing. They urged the students to seek arrest. One of the speakers said protest action taken "will be simple, nonviolent, unobstructive to the university and, most of all, Christian." The Rev. John P. Raynor, S. J., Marquette president, said the university was forming a committee of faculty, administrators and students to find ways to obtain more scholarships for Negroes and Black culture courses. At the same time, Father Raynor warned the university would not agree to the demand that a Black administrator be hired. He said the school would not hire a person solely on the basis of his color. "If any of our students persist, despite these efforts and commitment, to impede the orderly achievement of these objectives by disruptive demonstrations, I regretfully advise them that they no longer will be welcome at this university, and urge them to take prompt steps to withdraw," the priest said. "I now emphasize that this university will not be governed by coercion, nor will it respond to rash and loosely conceived program demands of such (protest) groups," he said.

According to a federal survey, Marquette, a Roman Catholic School operated by the Society of Jesus, has 49 Negroes among its some 7,000 undergraduates.

Milwaukee, Wisconsin (Associated Press). Marquette University administrators and leaders of a student racial protest used the first day of a 48-hour cooling off period for a series of separate meetings Friday. But the status of six Negro basketball players who made a short-lived threat of withdrawal was back in doubt. There were reports on the campus that Marquette, largest coeducational Roman Catholic university in the nation, was ready to hire a full time Negro administrator to recruit Negro students and faculty members as the demonstrators demanded. No one in authority would comment.

The athletes involved met privately Friday, then went into a closed meeting with school officials. George Thompson, Marquette's top basketball player, issued a statement early Friday—following a meeting with Coach Al McGuire—that the players had reconsidered the resignations offered Thursday night. The athletes were among 20 Negro students who said they would withdraw from school. The announcement came at a rally at the student union which culminated late Thursday night in the arrest of seven persons who refused to leave the building after closing. Two of the seven posted $50 bail Friday on disorderly conduct charges and were released. The others did not post bail and remained in jail. Following the early-morning statement on behalf of the athletes that they had decided to remain, the others said they would not change their minds. Thompson said the players reconsidered after the Rev. Bernard J. Cooke, chairman of the theology department and a widely-known scholar, asked for the 48-hour cooling off period. Father Cooke said he would resign if the university did not meet the demand for a Negro administrator.

University of Kansas

Lawrence, Kansas (Associated Press). All 15 Negro players on the University of Kansas Football squad boycotted spring practice Thursday to support demands for a Negro cheerleader, a Negro coach and some Negro professors. There was no immediate indication whether the boycott would spread to the track team. Five of the eight trackmen chosen to leave Friday for the Fresno, Calif., relays are Negroes. John Mitchell, assistant track coach, said Thursday night they would make the trip, as far as he knew.

A group of about 150 Negro athletes and students met Wednesday night and a spokesman said they decided to begin a "comprehensive boycott of all athletics" if they did not get "satisfactory answers" to their demands. The ultimatum was issued by the group after a university official had told the Negroes earlier Wednesday of plans to add a Negro girl as an alternate on the cheerleader squad. Three Negro girls were among 95 coeds who tried out for the Pom Pom (CQ) squad last month. The eight regulars and four alternates selected April 25 are all white. A letter protesting that there was discrimination in the selection of Pom Pom girls was presented to Chancellor W. Clarke Wescoe last week. The letter was signed by 57 individuals. The Negro group also added demands that the university employ a Negro professor to teach Negro history classes that would be open to all students, a Negro coach and more Negro professors.

Members of the protesting group, which includes non-athletes, met Thursday night with the KU human relations committee and learned that a Negro girl will be added to the cheerleader squad. "A vacancy has occurred on the Pom Pom squad through the resignation of one of the members for personal reasons," said William A. Kelly, associate dean of law and a member of the human relations committee.

Lawrence, Kansas (Associated Press). University of Kansas athletes have gained some results from a one-day boycott of spring football practice and a threat to boycott all athletics in support of demands for a Negro cheerleader, a Negro coach and more Negro professors. A university spokesman said Thursday night a Negro will be chosen to fill a vacancy on the pom pom girls' squad, a course in Negro history will be offered next fall, and the university always is looking for qualified Negro faculty members. The demand for a Negro coach is a matter for future consideration. John Greene, Negro student and former football player, said he thought the protesting group generally was satisfied with the answers. All 15 Negro members of the football squad triggered the action by boycotting Thursday's practice session, the 19th of the 20 spring practices allowed by the Big Eight.

University of Oklahoma

Norman, Oklahoma (Associated Press). University of Oklahoma athletic director Gomer Jones was scheduled to meet with Negro athletes today to discuss the problems that caused them to boycott Tuesday night's varsity "O" Club banquet. The Negroes stood quietly in the hall outside the ballroom where the banquet was held but refused to enter the room. When Jones entered, one handed him a petition. "It just said, We, the undersigned, join in boycotting the varsity "O" Banquet," Jones said. "It didn't give any reasons," he added.

The Negro athletes waited until the invocation for the banquet had been given and then quietly left. Jones said he didn't know what the complaint was, and none of the athletes could be reached for comment. No Negroes attended the banquet. It was the first indication that Negro athletes at OU were dissatisfied.

Norman, Oklahoma (Associated Press). Gomer Jones, athletic director of the University of Oklahoma, held a closed door meeting with about 15 Negro athletes Wednesday to hear complaints about their treatment at OU. Jones said he would need time to consider the complaints before issuing a reply. But he did say: "I consider this a friendly meeting from my standpoint. We discussed what the athletes considered mistreatment." The athletes said they had no plan to quit their sports or classes at OU. One request was for separate meetings with all the head coaches which Jones said he would try to arrange. Another was that the coaches did not treat Negro athletes with respect. One of the written requests presented to Jones said: "Why are there no Black counselors, coaches, trainers, secretaries and managers in the athletic department?" Other complaints were that Negro athletes were coerced to cut their hair short and shave off mustaches; Negro athletes were held responsible by many of the coaches when games were lost; Negro athletes were given less leisure time on trips than white athletes, and common courtesies were not extended to Negroes on campus.

Granville Liggins, Associated Press All-American Football Player, was identified as one of the principal spokesmen for the Negro athletes in the meeting with Jones. Liggins denied there had been any outside influence leading to the request for an airing of grievances. "We have banded together," Liggins said, "to present these grievances. There's no organization behind this."

Norman, Oklahoma (*United Press International*). Gomer Jones, athletic director at Oklahoma University, Monday that the Sooner athletic department believed in and endorsed the movement for equal opportunity, and he said he thought sports at OU had provided the quickest way for Negroes to secure social reform. Jones and Oklahoma's head coaches met with a group of Negro athletes Monday who boycotted an "O" Club banquet last week. Jones said after the meeting Oklahoma was "proud of its Negro athletes and of their feats." Jones distributed a three-page statement following the meeting, but refused a press conference. "Nothing can be accomplished by continuing this discussion with the press," Jones said. "The statement explains our full position on this matter."

In the statement, Jones said the university might be at fault in two areas— advising against interracial dating although it was not forbidden, and the need for employing additional Negro personnel throughout the university. However, he commented individually upon 20 of the 27 grievances listed by the OU Negro athletes, and explained the university's stand on them. He said in the future he hopes any athlete at the university, Negro or white, would feel free to approach either him or a head coach with any problem. "Now is the time for both our white and Negro groups to realize they have many mutual problems, and that they should exercise common sense in disposing of them," Jones said in the statement.

University of Michigan

Ann Arbor, Michigan (*Associated Press*). The University of Michigan promoted Dave Martin to head track and field coach today to take over July 1 when Don Canham steps up to succeed retiring H. O. "Fritz" Crisler as athletic director. The University also announced appointment of its first Negro to a varsity-level coaching job, naming Ken Burnley, a former Wolverine sprinter, as an assistant to Martin, who was elevated from assistant to the head coaching job. Also named as an assistant to Martin was Jack Harvey, two-time Big Ten Shotput champion.

At nearby Kalamazoo, meanwhile, Western Michigan University announced selection of two Negroes among three new varsity assistant coaches to be recommended to the Board of Trustees Friday. Negro students at both universities had demanded appointment of Negro coaches in demonstrations staged on the two campuses in recent weeks.

University of Southern California   *"And some saw the handwriting on the wall."*

Los Angeles, California (*Associated Press*). The University of Southern California announced Friday the appointment of Willie Brown, a former star football and baseball player at the school, as an assistant coach in both sports. He is the first Negro named to the coaching staff. Athletic Director Jess Hill said in a statement: "We have felt a need existed at the University of Southern California for another assistant football coach and an assistant baseball coach. Willie Brown is well qualified in both of these areas and we feel he will be a most capable addition to our coaching staff."

Appendix C:
The Black Record-Holders

Baseball

Black Batting Champions
(National League)

Player	Year	Average
Hank Aaron, Milwaukee Braves	1956	.328
Hank Aaron, Milwaukee Braves	1959	.355
Roberto Clemente, Pittsburgh Pirates	1961	.351
Tommy Davis, Los Angeles Dodgers	1962	.346
Tommy Davis, Los Angeles Dodgers	1963	.326
Roberto Clemente, Pittsburgh Pirates	1964	.339
Roberto Clemente, Pittsburgh Pirates	1965	.329
Matty Alou, Pittsburgh Pirates	1966	.342
Roberto Clemente, Pittsburgh Pirates	1967	.357

Black Batting Champions
(American League)

Player	Year	Average
Tony Oliva, Minnesota Twins	1964	.323
Tony Oliva, Minnesota Twins	1965	.321
Frank Robinson, Baltimore Orioles	1966	.316

BLACK MOST VALUABLE PLAYER AWARDS (NATIONAL LEAGUE)

PLAYER	YEAR	TEAM
Jackie Robinson	1949	Brooklyn Dodgers
Roy Campanella	1951, 1953, 1955	Brooklyn Dodgers
Willie Mays	1954	New York Giants
Don Newcombe	1956	Brooklyn Dodgers
Hank Aaron	1957	Milwaukee Braves
Ernie Banks	1958, 1959	Chicago Cubs
Frank Robinson	1961	Cincinnati
Maury Wills	1962	Los Angeles Dodgers
Willie Mays	1965	San Francisco Giants
Roberto Clemente	1966	Pittsburgh Pirates
Orlando Cepeda	1967	St. Louis Cardinals
Bob Gibson	1968	St. Louis Cardinals

BLACK MOST VALUABLE PLAYER AWARDS (AMERICAN LEAGUE)

PLAYER	YEAR	TEAM
Elston Howard	1963	New York Yankees
Zoilo Versalles	1965	Minnesota Twins
Frank Robinson	1966	Baltimore Orioles

BLACK HOME RUN CHAMPIONS (NATIONAL LEAGUE)

PLAYER	TOTAL	YEAR
Willie Mays, New York Giants	51	1955
Hank Aaron, Milwaukee Braves	44	1957
Ernie Banks, Chicago Cubs	47	1958
Ernie Banks, Chicago Cubs	41	1960
Orlando Cepeda, San Francisco Giants	46	1961
Willie Mays, San Francisco Giants	49	1962
Willie McCovey, San Francisco Giants	44	1963
Hank Aaron, Milwaukee Braves	44	1963
Willie Mays, San Francisco Giants	47	1964
Willie Mays, San Francisco Giants	52	1965
Hank Aaron, Atlanta Braves	44	1966
Hank Aaron, Atlanta Braves	39	1967
Willie McCovey, San Francisco Giants	36	1968

BLACK HOME RUN CHAMPIONS (AMERICAN LEAGUE)

PLAYER	TOTAL	YEAR
Larry Doby, Cleveland Indians	32	1952
Larry Doby, Cleveland Indians	32	1954
Frank Robinson, Baltimore Orioles	49	1966

AMERICAN TRACK AND FIELD RECORDS
HELD BY BLACK WOMEN

HOLDER	DISTANCE OR EVENT	TIME, HEIGHT, OR DISTANCE	YEAR
Wyomia Tyus	100-Meter Dash	11.0	1968
WyomiaTyus	100-Yard Dash	10.3	1967
Wilma Rudolph	200-Meter Dash	22.9	1960
Rosie Bonds	80-Meter Low Hurdles	10.8	1964
Mildred McDaniel	Running High Jump	5'9½"	1956
Willye White	Running Broad Jump	21'6"	1964
Earlene Brown	Four-Kilogram Shot Put	54'9"	1960
Earlene Brown	Discus Throw	176'10½"	1960

GENERAL WORLD TRACK AND FIELD RECORDS
HELD BY AFRO-AMERICANS

HOLDER	DISTANCE OR EVENT	TIME OR POINTS	YEAR
Jim Hines	100-Yard Dash	9.1	1967
Robert Hayes		9.1	1963
Charlie Greene		9.1	1967
Henry Carr	220-Yard Dash	20.3	1963
Tommie Smith		20.0	1966
Adolph Plummer	440-Yard Dash	44.9	1963
Tommie Smith	440-Yard Dash	44.8	1967
Otis Davis	400-Meter Run	44.9	1960
Lee Evans		43.8	1968
Lee Calhoun	120-Yard Hurdles	13.2	1961
Earl McCullouch		13.2	1967
Lee Calhoun	110-Meter Hurdles	13.2	1961
Earl McCullouch		13.2	1967
Rafer Johnson	Decathlon	8,392 pta.	1960
Hayes Jones Frank Budd Charles Frazier Paul Drayton	400-Meter Relay (each runner does 100 meters)	39 flat	1961
Charlie Greene Jim Hines Mel Pender Ronnie Ray Smith		38.2	1968
Otis Davis (member of team)	One-Mile relay (each runner does ¼ mile)	3.05.6	1960

GENERAL WORLD TRACK AND FIELD RECORDS
HELD BY AFRO-AMERICANS (CONT.)

HOLDER	DISTANCE OR EVENT	TIME OR POINTS	YEAR
Otis Davis (member of team)	1600-Meter Relay (each runner does 400 meters)	3.02.2	1960
Lee Evans (member of team)		2:56.1	1968
Wilma Rudolph	100-Meter Run	11.2	1961
Wilma Rudolph	200-Meter Run	22.9	1960
Willye White Ernestine Pollards Vivian Brown Wilma Rudolph	400-Meter Relay (each runner does 100 meters)	44.3	1961

TRACK AND FIELD ACHIEVEMENTS
OF BLACK U.S. OLYMPIC TEAM MEMBERS

ATHLETE	DISTANCE OR EVENT	RESULT & WINNING TIMES, DISTANCES	PLACE AND YEAR
George C. Poag	200-Meter Hurdles	Third	St. Louis, 1904
George C. Poag	400-Meter Hurdles	Third	St. Louis, 1904
J. B. Taylor (member of team)	1600-Meter Relay (each runner does 400 meters)	First—3.29.4	London, 1908
Dehart Hubbard	Running Broad Jump	First—24′5⅛″	Paris, 1924
Edward Gourdin	Running Broad Jump	Second—23′10⅞″	Paris, 1924
Eddie Tolan	100-Meter Dash	First—10.3	Los Angeles, 1932
Ralph Metcalfe	100-Meter Dash	Second—10.3	Los Angeles, 1932
Eddie Tolan	200-Meter Dash	First—21.2	Los Angeles, 1932
Ralph Metcalfe	200-Meter Dash	Third—21.5	Los Angeles, 1932
Edward Gordon	Running Broad Jump	First—25′¾″	Los Angeles, 1932
Jesse Owens	100-Meter Dash	First—10.3	Berlin, 1936
Ralph Metcalfe	100-Meter Dash	Second—10.4	Berlin, 1936
Jesse Owens	200-Meter Dash	First—20.7	Berlin, 1936
Matthew Robinson	200-Meter Dash	Second—21.1	Berlin, 1936
Archie Williams	400-Meter Run	First—46.5	Berlin, 1936
James DuValle	400-Meter Run	Second—46.8	Berlin, 1936
John Woodruff	800-Meter Run	First—1.52.9	Berlin, 1936

Fritz Pollard, Jr.	110-Meter Hurdles	Third—14.4	Berlin, 1936
Cornelius Johnson	High Jump	First—6'8"	Berlin, 1936
Jesse Owens	Running Broad Jump	First—26'5⁵⁄₁₆"	Berlin, 1936
Jesse Owens Ralph Metcalfe	400-Meter Relay (each runner does 100 meters)	First—39.8ᵈ	Berlin, 1936
Harrison Dillard	100-Meter Dash	First—10.3	London, 1948
Norwood Ewell	100-Meter Dash	Second—10.4	London, 1948
Norwood Ewell	200 Meter Dash	First—21.1	London, 1948
Mal Whitfield	400-Meter Run	Third—49.9	London, 1948
Willie Steele	Running Broad Jump	First—25'8¹⁄₁₆"	London, 1948
Herbert Douglass	Running Broad Jump	Third—24'9"	London, 1948
Lorenzo Wright	Running Broad Jump	Fourth—24'9"	London, 1948
Harrison Dillard Norwood Ewell Lorenzo Wright (members of team)	400-Meter Relay (each runner does 100 meters)	First—40.6	London, 1948
Mal Whitfield (member of team)	1600-Meter Relay (each runner does 400 meters)	First—3.10.4	London, 1948
Audrey Patterson	Women's 200-Meter Dash	Third—25.2	London, 1948
Alice Coachman	Women's High Jump	First—5'6¼"	Helsinki, 1952
Andrew Stanfield	200-Meter Dash	First—20.7	Helsinki, 1952
James Gathers	200-Meter Dash	Third—20.8	Helsinki, 1952
Ollie Matson	400-Meter Run	Third—46.8	Helsinki, 1952
Mal Whitfield	400-Meter Run	Sixth—47.8	Helsinki, 1952
Mal Whitfield	800-Meter Run	First—1.49.2	Helsinki, 1952
Reginald Pearman	800-Meter Run	Sixth	Helsinki, 1952
Harrison Dillard	110-Meter Hurdles	First—13.7	Helsinki, 1952
Jerome Biffle	Running Broad Jump	First—24'10"	Helsinki, 1952
Meredith Gourdine	Running Broad Jump	Second—24'8⁷⁄₁₆"	Helsinki, 1952
Harrison Dillard Andrew Stanfield (members of team)	400-Meter Relay (each runner does 100 meters)	First—40.1	Helsinki, 1952
Ollie Matson Mal Whitfield (members of team)	1600-Meter Relay (each runner does 400 meters)	Second—3.04.1	Helsinki, 1952
Bill Miller	Javelin	Second—237'8¾"	Helsinki, 1952
Milton Campbell	Decathlon	Second—6,975 points	Helsinki, 1952
Mae Faggs	Women's 100-Meter Dash	Sixth	Helsinki, 1952

TRACK AND FIELD ACHIEVEMENTS
OF BLACK U.S. OLYMPIC TEAM MEMBERS (CONT.)

ATHLETE	DISTANCE OR EVENT	RESULT & WINNING TIMES, DISTANCES	PLACE AND YEAR
Catherine Hardy Barbara Jones Mae Faggs (members of team)	Women's 400-Meter Relay (each runner does 100 meters)	First—45.9	Helsinki, 1952
Andrew Stanfield	200-Meter Dash	Second—20.7	Melbourne, 1956
Charles Jenkins	400-Meter Run	First—46.7	Melbourne, 1956
Lou Jones	400-Meter Run	Fifth—48.1	Melbourne, 1956
Arnold Sowell	800-Meter Run	Fourth—1.48.3	Melbourne, 1956
Lee Calhoun	110-Meter Hurdles	First—13.5	Melbourne, 1956
Josh Culbreath	400-Meter Hurdles	Third	Melbourne, 1956
Charles Dumas	High Jump	First—6'11¼"	Melbourne, 1956
Gregory Bell	Running Broad Jump	First—25'8¼"	Melbourne, 1956
Ira Murchison (member of team)	400-Meter Relay (each runner does 100 meters)	First—39.5	Melbourne, 1956
Lou Jones Charles Jenkins (members of team)	1600-Meter Relay (each runner does 400 meters)	First—3.04.8	Melbourne, 1956
Milton Campbell	Decathlon	First—7,937 points	Melbourne, 1956
Rafer Johnson	Decathlon	Second—7,587 points	Melbourne, 1956
Mildred McDaniel	Women's High Jump	First—5'9¼"	Melbourne, 1956
Willye White	Women's Running Broad Jump	Second—19'11¾"	Melbourne, 1956
Mae Faggs Margaret Matthews Isabelle Daniels Wilma Rudolph (members of team)	Women's 400-Meter Relay (each runner does 100 meters)	Third—45.4	Melbourne, 1956
Les Carney	200-Meter Dash	Second—20.6	Rome, 1960
Lee Calhoun	110-Meter Hurdles	First—13.8	Rome, 1960
Willie May	110-Meter Hurdles	Second—13.8	Rome, 1960
Hayes Jones	110-Meter Hurdles	Third—14.0	Rome, 1960
John Thomas	High Jump	First—7'¼"	Rome, 1960
Ralph Boston	Running Broad Jump	First—26'7¾"	Rome, 1960
Irv Roberson	Running Broad Jump	Second—26'7⅜"	Rome, 1960
Ira Davis	Hop, Step and Jump	Fourth—53'11"	Rome, 1960

Otis Davis (member of team)	1600-Meter Relay (each runner does 400 meters)	First—3.02.2	Rome, 1960
Rafer Johnson	Decathlon	First—8.392 points	Rome, 1960
Wilma Rudolph	Women's 100-Meter Dash	First—11.0	Rome, 1960
Wilma Rudolph	Women's 200-Meter Dash	First—24.0	Rome, 1960
Earlene Brown	Women's shotput	Third—53'10⅜"	Rome, 1960
Martha Judson Barbara Jones Lucinda Williams Wilma Rudolph (members of team)	Women's 400-Meter Relay (each runner does 100 meters)	First—44.5	Rome, 1960
Robert Hayes	100-Meter Dash	First—9.9	Tokyo, 1964
Mel Pender	100-Meter Dash	Seventh—10.4	Tokyo, 1964
Henry Carr	200-Meter Dash	First—20.3	Tokyo, 1964
Paul Drayton	200-Meter Dash	Second—20.5	Tokyo, 1964
Ulis Williams	400-Meter Run	Fifth—46.0	Tokyo, 1964
Hayes Jones	110-Meter Hurdles	First—13.6	Tokyo, 1964
Paul Drayton Robert Hayes (members of team)	400-Meter Relay (each runner does 100 meters)	First—39.0	Tokyo, 1964
John Thomas	High Jump	Second—7'1¾"	Tokyo, 1964
Johm Rambo	High Jump	Third—7'1"	Tokyo, 1964
Ralph Boston	Running Broad Jump	Second—26'4"	Tokyo, 1964
Ira Davis	Hop, Step, and Jump	Fifth—52'1¾"	Tokyo, 1964
Wyomia Tyus	Women's 100-Meter Dash	First—11.4	Tokyo, 1964
Edith McGuire	Women's 100 Meter Dash	Second—11.4	Tokyo, 1964
Marilyn White	Women's 100-Meter Dash	Third—11.6	Tokyo, 1964
Rosie Bonds	Women's 80-Meter Hurdles	Eighth—10.8	Tokyo, 1964
Willye White Wyomia Tyus Marilyn White Edith McGuire (members of team)	Women's 400-Meter Relay (each runner does 100 meters)	Second—43.9	Tokyo, 1964
Eleanor Montgomery	Women's High Jump	Eighth—5'7¾"	Tokyo, 1964
Willye White	Women's Running Broad Jump	Twelfth—19'8¾"	Tokyo, 1964
Earlene Brown	Women's Shotput	Twelfth—48'6¾"	Tokyo, 1964
Jim Hines	100-Meter Dash	First—9.9	Mexico City, 1968

TRACK AND FIELD ACHIEVEMENTS
OF BLACK U.S. OLYMPIC TEAM MEMBERS (CONT.)

ATHLETE	DISTANCE OR EVENT	RESULT & WINNING TIMES, DISTANCES	PLACE AND YEAR
Charlie Greene	100-Meter Dash	Third—10.0	Mexico City, 1968
Mel Pender	100-Meter Dash	Sixth—10.1	Mexico City, 1968
Tommie Smith	200-Meter Dash	First—19.8	Mexico City, 1968
John Carlos	200-Meter Dash	Third—20.0	Mexico City, 1968
Lee Evans	400-Meter Dash	First—43.8	Mexico City, 1968
Larry James	400-Meter Dash	Second—43.9	Mexico City, 1968
Ron Freeman	400-Meter Dash	Third—44.4	Mexico City, 1968
Willie Davenport	110-High Hurdles	First—13.3	Mexico City, 1968
Erv Hall	110-High Hurdles	Second—13.4	Mexico City, 1968
Leon Coleman	110-High Hurdles	Fourth—13.6	Mexico City, 1968
Ed Caruthers	High Jump	Second—7′3⅜″	Mexico City, 1968
Reynaldo Brown	High Jump	Fifth—7′¼″	Mexico City, 1968
Bob Beamon	Long Jump	First—29′2½″	Mexico City, 1968
Ralph Boston	Long Jump	Third—26′9½″	Mexico City, 1968
Art Walker	Triple Jump	Fourth—56.2	Mexico City, 1968
Jim Hines Charlie Greene Ronnie Ray Smith Mel Pender	400-Meter Relay	First—38.2	Mexico City, 1968
Lee Evans Ron Freeman Larry James Vince Matthews	1600-Meter Relay	First—2:56.1	Mexico City, 1968
Wyomia Tyus	Women's 100-Meter Dash	First—11.0	Mexico City, 1968
Barbara Ferrell	Women's 100-Meter Dash	Second—11.1	Mexico City, 1968
Margaret Bailes	Women's 100-Meter Dash	Fifth—11.3	Mexico City, 1968
Wyomia Tyus	Women's 200-Meter Dash	Sixth—23.0	Mexico City, 1968
Barbara Ferrell	Women's 200-Meter Dash	Fourth—22.9	Mexico City, 1968
Margaret Bailes	Women's 200-Meter Dash	Seventh—23.1	Mexico City, 1968
Jarvis Scott	Women's 400-Meter Dash	Sixth—52.7	Mexico City, 1968
Madline Manning	Women's 800-Meter Dash	First—2:00.9	Mexico City, 1968
Wyomia Tyus Barbara Ferrell Margaret Bailes Mildred Netter	Women's 400-Meter Relay	First—42.8	Mexico City, 1968

Basketball

BLACK SCORING LEADERS IN THE
NATIONAL BASKETBALL ASSOCIATION

YEAR	PLAYER AND TEAM	POINTS SCORED	AVERAGE
1959	Wilt Chamberlain, Philadelphia Warriors	2707	29.2
1960	Wilt Chamberlain, Philadelphia Warriors	3033	37.6
1961	Wilt Chamberlain, Philadelphia Warriors	4029	38.4
1962	Wilt Chamberlain, San Francisco Warriors	3586	50.4
1963	Wilt Chamberlain, San Francisco Warriors	2948	44.8
1964	Wilt Chamberlain, Philadelphia 76ers	2534	36.9
1965	Wilt Chamberlain, Philadelphia 76ers	2649	33.5
1968	Dave Bing, Detroit Pistons	2142	27.1
1969	Elvin Hayes, San Diego Rockets	2327	28.4

Football

BLACK NATIONAL FOOTBALL LEAGUE RUSHING LEADERS

YEAR	PLAYER AND TEAM	YARDS
1957	Jim Brown, Cleveland	942
1958	Jim Brown, Cleveland	1527
1959	Jim Brown, Cleveland	1329
1960	Jim Brown, Cleveland	1257
1961	Jim Brown, Cleveland	1408
1963	Jim Brown, Cleveland	1863*
1964	Jim Brown, Cleveland	1446
1965	Jim Brown, Cleveland	1544
1966	Gale Sayers, Chicago	1331
1967	Leroy Kelly, Cleveland	1205
1968	Leroy Kelly, Cleveland	1239

*NFL record

BLACK NATIONAL FOOTBALL LEAGUE SCORING LEADERS

YEAR	PLAYER AND TEAM	POINTS SCORED
1958	Jim Brown, Cleveland	108
1964	Lenny Moore, Baltimore	120
1965	Gale Sayers, Chicago	132
1968	LeRoy Kelly, Cleveland	120

BLACK AMERICAN FOOTBALL LEAGUE RUSHING LEADERS

YEAR	PLAYER AND TEAM	YARDS
1960	Abner Haynes, Dallas	875
1962	Cookie Gilchrist, Buffalo	1096
1963	Clem Daniels, Oakland	1098
1964	Cookie Gilchrist, Buffalo	981
1965	Paul Lowe, San Diego	1121
1966	Jim Nance, Boston	1458
1967	Jim Nance, Boston	1216
1968	Paul Robinson, Cincinnati	1023

BLACK AMERICAN FOOTBALL LEAGUE SCORING LEADERS

YEAR	PLAYER AND TEAM	POINTS SCORED
1960	Gene Mingo, Denver	123
1962	Gene Mingo, Denver	137

The Power Structure in American Athletics

Compare the preceding tables showing black achievements with the following lists that describes the situation in American sports today.

NUMBER OF BLACK OWNERS IN PROFESSIONAL FOOTBALL

National Football League	0
American Football League	0

NUMBER OF BLACK MANAGERS AND HEAD COACHES IN PROFESSIONAL FOOTBALL

National Football League	
Managers	0
Head Coaches	0
American Football League	
Managers	0
Head Coaches	0

NUMBER OF BLACK OWNERS IN PROFESSIONAL BASKETBALL

National Basketball Association	0
American Basketball Association	0

NUMBER OF BLACK MANAGERS AND HEAD COACHES IN PROFESSIONAL BASKETBALL

National Basketball Association
    Managers   0
    Head Coaches   1
American Basketball Association
    Managers   0
    Head Coaches   1

NUMBER OF BLACK OWNERS IN PROFESSIONAL BASEBALL

National League   0
American League   0

NUMBER OF BLACK BIG LEAGUE MANAGERS AND HEAD COACHES IN PROFESSIONAL BASEBALL

National League
    Managers   0
    Head Coaches   0
American League
    Managers   0
    Head Coaches   0

NUMBER OF BLACK PEOPLE IN POLICY-MAKING POSITIONS ON THE U.S. OLYMPIC COMMITTEE

    4*

NUMBER OF BLACK HEAD COACHES OF U.S. OLYMPIC TEAMS

    0

* Out of a total of 57. None of the four—Dr. Samuel Barnes, Stanley Wright, Ralph Metcalf, and Dr. Nell Jackson, the last two appointed as recently as May 21, 1969— have been in the vanguard of black militant movements. Many regard the recent appointments as an effort to forestall trouble during the 1969 summer track season.

Appendix D:
1968 National Black Power
Conference Statement

Brothers and Sisters:

Black Power!!

(I regret that I am not able to be here personally to give the address which follows. Due to a severe auto accident, I am stranded until the insurance settlement comes through. I have entrusted this sealed statement to Bro. Bill Gray of the More Bk. Store in San Francisco, California. It was his responsibility, so graciously accepted, to deliver this paper to either Omar Ahmad or Bro. Nathan Wright to be presented before a general meeting at the Black Power conference.)

Black Power Conference Address

My primary purpose is to report on the final status of the Olympic Project for Human Rights originating out of the Black Power Conference of 1966.

Let us first review the accomplishments of this phase of the athletic movement:

1. Several white racist organizations have either been completely shut down as athletic clubs or they have radically changed their "whites only" policies.
2. We have gained international recognition of the plight of black people in the U.S.A. We have shown that not even the most wealthy and most prestigious blacks are treated humanely in this racist society.

3. We have opened international avenues of communication and cooperation between Black African Nations and the Black Afro-Americans in America as witnessed by our cooperation and unity in getting So. Africa and Southern Rhodesia banned either in fact or in effect from the international Olympic movement.

4. We have removed the myth of allegedly how much sports have done for Black people.

5. We have exposed the white nationalism and racism instituted into the sports industry in all areas, amateur, professional, and collegiate.

6. We have found yet another way of educating Black people to the degree, extent, and intensity of racism in the U.S.

7. We have exposed the Olympic movement for what it is: a white nationalistic, racist, political tool of exploiting oppressive governments.

8. We have shown how Black people, by using their brains as well as their ballots and bullets can dramatize still further their degrading and humiliating status in this country.

9. We have brought the Black athlete out of the fantasy world of newspaper clippings and the athletic arena into the Black revolution to take their long vacant place as leaders and spokesmen for Black people rather than as puppets and dupes for the white establishment. We have also exposed certain toms and traitors to Black people who have been used willingly by the White and Negro racist due to their athletic achievements.

10. We have gotten world wide recognition of the plight of Black people without a single drop of Black blood being spilled.

Among the countries that we received documents of sympathy and unity from are:

Tanzania	Zambia
Nigeria	Russia
Uruguay	Cuba
Mexico	China
England	Yugoslavia
France	Czechoslovakia
Ireland	Guatemala
Guinea	and about a dozen others.

I wish to express the gratitude of Black people and the athletes to the following people who gave unselfishly to this phase of the movement:

1. The Family of the late Rev. Dr. Martin Luther King
2. Hon. H. Rap Brown
3. Dr. Louis Lomax
4. Mr. Floyd McKissick
5. Bro. Stokeley Carmichael
6. Mr. Sam Skinner
7. Mr. Dick Gregory and
8. the dozens of others who participated from time to time in the effort.

The majority of athletes will participate in the Olympics. WHY?

1. Of the 26 athletes who had an excellent chance of making the team, 12 and maybe 13 were willing to boycott under some circumstances. The remaining 13 were not willing to boycott under any circumstances. It was decided by the track and field athletes that they would go because:

A. Those who would not participate in a boycott could easily replace those who would. (For instance, Jim Hines—who has stated that he was going to run if no one but him ran—could replace Tommie Smith therefore rendering Smith's sacrifice unnoticed by the world.)

B. About 65% of the athletes voted to stick to a 65% rule (sixty-five percent must vote to carry a particular action). There was consensus on a protest at the game. The protest would be as follows:

1. No participation in victory stand ceremonies or victory marches;
2. Some athletes have decided to boycott at the games; and
3. Several lesser forms of protest shall be carried out by others, including a contingent of white athletes.
4. All Black athletes will wear Black armbands and demonstrate their support of the Black Power movement in some manner during the course of the Olympic Games.

The present phase of this athletic movement is drawing to a close. However, there are several proposed resolutions that the Olympic Committee for Human Rights requests action upon for the coming four years:

1. Be it resolved that an awards banquet for certain of the Olympic athletes be held as planned by the Olympic Committee for Human Rights in recognition of the tremendous contribution to the Black liberation struggle on the parts of men such as Brothers Lew Alcindor, Mike Warren, Lucius

Allen, Tommie Smith, Otie Burrell, and others. Tentatively, this banquet is scheduled for San Francisco around the first week in January. Further information will be forthcoming.

2. Be it resolved that a total move be organized against Negro and white racist athletic departments at the collegiate level for the purposes of utilizing athletics for greater political leverage in all phases of the Black liberation struggle. Under this resolution, the O.C.H.R. requests a call of boycotts and disruption where deemed necessary and in the interest of Black people.

3. Be it resolved that a total move against professional athletics be initiated in the Fall of 1968 and carried on henceforth for the purposes of increasing the stake of the Black community in one of the nation's most lucrative industries and also for the purposes of reducing the behavioral manifestations of racism against Black people in that industry.

4. Be it resolved that a general endorsement of an athletic boycott against all Mormon dominated schools shall be in effect from Fall 1968 until such time as the Mormon Church alters its avowed conviction that all Black people are by God doomed to a state of total moral, intellectual, and physical inferiority.

5. Be it resolved that immediate preparations shall get under way for the 1972 Olympic Games. Educational materials for Black athletes and the Black community shall be developed and a solid political program shall be developed.

6. Be it resolved that a Federation of Black Amateur Athletes shall come into being for the purpose of protecting the Black athletes from the ravages of exploitation. This is particularly urgent in light of several facts:

A. The NCAA and other amateur athletic unions have shown what is either a lack of capacity or lack of desire or both to protect the Black athlete;

B. Several Black athletes have been martyred as a result of their individual stands against injustice. The upcoming struggle will demand a forum from which unity can be projected.

7. Be it resolved that the Black Power conference categorically condemns all pretenders to the heavyweight crown of Muhammad Ali as traitors, hypocrites, or both.

In summary, this phase of this political movement originating out of the 1966 Black Power Conference has been a success. There are many things yet to be done. It is imperative that we push forward realizing all along, however, that one cannot free a slave against his will. All slaves must understand that freedom is not obtained by proving to the master how good and efficient a slave one can be. The System must be made as uncomfortable for the master as it is for the slave.

It is my fondest hope that these proposed resolutions will be passed in order that those individuals active in this program will have the backing to continue the work already begun in the interest of Black Liberation.

> *Black Power!*
> Professor Harry Edwards, Chairman
> Olympic Committee for Human Rights
> Kenneth Noel, Chief Organizer
> Olympic Committee for Human Rights

Appendix E:
Information Booklet Excerpts

OLYMPIC COMMITTEE FOR HUMAN RIGHTS
PROFESSOR HARRY EDWARDS—CHAIRMAN
DR. LOUIS E. LOMAX—CONSULTANT
REV. DR. MARTIN LUTHER KING—CONSULTANT
MR. FLOYD MCKISSICK—CONSULTANT
MR. KENNETH NOEL—CHIEF ORGANIZER

The purpose of this document is to familiarize you with 1) the aims of the proposed Olympic Boycott, 2) the evidence underlying the justification for the demands made, 3) the persons who have taken on the responsibility of organizing the Boycott, and finally 4) we hope to clarify some of the quotes and misquotes propagated by the press and other forms of mass media.

It is sincerely hoped that, regardless of your present position on the Boycott, you will read carefully the statements presented here. For in the last analysis, it is the position of persons like yourself that will determine the extent to which we are able to avail ourselves of this and other means of non-violent protest to further push back the barriers of racism and bigotry that threaten not only the survival of black people, but also the survival of American Society. Peace.

THE OLYMPIC COMMITTEE
FOR HUMAN RIGHTS

1. GOALS OF THE PROPOSED BOYCOTT
In a time when violent uprisings among the politically ineffective and poverty-stricken Afro-Americans of the United States are becoming common place, those of us who have managed to make some inroads into the

system have the responsibility of searching for new alternatives to violence for the effective expression of the plight of the masses of black people.

Last year, over 400 black men, women, and children were shot down in the streets during the course of "disturbances" and rebellions which "necessitated" police action and the calling out of armed troops. Untold millions were lost as blocks of property and real estate were destroyed last summer. Summer 1968 only promises more of the same.

The proposed boycott of the Olympic games would accomplish the following:

1. It would exceed rebellions and bloodshed as a means of dramatizing the plight of the masses of Afro-Americans in this society. Racists could no longer say that racial protests are the work of misfits, ingrates, and irrational malcontents. The racial issue in this country would at least become an issue that the U.S. would have to face before the world.

2. It would re-establish . . . the fact that no Afro-American really "makes it" in this society. (See the statements of documented evidence on the treatment of black coaches, Olympic Champions, and professional athletes in America included in this report.)

3. And it would afford the proven men of black society an opportunity to share in the preservation of this society and of the black race.

While the press has played up the proposed boycott as a *demand* or *directive* to individual athletes, it in fact has never been and is not now such. There is nothing to boycott now nor was there on November 23rd. The proposal was adopted for consideration of *all* athletes concerned and to develop the necessary strategy to organize such a program if necessitated.

Six other goals are involved in the boycott proposal. These too are to be evaluated by the individual athletes and the only factor binding on that athlete is his individual decision and conscience. These goals are:

1. Restoration of Muhammad Ali's title and license to box in this country;

2. Removal of the anti-semitic and anti-black personality, Avery Brundage;

3. Curtailment of participation by all-white teams from South Africa and Southern Rhodesia in the United States and in the Olympic games;

4. Two black Olympic coaches;

5. Two black people on the Olympic Committee;

6. Desegregation of the New York Athletic Club.

Arguments underlying the above goals:

The overriding goal (that of utilizing one of the few remaining nonviolent ways of effective expression of the plight of Negroes in the U.S.) should be self-evident. In a word, when people are suffering to the extent that they are laying down their lives in the streets, who is to say that *any* area is too sacred to be used as an avenue to relieve this suffering. Is an Olympic gold medal or the experience of participating in the Olympics of more sanctity than one human life—let alone 300 or 400 a year? Further, the factor which kept black athletes of Olympic caliber from being shot down in the streets of Newark or Detroit, or from being lynched like Emmett Till in Mississippi, was not their Olympic potential or their medals and trophies but . . . *the simple fact that they were not there.*

Evidence of the commonality of interest between black athletes and the masses of black people becomes apparent when one sees that even those Olympic Champions who have "proven themselves" in the games have been struck down when they have attempted to stand up as men or to express their own ideas and convictions. After their Olympic glory is no more than a lingering memory in their own minds and they are returned to the heap in which most black people live out their lives, they may begin to see their "accomplishment" in a broader perspective. Muhammad Ali, an Olympic Champion, was immorally and unjustly stripped of his title for no more than exercising his religious prerogative and refusing entry into the Armed Forces on religious grounds. Both of these acts are freedoms guaranteed by the Constitution of the United States. Jesse Owens was kicked out of amateur athletics for life after he refused to run a ninth straight race and expressed a desire to return home right after the 1936 Olympics. His greatest sins were that by his refusal to run, he lost money for the A.A.U. and he refused to follow the directives of a white man.

Dickie Howard, bronze medal winner in the 400 meter hurdles in the 1960 games, returned home to the U.S. to find that freedom at home was not what he thought it was. He was found dead from suspicious causes in a Los Angeles apartment on November 21, 1967.

The list could go on and on, but the story would be the same. The black Olympic hero does not become a Congressman like Bob Mathias, or a highly paid corporation public relations executive like Bob Richards, or even a member of the U.S. Olympic Committee in any policy making capacity, as Jesse Owens recently found out. These positions are not open to Afro-Americans. Even if they go into professional athletics they fall into a "quota" situation, so many blacks regardless of how many good ones are around, and no more. These professionals never become managers; one, Bill Russell, has become a coach [Now Two, John McLendon, Denver, A.B.A.], and few get to cash in on the commercial endorsements which may pay more than a professional athlete's salary.

And invariably the black athletes—professional and amateur—return to the status of "just another Negro," or worse yet a "has-been" who really never was and just didn't know it.

A boycott of the 1968 Olympic Games would succeed in denouncing the above-mentioned societal and athletic conditions and would go far to place a new emphasis and perspective upon the racial problem in the U.S. And, hopefully, new and dramatic action will be forthcoming. Even more important, it can be accomplished without bloodshed or rebellions. In this regard, the black athlete of Olympic potential may make his greatest contribution by *not* competing. The world knows (and has known for some time) that we can run and jump. Perhaps now the world can also be shown that we are men of conviction and dignity.

We can dismiss the argument that there is no place in sports for politics by simply noting the main reason why Jesse Owens is remembered: the fact of a political struggle that was going on between Hitler and the Allies during the 1936 Olympics and not the fact of his Olympic Championships.

The justice of the six secondary goals, as ABC sportscaster Howard Cosell, Dr. King, and many news columnists agree, are incontestable. They are readily obvious. They are so obviously valid that the press has not attacked these demands but has relegated its vitriol to attacks on the boycott proposal committee or those athletes expressing sympathy to the cause.

If this society and the captains of the sports industry of this country are seriously concerned about correcting the injustices suffered by blacks in this society, they can start by rectifying the conditions outlined in these six demands. It is obvious that the whole racial situation in this country cannot be cleared up by the onset of the 1968 Olympics. Therefore, it is only reasonable that the six demands expressed above be representative of an opportunity for the society and the sports world to show good faith. Since the demands are just, there is no excuse for these powers not rectifying the situations—if they are in fact sincere. Such correction would be sufficient indication of good faith to forestall the proposed boycott.

A brief discussion of the arguments underlying the six demands may further clarify these issues. The arguments are as follows:

1. Removal of Avery Brundage.

Brundage is a demonstrable anti-black and anti-Jewish personality. He *owns* and operates the Montecito Country Club in Santa Barbara, California. This club admits Jews on a quota system and has turned away several delegations requesting banquet space due to the fact that these delegations had black people in their aggregations.

Mr. Brundage's first comment when he heard word of the proposed boycott was, "We will just find white athletes who are just as good as the Negroes; they won't be missed." He added later, "The Olympics are the only chance on an international level for Jews, Negroes, and Communists to find recognition." Upon enlarging on his statement he unconsciously equated the three categories of people.

Several sportscasters have openly stated agreement with this demand. Howard Cosell referred to Brundage as ". . . an old dope who should have been retired 40 years ago for his incompetence let alone his racial attitudes." Mr. Brundage is unwelcome at the University Club in New York City today because of anti-semitic statements that he made there.

2. Muhammad Ali's Reinstatement.

Muhammad Ali was himself an Olympic champion. He was regarded as the "All-American Negro boy" until he became a convert to a religion of his choice—a right guaranteed by the United States Constitution. But his religion was not approved by *White America*. The press immediately began to crucify him. They found a hook upon which to hang their animosity when Ali decided against going into the Armed Forces. This too is a right guaranteed by the Constitution. (The law regarding the draft does not state that you *must* enter the Armed Services. It states that you must enter, qualify for exemption, or suffer the consequences of not entering.) Ali decided to either get an exemption status ruling or go to jail. The press and the white boxing world immediately called for his dethronement. Furthermore, they got it. (All of the non-white countries still recognize Ali as the Heavy-weight Champion of the World.) When did the Pentagon get into the boxing business? Ali did not win his title in the press or against the government, and morally and ethically these forces cannot take it away. If Gene Fullmer could keep his middle-weight Championship as a Mormon who dedicates himself each sabbath to the Mormon conviction that black people are by God doomed to a state of complete moral and intellectual inferiority, and if Sonny Liston could keep his title with a *history* of arrests as long as he is tall, then why cannot Ali keep his title? The difference between these cases is that Ali is a Black man who stood up for his convictions and a white dominated racist America cannot stand this.

We want the title back!

3. An end to discrimination at the New York Athletic Club.

The New York Athletic Club yearly puts on a big indoor track meet at Madison Square Garden where it grosses hundreds of thousands of dollars. Most of the headline stars are black. Yet the New York Athletic Club will not allow Afro-Americans to join the club or even be housed in its facilities. They take the receipts of these indoor games and they send the lily-white NYAC team across the country and around the world. The black athlete who makes this money for them, if he is lucky, will get a medal or a watch. We are asking that the club be opened up or no more black people will "perform" for the benefit of this white racist organization.

4. An end to competition against South Africa and Southern Rhodesia and a banning of athletes from these countries in competition within the political boundaries of the United States and in the Olympic games.

In Compton, California, in 1966, Lee Evans and Tommie Smith ran against Paul Nash, a white South African—*and they resented it greatly.* America does not hold emigration or exchange contracts with any country that does not allow white Americans to visit or enter its political boundaries. Yet this country brings white South Africans and white South Rhodesians over to the United States when no black athlete could go to these countries no matter how great an athlete he might be. What this government and this society is telling us is that *black people and their dignity doesn't matter.* We don't feel humiliation and insult. We are just performing animals without feeling, manhood, or intellect.

We are demanding that this country recognize us as men and human beings. We demand an athletic ban on South Africa and Southern Rhodesia.

5. Black coaches on the Olympic team.

Of all the black Champions that the U.S. has had, there has never been a black coach on the men's Olympic Coaching Staff let alone a head coach. If these coaches are chosen without regard to race, then one would have to imply that whites have a corner on quality coaching skills. This is obviously not true, since almost all of our women champions come from *black-coached* schools and a great many of our men champions come from such schools. (Examples of these schools are Tennessee A&M, Grambling, South Carolina State, and others.)

We want some black coaches!

6. We want blacks on the United States Olympic Committee. Many of our past Olympic Champions qualify for these posts. But as Jesse Owens found out, we don't qualify "due to rules, laws, and the method of nomination." These laws and rules are set by the Committee itself. If we can run for this country in the Olympics, then we can also qualify to be represented on the board that governs the Olympic Games Representatives for the United States.

We want black people represented on the United States Olympic Committee.

The above arguments represent, in brief, the foundations underlying the position of the Olympic Committee for Human Rights and the athletes who aligned themselves with the Committee.

We live in trying times. We must no longer allow this country to *use* black individuals of whatever level to rationalize its treatment of the black masses. We must no longer allow America to *use* a few "Negroes" to point out to the world how much progress she has made in solving her racial problems when the oppression of Afro-Americans in this country is greater than it ever was. We must no longer allow the Sports World to pat itself on the back as a citadel of racial justice when the racial injustices of the sports industry are infamously legendary. In a time when the oppressed black race is being annihilated in the streets, any black person who allows himself to be used in the above manner is not only a chump—because he allows himself to be used against his own interest—but he is a traitor to his race. He is secondly, and most importantly, a traitor to his country because he allows racist whites the luxury of resting assured that those black people in the ghettos are there because that is where they belong or want to be. Under such circumstances, this country and this government does less than it could to solve the racial injustices in America.

And finally, it is well acknowledged that Black athletes, with their awesome talents and incredible innovations, have the habit of turning sports into art forms, instituting style and grace where brute brawn and dull routine once reigned.

BUT NOW the Black athlete must go a step further. Still the innovator, he must utilize the endemic political, social, and economic aspects of sports for the greater and more profound purposes of freedom, justice, and equality for oppressed humanity.

Few would have dreamed years ago that scuffling, ragged boys, playing in ghetto streets and alleys, could grow to become world heroes or to utilize their uniqueness as an instrument to help elevate humanity. Black athletes must move sports up to a higher level.

WHETHER they boycott this year's Olympics because of Nazi-white South Africa (where millions of Blacks suffer an unspeakable slavery and degradation) or because they want the world to know that not all the gold medals in hell are worth glorifying America's disguised system of Black genocide, or whether they simply have too much pride and humanity to prance around in playful Olympics representing a nation engaged in destroying millions of innocent Vietnamese in a war all the world recognizes as the most inhuman in history, they must become, not simply "sports," but heroes of humanity.

They must brush aside the "holy" cries that sports should be a sacred arena, "off limits" to political issues. The life and death struggle to overthrow a hideous enslavement enables Black athletes to recognize the simple truth that there are no "sacred arenas." In whatever arena, cultural, religious, civic, economic, educational, political, an assault against the Old System must be waged and won.

AGAIN AND again, America sends all-white teams (that never win) to the Winter Olympics session. Even in most summer categories, such as swimming, gymnastics, etc., they prepare no Black athletes to participate and not a single Uncle Tom bothered to stomp through the country in protest. White America never complained about the lack of Blacks in Winter Olympics. So let them send an all-white team to its track and field events this summer. In fact, let the whites HAVE the Olympics.

It's time that Africa, Asia, and Latin America unite to form a new conference conceived and dedicated in the spirit of freedom, justice, and equality— and not representative of nations which practice slavery and the destruction of its Black populations while piously preaching "democracy."

The few Uncle Toms now traveling the country urging Blacks to dash into the Olympics in the old way may prevail upon some of our youths to participate for the "gold medals" and "glory."

HOWEVER, the medal of honor humanity will bestow upon those noble and advanced Black athletes, who sacrifice for a better world by their protest, will be emblazoned in the minds of mankind forever.

This would be the greatest innovation for the Black innovators to make.

Selected Bibliography

Axthelm, Pete, "The Angry Black Athlete," *Newsweek Magazine,* July 15, 1968.

———, "The Olympics Extra Heat," *Newsweek Magazine,* October 28, 1968.

Edwards, Harry, "Why Negroes Should Boycott Whitey's Olympics," *Saturday Evening Post Magazine,* March 9, 1968.

Esquire Magazine, "The Charge of the Faculty Brigade," September, 1968.

Green, A. W., *Recreation, Leisure, and Politics,* McGraw-Hill Publishing Co., New York, 1964.

Henderson, Edwin B., *The Negro in Sports,* Associated Publishers, Inc., Washington, D.C., 1949.

Life Magazine, "A Separate Path to Equality," December 13, 1968.

Look Magazine, "The Black and White Cowboys," January 7,1969.

Moss, Peter, *Sports and Pastimes Through the Ages,* Arco Publishing Co., Inc., New York, 1963.

NCAA-AAU Dispute, Hearings before the Committee on Commerce, United States Senate. Eighty-ninth Congress, First Session, United States Government Printing Office, Washington, D.C., 1965.

Olsen, Jack, "The Black Athlete—A Shameful Story," *Sports Illustrated Magazine,* July 1, 1968, Volume 29, No. 1, pp. 15–27.

———, "In An Alien World," July 15, 1968, Volume 29, No. 3, pp. 28–43.

———, "In the Back of the Bus," July 22, 1968, Volume 29, No. 4, pp. 28–41.

———, "Pride and Prejudice," July 8, 1968, Volume 29, No. 2, pp. 18–31.

———, "The Anguish of a Team Divided," July 29, 1968, Volume 29, pp. 20–35.

Russell, William, *Go Up for Glory,* Coward-McCann, Inc., New York, 1966.

Shaap, Dick, "The Problem Olympics," *Sports Illustrated Magazine,* September 30, 1968, Volume 29, No. 14.

———, "The Revolt of the Black Athletes," *Look Magazine,* August 6, 1968.

Scott, Jack, "The White Olympics," *Ramparts Magazine,* May, 1968, Volume 6, No's. 9 and 10.

Stump, Al, "The Man Who Would Destroy the Olympics," *True Magazine,* March, 1967.

The New York Times Magazine, "The Black Rebel Who Whitelists the Olympics," May 12, 1968, Section 6.

Thompson, Richard, *Race and Sport,* London Institute of Race Relations, Oxford University Press, New York, 1964.

Time Magazine, "Black Pride," October 6, 1967.

Afterword to the 50th Anniversary Edition

It is only with the perspective accorded by distance and consideration of developments over time that a more complete portrait of a history can be achieved. It is also the case that history and the lived past are not and could never be precisely repeated, replicated, or completely left behind. Past events and past advances prove a seminal prologue, as continuities, contradictions, and consequences carry over in some semblance, infusing present and future circumstances, influencing our definitions and perceptions of and responses to "reality"—even if this influence goes unrecognized. It is within the context of this long-view perspective that developments at the interface of race, sport, and society are best appraised and understood and that the connections between the past, present, and future are most reliably comprehended.

From the turn of the twentieth century until well into the post–World War II years, Black society was in a state of almost total institutionalized exclusion, an all-encompassing segregation-mandated "lock down" and "lock out" relative to involvement in American mainstream life and institutions. Sports of course were no exception. Despite having established a parallel Black sports institution that produced athletes and athletic performances demonstrably on par with and sometimes superior to those on display in mainstream sports (as illustrated in many Black versus White "exhibition" competitions), between 1900 and 1946, with a few notable exceptions, it was principally in the realm of international sports competitions that Black sports excellence was likely even to be recognized, much less (grudgingly) celebrated. Commensurately, by way of example, in the early 1930s, though the Negro press had repeatedly cited Jesse Owens as the "greatest [high] school boy athlete in the nation," his athletic exploits were not covered to any significant degree in the White mainstream press until he enrolled at Ohio State University and became an Olympic prospect. Similarly, Joe Louis had fought more than fifty professional fights before he became the subject of any coverage of note in the mainstream White media. Jesse Owens's performance at the 1936 Munich Olympics and Joe Louis's defeat of German Max Schmeling in their 1938 championship rematch, then, followed a pattern of Black athletes being recognized domestically for their demonstrated athletic prowess against international competitors. This was a pattern established as far back as Jack Johnson, who—after having been refused fights by White American heavyweight champions—defeated Canadian Tommy Burns in Australia for the heavyweight boxing championship title in 1908. Society-wide, American-style race-based apartheid and exclusion became the broader context that framed and fueled a persistent struggle to demonstrate Black athletic *legitimacy*, the intrinsic argument being "If we can compete against and defeat the best in the world in our sports, then why can we not compete against the claimed best in those same sports in our own country? Clearly, what we lack is not capability or demonstrable competence and competitiveness, but opportunity." This was as much a political statement as it was an athletic declaration because it challenged the legitimacy of the entire segregated racial structure of U.S. human relations. That sentiment also de facto marked the onset of the "First Wave" of Black athlete activism related to broader issues of Black freedom, justice, and equality in America.

With a growing political consciousness of intergroup issues that emerged in American society in the wake of World War II, combined with the advent of the Cold War between East and West and the competition it spawned for hearts, minds, and markets in the resource-rich, largely non-White developing nations, and with a heightened Black American impatience with racial segregation, the next phase of the struggle in sports, the "Second Wave" of Black athlete activism, was cast, even as the struggle for legitimacy continued.

From 1946 to 1965, the First Wave struggle in sports that had been forged to meet the challenges of demonstrating Black athletic legitimacy was expanded by Second Wave Black athletes to encompass an all-out struggle for *access*. Jackie Robinson and Larry Doby in Major League Baseball; Woodie Strode, Kenny Washington, Bill Willis, and Marion Motley in professional football; and Earl Lloyd and Chuck Cooper, who joined the NBA during the 1950–51 season, all contributed to paving a new path toward broadening democratic participation in American Sports.

By 1965, a "Third Wave" of athlete activism had emerged and joined the struggle, even as the struggles for legitimacy and access continued apace. Led by professional athletes such as Bill Russell, Jim Brown, Arthur Ashe, and Curt Flood, and epitomized by the actions of the 1965 American Football League Black All-Star football players, the newest phase of the struggle focused on compelling respect, dignity, and equality of treatment and justice for Black athletes in particular and for Black people more generally. Collegiate basketball players at U.C.L.A., Berkeley, Iowa, and St. Mary's College, world-class sprinters such as Tommie Smith and John Carlos, football players at San Jose State, the University of Washington, the University of Wyoming, Syracuse University, and at other colleges and universities, and even the Harvard University crew team joined in the struggle to compel respect, dignity, equality, and justice in sport and society. Yet other developments that contributed to all phases of the continuing struggle around developments at the interface of sport, race, and society could not have been anticipated, much less planned, and were at the time far from fully appreciated in terms of their import and seminal significance. A prime illustration of this point was the 1966 N.C.A.A. Championship basketball game between the all-White University of Kentucky team and the team representing Texas Western University, which started five Black players. When the Texas Western Miners defeated the Kentucky Wildcats, the racial significance of that outcome went largely unnoted and uncommented upon across much of the White mainstream sports press and was ignored for the most part by news organizations more generally. The victory was viewed and projected as neither historic nor seminal. *Sports Illustrated*, the "bible" of sports journalism, featured an extensive postgame story on the rise of Texas Western as a collegiate basketball power, but the story did not once mention race. The *New York Times*, the national "newspaper of record," gave top billing in its coverage following the Texas Western N.C.A.A. victory over Kentucky to the National Invitational Tournament game between BYU and New York University. Now, fifty years later, in retrospect the Texas Western–Kentucky game clearly marked the necessary onset of a turning point in the culture, stylistic character, and racial profile of, and the respect commanded by Blacks in collegiate—and by extension professional—basketball. (Parenthetically, that respect on the basketball court—at least insofar as the Texas Western players were concerned—eventually extended to their performances in the classroom. Of Texas Western's seven Black players, four eventually graduated. The other three came within a semester of achieving their degrees. Still, all manner of ridicule and derogatory comments concerning their assumed intellectual and educational deficits and deficiencies were directed at these Black players, e.g., "Their points per game average is higher than their average I.Q." Meanwhile, it did not come to light until well into the 1970s that of the five White starting players for Kentucky, four never earned their degrees.)

By the onset 1980s and into the 1990s, more change was already evident and underway—the early stirrings of a struggle for power. Initially, the focus was on the achievement of individual economic power epitomized by the aspirations and achievements of Earvin "Magic" Johnson and, later, by Michael Jordan. Earvin Johnson didn't want to be in movies like Jim Brown, Fred Williamson, or O.J. Simpson—he aspired to produce movies and own the theaters in which they were shown. Michael Jordan didn't just want to get endorsement contracts, he wanted to have ownership of the products that he endorsed and that were associated with his name. Johnson and Jordan didn't just want to be financially successful professional athletes, they wanted to own professional teams. LeBron James, among other active athletes today, continues that quest for "athlete-entrepreneur" economic power. But, with the onset of the twenty-first century, there was also a second path to power emerging, one that would give expression to a "Fourth Wave" of Black athlete activism.

Black athletes seeking economic power over the 1980s and 1990s appeared to place a single-minded concern upon the pursuit and safeguarding of their own individual economic interests unburdened by any presumption of social-political obligation occasioned by racial identity politics. Perhaps the most infamously memorialized sentiments expressed in that regard were those made by Michael Jordan in response to a request that he endorse a Black Democrat, Harvey Gantt (who had been the first Black student admitted to Clemson University), running in opposition to North Carolina's notoriously racist, right-wing senator, Jesse Helms ("Well, Republicans buy gym shoes too"), and by Charles Barkley in his scripted declaration in a product ad that "I am not a role model!" But to truly grasp the relevance of such comments, it is essential to correctly and fully understand the social-political context and climate within which they occurred.

By the early 1980s through the 1990s, not only had the prominence of the broad scale Black social-cultural and political movements of the 1950s, 1960s, and 1970s waned, but in the face of this decreased prominence there was the belief that the once powerful and persuasive Civil Rights Movement was dead. There were no prominent leaders with the definitional authority, charisma, or popular following of a Dr. Martin Luther King Jr. or a Malcolm X. There was no preeminent or coherent society-wide ideological framing or debate regarding the state or trajectory of race relations in American society. To the contrary, there was increasingly a mainstream acceptance of the presumption that not only was the Civil Rights Movement dead, it was also largely a victim of its own successes. America was presumed well on its way toward becoming a "post-racial" society—a disposition that would be perceived to be validated by the election of this nation's first African American president in 2008. Lacking a broadly accepted, energized, and viable Black social-political protest ideology or movement within which to frame their sentiments, high-profile Black athletes largely eschewed Black advocacy statements. There would be no shift in these circumstances until almost the onset of the second decade of the twenty-first century when there developed a resurgent, broad-scope Black protest movement and supporting ideology in the guise of the "Black Lives Matter!" movement, generating the bases for the emergence of a "Fourth Wave" of Black athlete activism.

With the onset of the Black Lives Matter movement—largely as a reaction to social media exposure of camera-phone video capturing the abuse and killing of Black men, women, and children by police officers—any semblance of legitimacy regarding athletes' attitudes of individual economic primacy and political insularity dissipated. Black professional and collegiate athletes began to find their political voices. More important, they began to leverage the political power potential inherent in their positions as high-profile athletes, particularly in professional and elite collegiate basketball and football. From the hoodie protest photo by Miami Heat players in 2012 to the actions of the University of Missouri Black football players who posted their group photo and statement of support for students protesting campus racism and discrimination in 2015, from the "Hands Up, Don't Shoot" gesture by five St. Louis Rams football players that same year to statements by LeBron James, Carmelo Anthony, Chris Paul, and Dwyane Wade at the ESPN ESPYs award program in 2016, and the protest actions of San Francisco Forty Niners quarterback Colin Kaepernick, Black-athlete protest expressions are precursors setting the course and trajectory of political developments at the boundary of sport, race, and politics going forward. In this regard, it is particularly worth noting how the *patterns of continuities and contradictions* evident in the processes and dynamics generating Black circumstances and subsequent protest actions at S.J.S.C. in the fall of 1967 came into play at the University of Missouri in the fall of 2015, forty-eight years later.

Black students at the University of Missouri had been experiencing circumstances and outcomes similar to those that confronted Black students at S.J.S.C. almost five decades earlier, circumstances and outcomes on the whole shared by Black students on other predominantly White campuses across the country. In 2015, Black student protests and expressions of concern over race-related issues were staged at universities as varied as Clemson, Yale, Princeton, Kansas, Occidental, Berkeley, and, again, San Jose State. What these persistent protest actions reveal is that today these institutions are little better prepared to be fully inclusive relative to African Americans in campus operations, community culture, and life than they were of Negroes fifty years ago. Not surprisingly, therefore, today Black-student demands in response to their circumstances bear striking similarities to those that I put forth at S.J.S.C. in 1967: increases in Black student recruitment and financial support; increases in Black faculty and administrators; curriculum changes that reflect the history, politics, and current realities of the Black experience in America; and programs that promise to change racially discriminatory and inhospitable campus social-culture climates. Some of the universities targeted by these Black student protests have likewise responded with regimens very much akin to those first promised and/or implemented at S.J.S.C. in 1967, including the appointing of "diversity officers" to monitor, report on, and resolve diversity-related issues on campus.

As with the S.J.S.C. movement, it took four to five years for developments to progress from initial stirrings of athlete political activism to collegiate Black-athlete demonstrations and threats of event boycotts over issues of racial inequities and injustice. And, most notably today, though the incidents were highly publicized in the mainstream traditional media, they were in most instances first disseminated and commented upon in a medium not available in 1967—online social media. The trajectory of broader sports institutional developments presaging the threatened University of Missouri athletes' football boycott can be dated from 2010 when the National Basketball Association (N.B.A.) Phoenix Suns wore jerseys emblazoned with "Los Suns" in protest of what the players believed to be draconian, if not outright xenophobic, immigration policies in the state of Arizona. Over the ensuing years protests escalated in both drama and number: athletes from around the N.B.A. threatened not to play games against the Los Angeles Clippers after the disclosure of tapes that revealed racist comments about African Americans and Latinos, including his own Clippers players, made by team owner Donald Sterling; L.A. Lakers and other N.B.A. players joined protests over police violence against Blacks; Ariyana Smith, a player on the (Galesburg, Illinois) Knox College women's basketball team, during the playing of the National Anthem at a game in Staten, Missouri (a few miles from Ferguson, where Black teenager Mike Brown was killed by a White cop) walked out to the flag with her hands up in the "don't shoot" gesture, dropped to the floor before the flag, and lay there for four minutes and thirty seconds in protest of the police killing of Brown, whose body was left lying in the street where he fell for four and a half hours; and football players at the University of Oklahoma collectively spoke out following racist chants by a campus fraternity, after a Black player's profanity-laced statement of outrage over the fraternity's behavior and words went viral over the social media. And unlike in 1967, even a historically Black institution had an incident of Black-athlete rebellion when the football players at storied Grambling University undertook a week-long boycott of the school's football program over the physical condition of athletic facilities, forcing cancellation of a scheduled game against Jackson State. By the time of the University of Missouri threatened football boycott, the *Fourth Wave* of Black athlete activism was fully underway.

Meanwhile, between 2010 and 2015 athletes and other sports figures were also becoming more politically active and outspoken concerning nonracial issues. Athletes in a number of sports, many still active, revealed that they were gay (most notably, Michael Sam and Kwame Harris in football; John Amaechi, Will Sheridan, Brittney Griner, Jason Collins, and Derrick Gordon in basketball; and professional sports executives Billy Bean of the Oakland A's and Rick Welts of the N.B.A. Golden State Warriors). Also, athletes such as Chris Kluwe, then a kicker with the Minnesota Vikings, came out forcefully in support of gay rights and gay marriage as early as 2012. Ed O'Bannon, a former U.C.L.A. basketball player fought an antitrust battle against the N.C.A.A. rule prohibiting its member institutions from compensating their athletes for use of these athletes' names, images, and likenesses, while a group of former Northwestern University student-athletes endeavored to form a collegiate athletes' union. (These acts of activism targeting collective economic interests could well establish a climate and create templates for further political protests, leading to yet another wave of athlete activism seeking unprecedented changes in *economic* relationships in collegiate revenue-producing sports.) By 2015, then, political developments in the larger society were fueling, giving impetus to, and ideologically legitimizing political activism that was already well this side of the social-political horizon within the sports arena.

Like the Black Power movement of the 1960s, as was stated, nothing has informed and framed Black athlete activism in the second decade of the twenty-first century as much as the Black Lives Matter! movement. Not surprisingly in the age of social media, Black Lives Matter! began as a hashtag created by three Black women that morphed into a slogan and then a movement name, a movement that spread and grew in adherents within sport without a formally named central leader or leadership organization, much as had the revolt of the Black athlete in the 1960s. A lack of formal structure or binding agenda or specific set of clearly defined goals, along with the political malleability and adaptability that this permitted, were functional assets of the Black Power movement. Black Power could portend and project almost any goal, from increased numbers of Black students on predominantly White campuses, to establishing Black studies curriculum, all-Black residential halls, and Black cultural centers for them once they arrived on campus. Similarly, Black Lives Matter makes no specific demands, has no set agenda and no central leadership or leadership organization. Black Lives Matter! can apply on the campuses of the Universities of Missouri, Oklahoma, and Princeton no less than on the streets of Ferguson, Missouri; Brooklyn, New York; and Baltimore, Maryland. But there are also critical downsides to this flexibility and adaptability. The Black Lives Matter movement can fuel, frame, inform, and even inflame activism, but with no definitive measures and markers of legitimate progress, as was the case with Black Power, it leaves its adherents open to a wide range of outcomes, including co-optation, confusing symbolism with substantive change, and pursuing goals that do not produce significant change in institutional culture, or in the control and application of power.

For instance, on the college campus, activist demands for the resignations of high officials within an institutional structure provide a case in point. At S.J.S.C. in 1969 Dr. Robert Clark resigned as president in the wake of the Black athletes' revolt on that campus. A new president was appointed by the same power structure and people who had hired and subsequently accepted the resignation of Dr. Clark. But the new president of S.J.S.C. knew less about the realities, dynamics, and mediation of racial issues on campus than Dr. Clark, who had learned a great deal in that regard after working to surmount those challenges daily for more than two years. Predictably, conditions slowly drifted back toward status quo conditions existing prior to the protest movement that arose from the athlete boycott. Over time, as non-athlete student numbers rose in the wake of their targeted recruitment, and as institutional investments in revenue-producing sports continued to increase, athletes were more "siloed" socially, academically, and politically by the Athletic Department and the university than ever before, thereby reducing the risk of their involvement in campus issues. Also, in their very act of meeting expressed student demands, even when with the best of intentions, educational institutions often succeed in nothing so much as affirming and reinforcing the already-entrenched images and perceptions of minorities as "the other," as largely "outsiders" who cannot compete or function normally without special programs, protections, and support systems. So, ironically, universities such as S.J.S.C., compelled to confront and pursue correction of anti-Black exclusion, discrimination, and other race-related issues under threat of protests and Black athlete boycotts, in the final analysis often end up compounding the very problems that they seek to resolve. As successive cohorts of students enroll and graduate, as the original issues precipitating corrective actions and the protest movements taken to secure them fade from common knowledge and popular awareness, the hard-won programs and support systems targeting Black student issues and interests come increasingly to be perceived within the larger campus culture as either no longer warranted or as "special treatment" for a group "apart," a group either unduly privileged or one that otherwise would not be able to compete. Over time, again as was the case at S.J.S.U., in either case institutional supports for such corrective measures begin to erode. Over the course of successive administrations, most such supports either no longer function as viable, substantive programs or, worse, are discontinued altogether. Typically, decisions leading to gradual retrenchment and reinstitution of the status quo are the prerogative of university "power structures," to which the Black student protestors and their athlete supporters, even at the height of their influence, have little or no access or input. So, at S.J.S.U. in 2015 Black students were again engaged in a campus protest movement with sweeping goals and demands almost identical to those put forth there in the fall of 1967. On the whole, the one major difference has been that students today have access to social media, the greatest tool of protest organization in history. Only time will tell if the protest movements today at S.J.S.U., the University of Missouri, and or other campuses will approach the challenges they face with more wisdom, vision, and effectiveness—and whether, in the end, they will fare any better long term, with or without leveraging the power potential of Black athletes.

Compounding the complexity of activist movements in sports going forward will be largely uncontrollable, often unanticipated developments that emanate from beyond the arena and have consequences that impact the sports in ways that are substantially unavoidable. In past eras, racial segregation framed the experiences, political dispositions, and outcomes of *First Wave* Black athletes; the "Cold War," racial desegregation policies, and a burgeoning Civil Rights Movement provided social-political scaffolding for *Second Wave* Black athlete activism; contentious political, cultural, and inter-generational society-wide divisions over the conduct and continuation of the Vietnam War and a high profile Black Power Movement framed the *Third Wave* revolt among Black athletes in the late 1960s; and the Black Lives Matter! Movement, camera phone technology, and social media gave impetus to the *Fourth Wave* of athlete activism. As we enter 2017 and the beginning of a new presidential administration, campus protest and mass popular demonstrations are already underway in opposition to president-elect Donald Trump and his proposed policies, particularly insofar as they deal with the circumstances of certain groups, i.e., women, Muslims, Latinos, and African Americans. In some cases, athletes and coaches have joined in the outcry, expressing concern about the outcome of the election and, going further, refusing to stay at or billet teams at hotels associated with Trump real estate interests or to patronize businesses that sale or feature products that bear the Trump name.

But a word of caution is in order here: there should be no expectation of even a quasi-unified or uniform activist response or disposition in sports relative to broader-scope societal developments no matter the extent to which they might be rightly deemed draconian or even detestable and deplorable. Again, it is not enough to simply be "right" if one is to persuade others to the "right side of history" in a struggle—including some "others" from among those on whose behalf the struggle is being waged. Struggles, then, can—and usually do—become complicated, even messy affairs. Sports figures, like any other grouping of individuals defined collectively by some limited and largely circumscribed set of features and characteristics (such as sports involvement) are in fact highly diverse in their perspectives, in their perceived self-interests, and in their political awareness and dispositions. Creating and sustaining some degree of functional unity in response to political circumstances is always the first challenge confronting those who would forge a movement among athletes—Black, White, or otherwise. There are seldom, if ever, any straightforward, universally agreed upon pathways of advancement in any conscientiously undertaken struggle. This reality is unlikely to change in the future, irrespective of how urgent or "right" the struggle might be.

And finally, I must emphasize that nothing stated here should be construed as discouragement, disenchantment, or disaffection on my part relative to athlete activism or the protest actions of Black students and athletes and their collaborators on and off the campus. It cannot be overemphasized that freedom, justice, and equality must reside, in substantial part, in the hearts and minds of the people. It is The People who initiate and who lead change efforts, not the courts, or the legislators, or the governors, and not the presidents, or other executive-branch office holders or appointees—on or beyond the campus. Injustice and inequality will reign unchallenged and unchecked only so long as there is no organized effort by the people to compel a different course. In this regard, social, cultural, and political movements are critical, not because they always succeed, or because the gains that they achieve endure, but because they compel society to confront and engage key challenges and contradictions.

There have been six great movements over the course of American history: the abolitionist movement against slavery; the women's suffrage/liberation movement, the labor movement, the civil rights movement, the environmental movement, and the gay rights movement. Not one of these movements was initiated or had its basic concepts, methods, and goals first articulated by an elected or appointed official in conjunction with mandated duties. Not one of these movements precipitated initially out of a government policy. Freedom and justice "live" only partially in our laws and in our founding documents. These provide the scaffolding and foundation principles guiding our institutions. The noble and much cited principle that "All men are created equal" can be enshrined in the most cherished and honored civil documents of a slaveholding society. The principle of "equal justice before the law" can be chiseled into the stone facades above courthouse doors in a society that arrests, prosecutes, incarcerates, and executes the poor and minorities in grossly disproportionate numbers. Movements are, therefore, an imperative of democracy. This is the true meaning and relevance of the opening line of the Preamble to the United States Constitution: "We the People of the United States, in order to form a more Perfect Union . . ."—not we the courts, or we the elected officials, and so on. So it has been from the outset in this nation, and so it is today. The challenges of achieving that "more Perfect Union" have always, at core, been fundamentally the burdens of "We The People." And no challenge reflects the ongoing reality, magnitude, and consequences of such burdens more than racism.

The sentiment that "slavery is America's original sin" has been declared and reiterated so often down through the years that it has almost become an axiom, virtually an article of faith. I've had a problem with this notion going back to my earliest days in college, when I was reading biographies on the likes of John Brown and Frederick Douglass, fiction such as *Uncle Tom's Cabin* and *Gone With The Wind*, and books on the Civil War written from the perspectives of both sides of that conflict. My first issue with the idea that slavery was America's original sin is that it conveniently consigns the "original sin" substantially to the past. If slavery was the original sin, and slavery has been eliminated and is behind us, then this nation's "great sin" is likewise behind us—as Black people are so often reminded when some among our White contemporaries declare in effect that "slavery has been over for 150 years and I never enslaved anybody. It's in the past and doesn't have anything to do with me. You need to get over it."

The second problem I've always had with the idea of slavery as America's "original sin" is that it totally ignores the question of how America came to institute slavery in the first place, how this society came to support and defend it. The enslavement of Black Africans and their progeny in this country didn't "just happen," it was deeply rooted in a pervasive ideological and social-pathological strain of White supremacist racism. And it is this virulent White supremacist racism that is America's "ORIGINAL and CONTINUING SIN." It was White supremacy that enabled European adventurers, immigrants, and refugees to come to these shores in the fifteenth and sixteenth centuries and claim to have "discovered" a new land—with people ashore watching them get off their boats. Slavery—along with genocidal policies and actions against Native American populations—was simply an early institutional manifestation and expression of that original sin. White supremacist racism, then, was the core "sin" and evil that was at the foundations of slavery, a sin that has had the demonstrable capacity to evolve, to transcend history, and to carry over into different eras. It has moved with America, never left behind. It was the driving force behind racial segregation, lynching, and other forms of anti-Black injustice, inhumanity, and outright barbarism. It is still a commanding influence generating so much of the brutality and injustice perpetrated in Black communities across America. America may well have put legal slavery behind us, but its commitment to a deeply rooted, all-too-pervasive White supremacist racism that rationalized, justified, and sustained slavery is still very much with us—and all the more insidious for its chameleon-like capacities to adapt to modern contexts. In combination with chauvinistic patriarchy, White supremacy is the foundation ideology behind White male privilege and power in America—and both chauvinistic patriarchy and White supremacy were fundamental to generating the necessary political appeal to White voters who in the majority elected Donald Trump to the presidency of the United States.

Today, White supremacist racism remains this nation's most corrosive, divisive, and volatile institutional, political, and social-cultural burden, and it must be vigorously confronted and vociferously addressed in every realm and within every context of American life. This means that there must be movements against White supremacy and the racism-based bias and outcomes it fosters. Silence is evil's greatest and most consistently dependable ally. Fear is evil's most ubiquitous and enduring tool. But enshrined in our

National Anthem are the words "land of the free and home of the brave," not "land of frenzied and home of the afraid." We cannot, must not, stand silent and afraid in the face of the White supremacist challenge. Under the circumstances, even given the all-but-impossible odds against any single movement effort achieving total or even lasting success against this evil, there are no grounds—most certainly not the odds—and no justification to forgo the struggle against it, the struggle that must be.

I frequently have been asked if I am saddened, disappointed, or discouraged by the need for athlete activism and campus movements today, with demands virtually indistinguishable from those that I fought for nearly fifty years ago. The answer is no, quite the contrary. We should neither be surprised nor dismayed over the facts that battles thought won continue to be waged, or that there are new battles being fought to sustain gains thought secured. President Lyndon Johnson's signing of the Civil Rights Act of 1964 and the Voting Rights Act of 1965 into law neither marked the end of battles for civil rights and voting rights nor brought an end to police profile stops of Black and brown people, nor stopped voter-suppression efforts in states across this nation. *Roe v. Wade* did not end the struggle for women's rights to legal, safe, and accessible medical services. Not even movement gains in sports are secure from retrenchment pressures. So almost fifty years after the O.P.H.R. was initiated, I received the following on January 26, 2016:

> Trademark rights: This new trademark application falls within the same statutory prohibitions, namely that Olympic trademarks may not be used by any third party without permission from the USOC.

> Use of this mark, OLYMPIC PROJECT FOR HUMAN RIGHTS & WREATH DESIGN, on athletic apparel and uniforms is highly likely to create the mistaken assumption that any products or services associated with this mark are

officially connected with or sanctioned by the USOC. The USOC object to any and all use of the false impression it produces.

The USOC would like to resolve this matter amicably. Thus, we request that you withdraw U.S. Trademark Application Serial No. 85/899683 and provide your assurance that you will select an alternate name for both the clothing and initiative.

We would appreciate a reply to this letter by no later than February 1, 2016. If you would like to discuss this matter directly or would like assistance withdrawing the trademark application on-line, please feel free to call me.

The name "Olympic Project for Human Rights" and the O.P.H.R. button that I designed and distributed nearly fifty years ago promoting and publicizing that political effort have been recognized and in many cases memorialized both nationally and internationally as the name and insignia of the most dramatic and iconic African American protest movement against racism in sports and society over the last half of the twentieth century. Worldwide, more than a score of books and literally hundreds of articles have been published that have focused in whole or in part on the O.P.H.R. movement and its goals, tactics, and achievements. There have likewise been hundreds of educational programs and projects, lectures, seminars, workshops, and conferences over the decades that were organized for the purpose of examining the O.P.H.R. and the historical legacy of that movement. The O.P.H.R. button and the movement that it has long represented have even been memorialized in exhibits at the Smithsonian National Museum of African American History and Culture. Most famously, of course, Tommie Smith, John Carlos and Peter Norman wore O.P.H.R. buttons on the awards podium during the playing of the United States National Anthem at the 1968 Mexico City Olympic Games—as I had done throughout 1967 and 1968 while organizing and promoting the O.P.H.R. Over the decades since the 1968 Olympic Games, the name "Olympic Project for Human Rights" and its most recognized insignia, the O.P.H.R. button, have been memorialized on statues, in historical and educational exhibits across the country, and on countless posters, book jackets, and magazine covers. And there has not been a single case of the O.P.H.R. or the O.P.H.R. button being confused with or construed as being associated with a United States Olympic Committee project, program, sponsored activity, or item. To the contrary, it has been universally recognized that the O.P.H.R. and everything associated with it was in part organized specifically *in opposition to* the U.S.O.C., its policies, and its practices in 1968. The fact that I do not now and have never had any interest in using these emblems of struggle to promote or sell apparel and other merchandise for profit is beside the point. (But just to make the intent of my trademark clear, with the fiftieth anniversary of O.P.H.R. movement fast approaching, I wanted to make sure that no other interest—not even the U.S.O.C.—would be able to turn these insignia of struggle into merchandizing and marketing tools). That the U.S.O.C. would threaten to legally challenge my use of the O.P.H.R. name and its representation on the O.P.H.R. button in 2016 could be taken as an attempt to control and contain today what it could not crush in 1968, or perhaps worse, as an indication and reflection of gross ignorance of U.S.O.C. history within the organization—history lost, forgotten, denied. It's too early to tell. But, clearly, even the O.P.H.R. struggle continues.

But still other developments must also be factored into the mix when assessing the history of movements and related developments over time. What is to be made of the fact that S.J.S.U. has erected a 24-foot-tall statue of Tommie Smith's and John Carlos's 1968 Olympic victory-stand protest, or that on February 11, 2016, I received the following letter from the office of the president of S.J.S.U., my alma mater and the only institution with which I have ever been affiliated, to terminate me (in 1968) in response to my activist activities:

> Dear Dr. Edwards:
>
> I am pleased to extend the invitation to you to be our Commencement Speaker on Saturday, May 28, at the San Jose State University Annual Commencement Ceremony, and to be our Honorary Doctor of Humane Letters (L.H.D) Degree recipient. Commencement is the most important public event of the academic year, celebrating everything that the university is and does, as we confer degrees on all those who have completed their academic requirements during the preceding year.
>
> Having an outstanding alumnus as Commencement Speaker and Honorary Degree recipient will make our Commencement Ceremony truly memorable for our graduating students and their families, as well as faculty, staff and guests who will attend.
>
> The Board of Trustees of the California State University approved San Jose State's request to award an honorary doctoral degree to you on behalf of both San Jose State University and the California State University. The California State University has an extensive process for approving and awarding honorary degrees. It will be a honor for the campus to make this presentation on behalf of all of those for whom you have labored in the past, and those who will benefit from your achievements in the future.

How should the symbolism of statues, honorary degrees, and institutional acknowledgement that those who waged a struggle almost fifty years ago were on the right side of history all along, that they had fought the good fight, that they contributed? How should these things be weighed against the reality of the absolute imperative of continued struggle? It is, again, too early to tell. Today's Black Lives Matter! movement—no more so that the Black Power movement—most certainly provides no definitive answer to this question. And, in some respects, the question in the final analysis might prove to be all but irrelevant. Protests, boycotts, and marches against racism and exclusion must continue—even in the wake of the most heartfelt and sincere substantive and symbolic gestures of recognition and validation to past struggles (including SJSU's commitment to establishing a new "Institute for the Study of Sport, Society, and Societal Change"). And if these struggles today do not take place most legitimately on our campuses, within the racism-afflicted cultures and structures of our institutions of higher education—then where? Put most simply, then, the challenges to achieving the promise of America—that more Perfect Union—are diverse and dynamic; our struggles, therefore, must be multifaceted and perpetual, and THERE ARE NO FINAL VICTORIES! Only the struggle, and the people and the nation on whose behalf it is waged, endure. All else ultimately is reduced by time and ever-shifting circumstances and evolving challenges to the temporary and ephemeral. All pretense of permanence in the gains and achievements of struggle is always in some substantial measure illusion and self-delusion. It is not that goals cannot be achieved or that sacrifices and costly effort in a struggle to compel change are folly and utterly futile. Over some specific era or frame of time, in terms of some specific constellation of issues, *Hard Won Gains Matter* and can make a tremendous difference in the lives of the people. This is why each generation must fight its battles, make its contribution to the struggle. What is more, struggle itself is redemptive. In the end, if, after all is said and done and despite our struggles, we are still not "saved," it will be the very fact that we did struggle that will unequivocally establish and communicate that we were worth saving, that our history, our contributions, and our lives mattered—oppositional history and all else to the contrary notwithstanding. And on that basis alone, subsequent generations will find incentive and reason to continue the struggle. In the meantime, the movements of "We the People" will rise and wane, fade and pass away with each new generation like the morning mist before the rising sun of a new day. But still, the struggle continues. Such are the lessons of biography and history informing my perspectives, perspectives born of fifty years of experience on the front lines of the struggle around issues at the interface of sport, race and society—a struggle with which today I am not only at peace, I am pleased.

* * *

Haki R. Madhubuti, then the poet don l lee, wrote a poem in homage to Tommie Smith and John Carlos that should not be construed as just a curious "left over ending," despite its placement by an editor in the original edition of this book. This poem highlights a moment of athlete activism that changed perceptions and understandings of human relations in American sports:

BLACKRUNNERS / BLACKMAN
OR RUN INTO BLACKNESS

(for brothers tommie smith & john carlos—super-sprinters—
but most of all blackmen)

u beat them
brothers;
at their own game.
   (out ran the world-runners)
whi-te boys
& others
had a dust meal.

u beat them.
now
in this time in space
the rule-makers
are also
the vanquished

anyhow/way
we can't eat gold medals
& sportsmanship is racism
in three syllables.

u beat them brothers
and u/we
will beat them again.
they
just don't know
that
u've/got friends
&
we know how to
fight dirty

Throughout my activist career, I have been committed to the proposition that activism without scholarship is conducive to nothing so much as chaos. It is within this context that I offer this "Blueprint for Educational Achievement." And it is an honor and a privilege to share this space at this place in this book with Haki /don l lee and hopefully between the two of us inspire, illuminate, and pave a path to continued informed struggle.

A "BLUEPRINT" FOR EDUCATIONAL ACHIEVEMENT
(Lessons from the life and calling of a once-failed student)

Owing to academic deficiencies, I attended a community college for a semester. I did not qualify to enroll in any of the four-year colleges offering me an athletic scholarship in football, basketball, or track and field. Three-and-a-half years later, I graduated with honors and a B.A. in Sociology from San Jose State University and accepted a Woodrow Wilson Fellowship to attend Cornell University, where I earned both an M.A. and a Ph.D. before later joining the sociology faculty at the University of California at Berkeley. Outlined below is what more than fifty years of experience as a student and teacher has taught me relative to meeting the challenges of educational development: a "blueprint" for academic achievement and success.

    I.   **Follow your bliss.** Seriously explore and consider paths that might lead not just to achieving a career interest but to realizing **your calling**—that educational option and emphasis that **for you** lies at the confluence of **talent, passion, productive potential,** and **opportunity.**

    II.   **Cultivate the habit of high expectations of yourself and of every effort** that you undertake in pursuit of your educational goals.

    III.   **Respect the challenges and demands of your calling by learning to dream with your eyes open.** The achievement of a calling **always** means meeting demands and surmounting challenges—known and unanticipated. There will be routine educational requirements and there will be those educational "mountains and valleys" that you never could have fully foreseen.

    IV.   **Learn to "behave as if."** Cultivate the habit of behaving, of "acting" as if you are **already** an outstanding, accomplished student. Ask yourself at every turn, "What would a committed student choose to do at this juncture, in this situation, at this 'fork in my path'?" Every outstanding student I have ever encountered shared my own experience of having **thought** like, **worked** like, and made **choices** like an outstanding student long before they became outstanding students.

V. **Commit to a strategy, practice, and disciplined program of hard work.** I have often been asked if there is a "shortcut" to educational achievement and success. **Hard work IS the short cut—** every other path is more difficult. Maximize the results of your hard work—organize, prioritize, and have a plan for meeting the challenges of your calling.

VI. **Persevere. Stay on course by employing a strategy of "living in anticipation of tomorrow."** Living in anticipation of tomorrow means cultivating and abiding by the **understanding** that what you do today never fully recedes into the past with the passage of time. Rather, your commitments, actions, and experiences, in some substantial part or measure, advance in life with you, strongly influencing who and what you are becoming.

VII. And, lastly, **learn and abide by the work-rest cycle of your mind and body.** When fatigue sets in, even the most inspired and committed student can become dull and increasingly less educationally productive. On the other hand, **hard work followed by a well-earned period of rest and "re-creation" often reinvigorates and re-energizes educational effort and even insight. Rest and re-creation make critical contributions toward maximizing the productivity of hard work.**

Index

HARRY EDWARDS is Professor Emeritus of Sociology at the University of California, Berkeley. He was the architect of the 1968 Olympic Project for Human Rights and his scholar-activist career since has focused on the role and potential of sports in fostering social change. He is a consultant with a number of NFL and NBA franchises and with several NCAA Division I conferences and basketball and football teams. His other books include *The Struggle that Must Be: An Autobiography*.

Sport and Society

Sex Testing: Gender Policing in Women's Sports   *Lindsay Parks Pieper*
Cold War Games: Propaganda, the Olympics, and U.S. Foreign Policy   *Toby C. Rider*
Game Faces: Sport Celebrity and the Laws of Reputation   *Sarah K. Fields*
The Rise and Fall of Olympic Amateurism   *Matthew P. Llewellyn and John Gleaves*
Bloomer Girls: Women Baseball Pioneers   *Debra A. Shattuck*
I Fight for a Living: Boxing and the Battle for Black Manhood, 1880–1915
Louis Moore
The Revolt of the Black Athlete: 50th Anniversary Edition   *Harry Edwards*

REPRINT EDITIONS

The Nazi Olympics   *Richard D. Mandell*
Sports in the Western World (2d ed.)   *William J. Baker*
Jesse Owens: An American Life   *William J. Baker*

The University of Illinois Press
is a founding member of the
Association of American University Presses.

University of Illinois Press
1325 South Oak Street
Champaign, IL 61820-6903
www.press.uillinois.edu